THE BEST AMERICAN

NONREQUIRED
READING™
2008

■

EDITED BY

DAVE EGGERS

INTRODUCTION BY

JUDY BLUME

MANAGING EDITOR

ELISSA BASSIST

HOUGHTON MIFFLIN COMPANY
BOSTON • NEW YORK
2008

www.houghtonmifflinbooks.com

ISSN: 1539-316x
ISBN: 978-0-618-90282-8
ISBN: 978-0-618-90283-5 (pbk.)

Printed in the United States of America
DOC 10 9 8 7 6 5 4 3 2 1

CONTENTS

INTRODUCTION

Featuring an interview with Judy Blume

THE BOOK YOU'RE HOLDING is part of a series which every year
seeks to compile a varied and unexpected anthology of fiction, nonfiction, essays, journalism, comics, and humor. The books in the
Nonrequired series are still assembled in much the same way they've
always been — passionately and unscientifically. This anthology, part
of the *Best American* juggernaut that includes everything from the
original *Best American Sheetrock Poetry* to the newest addition, the
*Best American Canadian Marsupial Short Fiction Featuring Lewd Wood-
working*, is considered the best of them all, chiefly because ours usually features the highest volume of cursing.

The *Best American Nonrequired Reading* is edited in the basement
of a building in the Mission District of San Francisco with the help,
this year, of managing editor Elissa Bassist and, as always, with a
group of high school students from all over the Bay Area. Each Tuesday night, these students, eighteen of them this time around, meet to
read and discuss and debate the merits of everything they find written in English and printed on paper. We try to read everything. We
certainly read all the journals, magazines, comics, weekly newspapers, and blogs that are sent to our office through the mail or web.
We spend many months in the read-and-debate stages, and then we
spend the late spring in the finalizing stages, and this year, we were
given the opportunity to actually design and typeset the entire book
ourselves, all from that same — okay, sort of dingy — basement. In

our roundabout and willy-nilly way, we try to compile a collection that strikes a balance between the heavy and less-heavy, and which speaks eloquently about what it's like to be alive right now.

Speaking without any objectivity at all, the editors want to say that this year's is one of the best collections the *Nonrequired* series has yet produced. Every single piece in this anthology, we think, is a show-stopper, and we hope you'll find many new voices and styles herein.

Every year, the *BANR* students are asked to nominate a cover illustrator and a guest introducer for the collection. This year's cover artist, following in the footsteps of the likes of Daniel Clowes, Art Spiegelman, and Adrian Tomine, is the extraordinary graffiti artist Barry McGee. Some of the students knew his work from the abandoned buildings of San Francisco, and some had seen his work in museums and galleries. In either case, he's done an astounding cover for us, which reflects the eclectic nature of this collection, and which features a head, on the bottom right, that apparently looks like someone on the editorial end of this book.

For the collection's guest introducer, we sought someone who has a unique voice, a history of groundbreaking accomplishments, and a keen interest in reading widely and catholically. In the past, these introducers have included Zadie Smith, Beck, Matt Groening, Sufjan Stevens, and Viggo Mortensen. This year, the students nominated an author who similar committees might have chosen at any time in the past thirty or so years. That she remains so relevant to teenagers in 2008 is a loud and clear statement about how brave she's always been as a writer, and how originality, candor, and integrity have great staying power, even among the fickle and questionably dressed young people who labor over this book.

In an effort to keep the collection moving in new ways and avoid litigation, we decided to give these same students the opportunity to ask questions of our guest introducer, the unimprovable Judy Blume.

How do you feel when you read a headline or title of another story that starts with "Are you there, God? It's me . . ."
Judy Blume: Oh my God, there are so many of them these days. I suppose I should feel flattered. But it's actually pretty weird. The

latest I've seen is *Are You There, Vodka? It's Me, Chelsea* by Chelsea Handler. What can I say?

There's actually a piece in this collection called Are You There God? It's Me. Also, a Bunch of Zombies. *Is this the first time someone has adapted one of your titles to apply to the undead?*

JB: As far as I know this is the first time my title has been adapted to apply to the undead. Let's hope it's the last? I've told my husband I think I should have a headstone someday that reads:

ARE YOU THERE GOD? IT'S ME . . .
JUDY BLUME

Or would that be too odd?

Is now a good time for a teenager to grow up?

JB: Is any time a good time?

What's different about being a teenager now and when you were a teenager?

JB: Everything — and nothing. I was a teenager in the '50s, a decade I think of as bland and boring. Or maybe I was bland and boring. No, really — most of us didn't think out of the box. I grew up in Elizabeth, New Jersey, and went to an all-girls public high school (both high schools in town were segregated by sex). My mother's advice was: *Go to college, get a degree in education in case, God forbid, you ever have to get a job — and while you're at it, find a husband, a professional man with a good future. Wind up with a house in the suburbs and a couple of perfect children.*

Are you gagging yet? Because I really did that. Oh — and I almost forgot a piece of really important advice (no joke) which still makes sense — *Don't get pregnant before you're married (or prepared to be responsible for yourself and your child) and ruin your life.* Turns out three of my top classmates *were* pregnant at graduation, and yes, their lives were changed forever. No legal abortion then.

We read in our feminist lit classes that there was, for a while, a tough relationship between the "career women" and stay-at-home moms. Did you ever get frustrated with your peers who were more content to stay within traditional gender roles?

JB: There was a time when we were told we could have it all — career, kids, marriage (this was in the late '60s and '70s, after I'd married and had kids). The mistake, I think, was in feeding girls the idea that they had to have it all at the same time. That's not always possible. Most of the women I know have found work they care about. Maybe they found it after their kids were in school. Maybe after their kids grew up. I felt resentment from many of my young neighbors (married with children, living in the suburbs) when I began to write. Looking back I think it had to do with their wish to get out of the house and have a career too — something not easy to admit at the time. Traditional '50s husbands needed to prove they could provide for their families. They didn't want their wives to work because it reflected badly on them. All this began to change as I hit thirty. So sure — go for it all if you want it. Just don't beat up on yourself if you can't pull it all off at the same time.

What is the first thing that comes to mind when you hear "books for teenage girls"?

JB: I hate categorizing books. Good books are good books. I know what you mean, though — there are so many books published today aimed at teenage girls, and too many are told in similar voices. I always hope, when I open a new one, I'll find something fresh and original — and sometimes I do.

When I started to write I was determined to write books that kids wouldn't use for book reports in school. I wanted only to write "nonrequired" books. Books that kids would curl up with and keep private. Books they'd want to read. It's funny, because third and fourth grade teachers all over read the *Fudge* books aloud to their classes. And I've discovered, I don't mind at all.

Okay, now we have to get serious with some of these questions. On the next page, we've provided photos of all the student members of the committee. Now, of all the students pictured below, who looks the most likely to enjoy the music of Burt Bachrach?

JB: Since I was a Bachrach fan (he was so new back in the days of

Carlos Cheung   Carmen DeMartis   Josh Freydkis   Yael Green   Katie Henry

Sayra Hernandez   Sophia Hussain   Arianna Kandell   Bora Lee   Terence Li

Tanea Lunsford   Osvaldo Marquez   Nina Moog   Elizabeth Rodriguez   Marley Walker

Naomi K. Wernham   Eli Wolfe   Iris Zhang

Alfie), I'm going with Bora and Josh. I'll bet they'd look great in '70s style. Maybe the three of us could do backup?

Who wouldn't you trust to babysit your granddaughter?

JB: If I had a granddaughter, there's no way I'd let Eli watch her.

We've been trying to get Osvaldo to go by the nickname "Oz." Do you think that's a good nickname for him?

JB: I loved all the *Oz* books when I was a kid. So the name has appeal for me. But I think it should be up to Osvaldo. And whatever you do, don't call him Ozzie.

Does it make him seem mysterious, like the magical land where the Wizard lives? Or will people expect him to wear green all the time?

JB: Forget the green. Go with the mystery.

Tanea needs a nickname, too. You have any ideas?

JB: How about that old standby Anea-tay?

Tanea plans to be a writer. Can you provide one do *and one* don't *for her?*

JB: *Don't* let anyone discourage you. *Do* write without fear.

So many young people read your books at a very sensitive point in their lives. You must get so many letters from young readers who are confused about their place in the world, bewildered by their parents and family, and who look to you for answers. Can you talk about any letters like that, and how you answer them?

JB: I once spent three years putting together a book of letters (*Letters to Judy: What Kids Wish They Could Tell You*) from my readers. It was emotionally draining, not just because I tried to tie them together with autobiographical material, but because of the letters themselves. At one point I had to go to a therapist to find out how I could keep writing fiction while being responsible (and responsive) to my readers. I was so involved with a couple of kids (I wanted to save them) that the therapist had to teach me how to step back while still being there for them. Over the years there have been seven kids who started to write to me at age twelve — kids with tough lives — who still write to me today and they're in their twenties and thirties now. Most of them are okay. Some are parents. I still try to answer the really serious letters myself.

Was it important for you to put positive moral values in your young adult books?

JB: I don't think the best stories come out of a place where the author is determined to put in positive moral values. I mean, whose values? I'm happy when my characters behave in an ethical way. But they're not always going to. An exception was *Forever* . . . I wanted to show two decent teens taking responsibility for their actions. But really, I'm just telling stories. I hope my readers will come away thinking. I hope they find something in my books they can relate to, something that illuminates life for them.

What was the first book you read where you felt changed, moved, like your world had been expanded?

JB: It could be Anne Frank's *Diary of a Young Girl*. I was thirteen or fourteen when the book was published and my mother handed it to me. My mother was a reader, but she never talked to me about anything important. She didn't know how. She wasn't comfortable as a parent. Instead, from time to time she'd hand me a book. (This was long before the book was assigned reading in middle schools.) I totally identified with Anne. I was a Jewish girl in New Jersey, but I could just have easily been born in Berlin. Anne's story could have been mine, could have been any of ours. Isn't that what gets us? The universality of it? Talk about a book that you never forget! That may be the first book that left me shaken and in tears.

Has writing fiction diminished your ability to enjoy reading fiction — like the way sausage-makers no longer like to eat sausage (or so we've been told)?

JB: Only when I'm writing. Make that only when I'm writing intensely — meaning once I'm past the first draft. I hate writing first drafts. It's the worst part of the process for me. I'm a rewriter. A reviser. When I'm caught up in my characters and their story, I can't allow myself to get involved in the lives of other characters — and reading fiction for me means being caught up in the lives of the characters. I know a book has meant something special to me when I keep thinking about it, long after I've finished reading the last page. As a writer, that's what I hope my readers will do.

I can read in short bursts when I'm writing — articles in *The New Yorker,* pieces in an anthology like this one — but I have to be very careful. Once, when I was writing a novel (*Smart Women*) I made the mistake of starting to read a book, *Dad*, by William Wharton. I'd read his first novel, *Birdy* (recommended by my daughter, the most voracious reader in our family) and was anxious to read his second. But once I started, I couldn't stop. I read it straight through. Which would have been okay except it left me so insecure about my own writing — *What am I doing? I can't write this well. I'll never be able to write this well. I might as well quit now —*

I couldn't write a word. I put away the novel I was trying to write and couldn't pick it up again for close to three months.

How often do you put down a book, never to finish it? And do you feel a sense of guilt, as if that put-down book is weeping silently on the shelf where you've placed it?

JB: I rarely put down a book once I actually begin. Which doesn't mean I don't taste a lot of books I never actually read. I do. And many times I mean to go back and read from the beginning. And no, I don't think we need a support group for these books because the book I decide to put down could be the book you read from cover to cover in one gulp.

My best friend (we met in seventh grade) tastes books by reading the last page first. As a writer (even as a reader) this drives me crazy. But no amount of arguing will change her mind.

Can you look at the Rorschach images below and tell us what comes to mind for each? Do any of the images make you hungry or feel faint? Would any of them benefit from the nickname "Oz"?

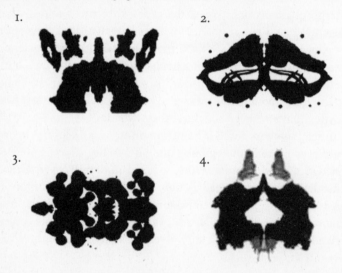

I. 2.

3. 4.

JB: I hope these are in the right order.

1. A girl's head/hair with her secret, unprintable thoughts above.
2. Laughing guy, braces on his teeth, scattered zits.
3. Monster Attack — primitive weapon going through and coming out on the other side. This one could be called "Oz Strikes Again."
4. Elephants in red party hats kissing while resting their front feet on red drums.

None of the images make me feel hungry, probably because I just finished lunch.

What were you reading in middle school?

JB: By sixth grade I'd pretty much given up on children's books. There were no YAs then (except for *Seventeenth Summer,* a book we all devoured in ninth grade). I'd loved the *Betsy-Tacy* books by Maude Hart Lovelace when I was younger, along with *Alice in Wonderland* (my aunt gave me a beautiful edition with pages thinner than waxed paper). I devoured *Little Women,* went through all the *Oz* books, and for a while, was buying a *Nancy Drew* mystery every week at the Ritz book shop with my twenty-five-cent allowance.

But when we had to give oral book reports in class, rather than read a book I wasn't interested in, I'd invent a book. That's right — I made up a title, an author's name, characters, and a theme. (To this day I hate to be asked about themes.) I still can't believe I stood up in front of the class and presented these reports. (Up to fifth grade I'd been shy and quiet.) Most of my invented books were about Dobbin, a horse, because that's what I thought my teacher expected me to be reading — horse books, like the other girls in my class. But I had no interest in horse books. I had interest in sex and the secret world of grownups. So I was reading from my parents' bookshelves. They never told me any book was off limits. They loved to read themselves. Reading was a good thing, not something to be afraid of. Did they know I was reading Ayn Rand's *The Fountainhead,* Saul Bellow's *The Adventures of Augie March,* and a book of short stories by John O'Hara? I couldn't have understood half of what was in those books, but I found a certain satisfaction in them. Later I found *The Catcher in the Rye* on the bottom shelf. And an illustrated copy of *Lysistrata.*

I got As on my invented book reports, but not when I was reporting on a *real* book.

Were you like any of the characters in your books?

I was like my character Sally Freedman. I had a lot of imagination. Often, what I imagined was worse than reality. *Starring Sally J. Freedman as Herself* is my most autobiographical book. My fourth-grade teacher, who I fictionalized in *Sally J.*, recently died. I met up with her when *Double Fudge* was published and she came to a talk/signing in the Miami area. It was a thrill to introduce her to the audience.

My sixth-grade experience was like Margaret's in *Are You There God? It's Me, Margaret*. And yes, I did those breast-enhancement exercises. (And no, they didn't work for me.)

How do you start your day or morning? Pop-Tarts? Jogging uniform? Cold shower? Do you perform any rituals before or after you write?

JB: First a two-mile fastwalk (shlumpy clothes, no jogging uniform, but good shoes). Then breakfast. I love breakfast. No, not Pop-Tarts — cereal with bananas and blueberries. Then the (not cold) shower, then to work.

I used to have to clean out all my closets and drawers before I could begin a new book. I'd think up excuse after excuse because beginning is the hardest part for me. I still think up excuses but they have less to do with cleaning out closets.

Describe the chair you sit on when you write.

JB: I live in three places and have different chairs in each. My favorite is in Key West, where I am now. It's vintage leather (a dark aubergine color) with steel arms, feet, and casters.

On Martha's Vineyard, where we spend summers, I work at a picnic table I bought for ten dollars at a yard sale almost twenty years ago. It's painted white, and it's too small for a desk so I spread my papers out on the adjacent bed. My chair is one of those twenty-dollar numbers that come in different colors. Actually, it's very comfortable.

What do you spend your paycheck on? Any airplanes made of solid gold?

JB: Sorry, no airplanes made of gold, although my daughter was a commercial airline pilot — does that count? I don't spend it on cars (my grandson can't believe that I drive around in an old Jeep Wrangler). I do have a thing for nice houses — I'm a nest builder.

Favorite Central American country?

JB: Help! I've never been to a Central American country.

Can you draw a blue duck for us?

JB: No.

That was going to be a trick question, since this section is in black and white. Get it?

JB: Oh. Okay, moving on . . .

Can you draw yourself as a teenager?

JB:

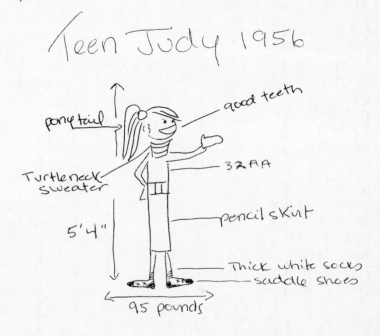

Recent bumper sticker you liked?

    JB: I just saw an ad for one that says *Coexist.*

Where do you see your writing in the next ten years?

    JB: Will I still be writing? If the stories keep coming, yes. Do writers ever retire? Still trying to figure that out. In ten years I'll be . . . (Well, you know I was born in 1938, right?)

Would you happen to have a picture of yourself in a buccaneer outfit?

    JB: Let me see. How's this?

Thank you very much, Judy Blume.

BEST AMERICAN FRONT SECTION

FROM POLICE BLOTTER ITEMS to champion dog names to dozens of end-of-the-world lamentations, the Best American Front Section is the best of the front sections that exist in books like this that you know of. There was a movie named *Tron* released in 1982; it starred Bruce Boxleitner and changed everything.

Best American Police Blotter Items from Kensington, California

FROM *www.aboutkensington.com*

Kensington is an unincorporated community in the San Francisco Bay Area. It is 81.77 percent white and 10.58 percent Asian. Kensington features a median income of $71,278, a poverty rate of 1.7 percent, no post office, and a notoriously bored police force.

A man of "foreign appearance" was reported as being suspicious. He was from Africa visiting a friend.

An Oberlin Ave. couple argued over her purchase of a new kitchen table. He complained to police they always agreed on purchases before making them, but she said she knew he would disapprove so she bought it without telling him. The police listened patiently.

A woman living on Purdue Ave. complained to the police that her neighbor's tree was obstructing her view. Apparently the owner of the view had been topping the tree for years, but the owner of the house had given the house and tree to her daughter, who refused to let the neighbor cut the tree. Civil law suits are being threatened.

A woman who works on Arlington Ave. reported her car was stolen. Seems that her husband had parked it in the BART parking lot and had forgotten about it. They remembered the next day.

A Lake Dr. resident was concerned when they were approached by two teenagers asking for directions to Trinity Ave. They pointed them in the wrong direction, toward Grizzly Peak, and then called the police.

A driver on Highland Blvd. found that someone had placed two tampons on their car. The police recorded it as a suspicious event.

Two people on Columbia Ave. got into an argument about the quality of a language translation of a children's book, which one had done for the other. Police informed them that this was a civil dispute and advised them to settle it amicably or to seek legal counsel.

Neighbors reported a noisy party at 11:30 at night. Police found a couple of families sitting around a fire pit in the backyard of a house on Ardmore. Sometimes people talking in their gardens can be disturbing to neighbors.

A woman on Highgate Rd. called police because she thought that her neighbor had deposited dog poop in her driveway. She claimed to have seen the neighbor looking at her car. A police officer described this ongoing neighborhood situation as a "maturity issue." It is uncertain if he meant that the complainer has not yet grown up or is too old to know what she is doing.

An argument between two brothers escalated until police were called to intervene. It seems one was refusing to clean his room.

A deer cornered a man walking his dog one evening near the Carmelite Nuns Monastery just off Rincon. The deer had man and dog trapped up against the monastery door and would not let them escape. Hoping for a response from the front door, there was nun [*sic*]. The man called police on his cell phone; they found the deer to be continually aggressive. By flashing the police car lights and sounding the siren, police were able to distract the deer and escort the man and dog to the safety of the road, keeping the police car between the wild beast and its quarry.

Ten African American men, wearing suits and ties, on Coventry Rd., were reported to police, who discovered they were Jehovah's Witnesses, spreading the word of God. As they were not selling anything or asking for money, they were allowed to go on their way.

School staff noticed a stranger in the bathrooms at Hilltop School. Police found the lady somewhat confused; at first she thought she was a member of a police SWAT team, but then she decided she wasn't. Police gave her a ride to BART, so she could get home.

A person was reported as being suspicious because he was seen sitting on a step on Ardmore Path and eating a sandwich.

A person on Coventry Rd. reported a suspicious person, after a passerby looked at their home for a few seconds when walking past.

A dispute was reported on Grandview Dr. because a mother wouldn't give her sixteen-year-old daughter the cell phone charger.

Someone going for an interview parked their large BMW in the Sunset View Cemetery parking lot. They returned to find that thieves had made off with a $2,100 Gucci purse, $600 in cash, an $800 camera, $50 lip gloss, a $50 stereo, debit cards, and a junky $10 pair of sunglasses. The keys had been left in the car.

A truck was reported stolen from a Clarence residence. Officers determined it actually had been repossessed.

A suspect was arrested for shoplifting from Tops on Orchard Park Rd. after he pushed a cart filled with $160.17 of assorted merchandise into the parking lot without paying for anything. Eggs, juice, cake mix, frosting, and pork chops were among the goods which the suspect allegedly attempted to steal.

A man took a set of car keys from his ex-wife and left. He said he was upset the vehicle was being sold and just wanted to drive it.

An officer noticed a vehicle pull into an auto service facility on Seneca St. and drive around the back of the building although the business was closed. The driver said he was looking for a place to fix his girlfriend's son's dump truck.

A check was requested on Island Park on Main St. for a middle-aged man that was on the ground moaning. He was practicing yoga.

Best American Things for Sale That This Man on the Internet Will Sell You

FROM *www.davidhorvitz.com*

David Horvitz of New York has created a unique website on which one can pay him to perform various services. The following is a list of items for sale. The grammar is his, and these offers are real.

If you give me $1,626 I will go to the small Okinawan island called Iriomote and send you an envelope filled with star-sand (don't worry, I've been there before, I know where to go). I will send it from there.

If you give me $75 I will go see a psychic and ask them for advice on my life. I will send you a write up of what happened and documentary photographs.

If you give me $1,689 I will go see a psychic, ask them where in the whole world I should go to, and then I will go there. I will mail you documentation of this from where ever it is I go to.

If you give me $9,999 I will go see a psychic and ask them where I SHOULD NOT go to in the whole world. I will then go there and mail you documentation of it from there.

If you give me between $100 to $400 I will find a moon tree and kiss it for you. Do you know what a moon tree is? In 1971 Stuart Roosa was the Apollo 14 Command Module Pilot while his comrades were down on the moon. Stuart, a former smoke jumper, had brought with him hundreds of tree seeds. He wanted to take them to the moon. He wanted to do this because he knew that when he planted the seeds on Earth they would grow as tall as they could because they would want to return to the moon. I will send you a photograph of me kissing a moon tree.

If you give me $3 I will send you an empty envelope. It is like sending you nothing. Or at least, it is sending you something that has traveled a journey that is the distance from me to you.

Jenn Wong has an empty envelope mailed from New York to New York.

Philip Hucknall has an empty envelope mailed from New York to Glasgow.

Chad Cheney has an empty envelope mailed from New York to Battle Ground, WA.

If you give me $30 I will walk around New York, and the first homeless person I see I will buy him or her whatever he or she wants to eat (as long as it is less than $30). I will mail you back the exact change (minus the PayPal fee and the cost of the postage stamp) with the receipt for the food and the name of the person who ate it.

Kris Efland bought a really big Kentucky Fried Chicken meal and an orange drink from Nedick's for Regional Keith on W. 33rd and Broadway on February 24, 2008.

Joie Mikitson bought a bunch of groceries from Park Avenue Food Court for Francis on E. 10th and 4th Ave. on February 25, 2008.

Bart Schouten bought a pizza full of every topping except anchovies from Johns' of Bleeker Street for Marvin who was in the Houston train stop for the 1 on February 28, 2008.

Bart Schouten bought two slices of pizza and a bag of groceries for a man in the F station on 2nd Ave. on February 29, 2008. The situation was too awkward to ask for his name.

Michael bought two bags of food from Whole Foods for Joey who was sitting on Houston on March 2, 2008.

Gary Rutz bought three slices of pizza, cheese cake, and a coffee from Ray's Pizza for Nathon on Houston and Orchard on March 2, 2008.

Paul Hoffman bought Kentucky Fried Chicken and coffee from Dunkin' Donuts for Basima and Bill outside of Grand Central on March 3, 2008.

Lisa Philpotts bought a large bag of food from Citarella for Bookie, who was sitting outside, on March 3, 2008.

If you give me $1 I will sit in silence and think about you for one minute. I will send you an email when I start this, and I'll send you another email when I'm done.

I thought about Moisés Horta from 4:22 A.M. to 4:23 A.M. on February 14, 2008, in New York.

I thought about Vijaychandran Veerachandran from 7:08 P.M. to 7:09 P.M. on February 22, 2008, in New York.

I thought about Chantee Derek Damron from 7:37 P.M. to 7:38 P.M. on February 23, 2008, in New York.

I thought about Andrey Kosarev from 1:21 A.M. to 1:22 A.M. on February 25, 2008, in New York.

I thought about Aaddrick Williams from 1:26 A.M. to 1:27 A.M. on February 25, 2008, in New York.

I thought about Cheeseburger Brown from 12:14 A.M. to 12:15 A.M. on February 26, 2008, in New York.

I thought about Jeff Gordon from 12:18 A.M. to 12:19 A.M. on February 26, 2008, in New York.

I thought about James A. Calwell III from 12:23 A.M. to 12:24 A.M. on February 26, 2008, in New York.

Gary Rutz purchased three minutes worth of thinking about him. I thought about Gary from 2:24 A.M. to 2:27 A.M. on February 27, 2008, in New York.

I thought about Hailina Alter from 2:34 A.M. to 2:35 A.M. on February 27, 2008, in New York. Hailina lives in Perth, Australia, the farthest place away from me!

I thought about Jim Darrough's stepmother, Arleen, who passed away on February 24, 2008, at 3:32 A.M. Pacific Time. Jim was holding her hand at this time. I thought about Arleen from 1:18 A.M. to 1:19 A.M. on February 28, 2008, in New York.

I thought about Erok Johnson from 3:02 A.M. to 3:03 A.M. on February 29, 2008, in New York.

I thought about Luca Kunz from 3:15 A.M. to 3:16 A.M. on February 29, 2008, in New York.

I thought about Emily Jenkins from 10:44 P.M. to 10:45 P.M. on March 2, 2008, in New York.

I thought about Gold Joinee Abad from 2:25 A.M. to 2:26 A.M. on March 4, 2008, in New York.

If you give me $10 I will take a photograph of the sky just for you . . . I will also delete the file so that you will have the only existing copy of that photograph. It's just for you.

Gary Rutz has a sky from March 3, 2008.

Allison Godat has a sky from March 3, 2008.

Marcelo Kertesz has a sky from March 3, 2008.

Rachel Gluzband has a sky for March 4, 2008.

Brittany Liggett has a sky for March 5, 2008.

Katy Nelson has a sky for March 5, 2008.

This one is really serious. I'm scared to do this. But I think I have to. If you give me $10 I will think really hard of someone who I need to apologize to. I will write them a letter of apology. I will make two copies of the letter. I will send one to you and one to the person who I am apologizing to.

Hana Hutchings owns an apology letter to Laura Pearson.

Hyunhye Seo owns an apology letter to Uta Barth.

Brent Goldman owns an apology letter to Jim Isermann.

Kevin Lawler owns an apology letter to Zach Houston.

Stephan Burgess owns an apology letter to Mylinh Nguyen.

Dan Baird owns an apology letter to Jamie Stewart.

Jonathan Feinburg owns an apology letter to Naseem Bazargan.
Alex DeCarli owns an apology letter to Rheal Lewitski.
Jessica Shade owns an apology letter to Jasmine Little.
Simon P. Hayes owns an apology letter to Dori Hana Scherer.
Luca Kunz owns an apology letter to Mana Pirnia.
Lindsay Martin owns an apology letter to Michael Smoler.

If you give me $5 I will write down a secret and mail it to you . . .
This is something you cannot tell anyone.

Nick Ripley owns a secret of mine.
Tomas James Russell owns a secret of mine.
James J. Panegasser owns a secret of mine.
Brian Scranage owns a secret of mine.
Lous D. Walch owns a secret of mine.
Chris Creel owns a secret of mine.
Emma Bolton owns a secret of mine.
Katie Harpestad-Spatuzza owns a secret of mine.
Baudoin Van Humbeeck owns two secrets of mine.
Hannah Chura owns a secret of mine.
Hailina Alter owns a secret of mine.
Gary Rutz owns a secret of mine.
Brent owns a secret of mine.
Tim Quijano owns a secret of mine.

Best American Facebook Groups

FROM *www.facebook.com*

Facebook groups are gatherings where members can share a similar inter-
est, thought, idea, desire, action, memory, hatred, love, wish, or dream.
The goal in joining "groups" is to catalogue all of one's intricacies in a
compact list. This list appears on one's profile as a series of links, which
can be clicked to show more about the group. The following are some of the
more specific groups currently looking for new members.

I Thought You Were Hot Until I Clicked on "View More Pictures"

I Feel Bad When I See Kids on a Leash

If This Group Reaches 15K, Kevin and I Will Have a Pinecone Eat-Off

Catholic School Screwed Me Up, but I'm Still Sending My Kids There

A Bowl of Fruit Punch Just Busted Through My Fucking Wall

I Am Canadian, Therefore I Live in an Igloo and Ride Polar Bears to School

I Beat George W. Bush on the SATs

I Laughed When Rick Santorum's Kids Cried at His Concession Speech

If It Were Really Raining Men, the Ground Would Be Very, Very Bloody

Gay Marriage Killed the Dinosaurs

Beer Pong Is a Game, Beirut Is a War-torn City in Lebanon

Disney Gave Me Unrealistic Expectations about Love

I Feel Relatively Neutral about New York

Collegeboard: A Money-Grubbing Monopoly That Makes Microsoft Seem Like a Charity

Facebook: Where Stalkers Unite

When I Was Your Age, Pluto Was a Planet

When I Was Your Age, There Were Only 150 Pokemon

I Wish My Homework Was Asexual So It Would Do Itself

I Judge You When You Use Poor Grammar

Writing Papers Single-Spaced First Makes My Double-Spaced Result Climactic

Every Time I Walk into Math Class a Little Part of Me Dies

Dear Pennsylvania: Get the Fuck Out of the Left Lane. Love, New Jersey.

I Am a Boy Scout, Therefore I Am a Pyro

I Like Pretending to Text in Awkward Situations

Legalize Dueling

If This Group Reaches 150,000 Members I Will Name My Son Batman

Every Time I Find Out a Cute Boy Is Conservative, a Little Part of Me Dies

Automatic Doors Make Me Feel Like a Jedi

I Have to Sing the ABCs to Know Which Letter Comes Before the Other

The Remus Lupin and Nymphadora Tonks Memorial

I'm Saving Myself for Wild, Passionate, Awkward Honeymoon Sex

Real Friends Kill Friends Who Become Zombies

If 500,000 Join This Group I Will Change My Middle Name to Facebook

It Wasn't Awkward Until You Said "Well, This Is Awkward." Now It's Awkward.

If 1,000,000 People Join, Scotland, Ireland & Wales will INVADE ENGLAND

There's a Good Chance I'm an Alcoholic, but Meh, So Are All My Friends

My Mom Makes Me Clean Up for My Cleaning Lady

My High School Mascot Was a Condom

I Change the Date on Homework So My Teachers Don't Think I Procrastinate

That Waldo Is a Tricky Son of a Bitch

For Every 10,000 People Who Join This Group, I Will BREAK ONE BONE IN MY BODY

If I Fail My Exams, It's Facebook's Fault

Do You Believe in Love at First Sight, or Should I Walk by Again?

Someday I Will Marry a Man Old Enough to Be My Father

If Wikipedia Says It, It Must Be True

When I Found Out the Disney "D" WAS a "D," It Blew My Mind

All I Need to Know in Life, I Learned from Musical Theatre

I Refer to People by Nicknames They Will Never Know

Carol Never Wore Her Safety Goggles. Now She Doesn't Need Them.

For Every Person That Joins This Group . . . It Will Be One Person Larger

The Beyoncé Knowles Institute for Health and Science

The Beard and Unusually Attractive Moustache Appreciation Group

Friends Don't Let Friends Invade Russia with Winter Approaching
EVERY TIME YOU GNARLY SOCALERS CREATE A
  "I HATE NORCAL" GROUP, I REP HARDER
Resistentialists Unite!
Who Needs College When You Have Wikipedia?
I'm Asian, You're Asian, Let's Compare Grades!
Captain Planet Taught Me to Recycle!
I Wish Morgan Freeman Narrated My Life
I Stay Up Late and I Don't Do Anything Productive
Stop Losing Your Fucking Phones
Mr. Miyagi Taught Me How to Fight
. . . So Apparently I'm Going to Hell
I Wikipedia Things I Don't Care about and Work Them into My
  Conversations
You're Not Allowed to Talk about Facebook outside Facebook
If You're OCD and You Know It Wash Your Hands!
A Realistic Assessment of How Many Twelve-Year-Olds You
  Could Beat Up . . .
I Had a Leash When I Was Little
Eighth Graders Need to Back Off Ninth-Grade Guys Especially
  Other People's BFs
I Flip My Pillow Over So I Can Feel the Cold Side When I'm
  Sleeping
I Wasn't Aware That Sexy Ever Left
I Would So Have Sex in the Darkroom
Anti-Snow and Most Things Cold
People Who Suck at Telling Stories Because They Get Distracted
  and Forget the P
Being Bilingual Obviously Makes You a Better Person
I See That You Are Gangster. I Am Pretty Gangster Myself.
I Love How We're Friends on Facebook, but We Don't Actually
  Talk in Person
We Have All Directly or Indirectly (Through Each Other)
  Hooked Up
Every Time I Watch *Titanic* I Hope It Doesn't Sink This Time
When I'm Super Bored, I Go on Facebook and Join Tons of
  Pointless Groups

Best American *New York Times* Headlines from 1907

FROM *the archives of* The New York Times

The New York Times, *founded in 1851, has immaculate archives of every issue published since September 18, 1851. The online archive is searchable by date, author, and subject. In 2007, we searched the December 1907 archives to see what was making headlines one hundred years ago.*

Lightning Set Fire to Gas — Man is Burning

Capt. Winslow to Wed Miss Carrington, who Hit Him with Ball

OKLAHOMA BEER IN SEWER: 2,300 Barrels, Finished After Statehood, are Confiscated

Roosevelt Home Again: Didn't go for Basket Ball, but Had a Good Time, He Says

Bears Loose in a Store — Clerks and Shoppers Panic

Optimism in Berlin — Expectation that American Situation will Improve in the Coming Year

CHINESE KNOW TOO MUCH; Government Stops Instructing Them on Constitutional Government

The Descent of An Electric Ball will Mark 1908 To-night

SUMMER BASEBALL MOST SERIOUS EVIL; More Prone to Abuse than Any Other Sport

PRESIDENT'S QUIET SUNDAY — He Goes to Church, Greets Neighbors, has Shot only Rabbits

HIS BOOTY WAS DYNAMITE: Tramp Finally Laid it Aside and Flinders Suspected a Plot

Is New York Becoming a City of Canyons and Ravines?

Crack Runner Easily Beats Williams on Broad Track

RUM WINS BY 11 VOTES — Union Rejects Prohibition

WON METALS, LOST HUSBAND: The Divorced Woman Roller-Skater Champion

"Old Figgers" May Win if Foraker Defeated by Taft

Have You a Fetich? Most of us Have

Some Favorite Southern Dishes: The Instinct to Obey

FRENCH IMPOLITE TO THEIR WOMEN: League of Men Formed to Reform Their Fellows. TASK WILL BE DIFFICULT.

Women's Suffrage in Australia Followed by Disastrous Results; Men Demoralized

Buried 21 Days, Miners Cheerful

SORRY THE FLEET SAILED: Archbishop Glennon Preaches Against Cruises.

Man Pours Molten Lead into Own Ear: Believed to Have Been Reading Hamlet

Best American Last Sentences of Books of 2007

Members of the Best American Nonrequired Reading *Committee spent three hours in a bookstore, opening 2007 books and copying down the last sentences. This represents only a fairly random sample of titles published in 2007; it is not definitive.*

SHERMAN ALEXIE, *The Absolutely True Diary of a Part-Time Indian*
We didn't keep score.

SHERMAN ALEXIE, *Flight*
Please, call me Michael.

TARIQ ALI, *A Banker for All Seasons*
You'll never get on in life if you take any notice of what people say about you.

MARC ARONSON, *Race*
That pause, that instant of reflection, is the gift given to us by those people of courage who resisted the prejudices of their day; that precious chance to question ourselves is precisely what makes us, all of us, members of the human race.

MAUDE BARLOW, *Blue Covenant*
In Africa, they say, "We don't go to water ponds merely to capture water, but because friends and dreams are there to meet us."

VERONICA BENNETT, *Cassandra's Sister*
"I can do the first, but not the second," said Jane, and closed her eyes.

BENAZIR BHUTTO, *Reconciliation: Islam, Democracy, and the West*
It is time for reconciliation.

MIKITA BROTTMAN, *The Solitary Vice: Against Reading*
What do you think it will be?

JOSEPH BRUCHAC, *The Way*
There is peace within me as I follow THE WAY.

MICHAEL CHABON, *Gentlemen of the Road*
And then they took the first road that led out of the city, unmindful of
whether it turned east or south, their direction a question of no interest to either of them, their destination already intimately known, each
of them wrapped deep in his thick fur robes and in the solitude that
they had somehow contrived to share.

MICHAEL CHABON, *The Yiddish Policemen's Union*
"Brennan," Landsman says. "I have a story for you."

JEROME CHARYN, *Johnny One-Eye*
Peacetime was but a sweet deception, a winter without black drum-
mer boys — there was no end to revolution.

J. M. COETZEE, *Diary of a Bad Year*
Good night, Señor C, I will whisper in his ear: sweet dreams, and
flights of angels, and all the rest.

CAROLINE B. COONEY, *Diamonds in the Shadow*
He came from a family of good teachers.

LAMA SURYA DAS, *Buddha Is as Buddha Does: The Ten Original
Practices for Enlightened Living*
May all that has been prayed for and here affirmed
be realized and accomplished by one and all!

JANICE M. DEL NEGO, *Passion and Poison*
Come out, come out, wherever you are.

KELLY EASTON, *Hiroshima Dreams*
Matt tugs me in close as one explosion after another bursts open,
lighting the upturned faces on the shore, raining over the water, like
everyone having the same dream of night and falling stars.

STEVE ETTLINGER, *Twinkie, Deconstructed*
At least now you know what you're eating.

SUSAN FALUDI, *The Terror Dream: Fear and Fantasy in Post 9/11 America*
September 11 offers us, even now, the chance to revisit that past and reverse that long denial, to imagine a national identity grounded not on virile illusion but on the talents and vitality of all of us equally, men and women both.

ATUL GAWANDE, *Better*
See if you can keep the conversation going.

WILLIAM GIBSON, *Spook Country*
She put the helmet on, turned it on, and looked up, to where Alberto's giant cartoon rendition of the Mongolian Death Worm, its tail wound through the various windows of Bigend's pyramidal aerie like an eel through the skull of a cow, waved imperially, tall and scarlet, in the night.

ALAN GRATZ, *Something Rotten*
"You never do get used to the smell."

DAVID HAJDU, *The Ten-Cent Plague: The Great Comic Book Scare and How It Changed America*
Me and my brother and a lot of people in our generation never got over it.

CHRISTINE HAROLD, *OurSpace: Resisting the Corporate Control of Culture*
This collective autonomy is made possible only by imagining publics not as embattled and atrophied, but as fluctuating, pervasive, and full of creative potential; not as bodies defined by opposition, but as interconnected and active agents who strategically navigate the vast resources of commercial culture and make them their own.

CHRIS HEDGES, *I Don't Believe in Atheists*
And in their words we see the limits of reason and the possibility of religion.

CHRISTOPHER HITCHENS, *God Is Not Great*
To clear the mind for this project, it has become necessary to know the enemy, and to prepare to fight it.

DERRICK JENSEN AND STEPHANIE MCMILLAN, *As the World Burns: 50 Simple Things You Can Do to Stay in Denial*
You might get that chance.

DAVID CLAY JOHNSTON, *Free Lunch: How the Wealthiest Americans Enrich Themselves at Government Expense (and Stick You with the Bill)*
Reform begins with you.

LIEVE JORIS, *The Rebels' Hour*
If anything happens to my family, I'll hold you responsible.

BARBARA KINGSOLVER, *Animal, Vegetable, Miracle*
A nest full of little ding-dongs, and time begins once more.

STEPHEN KINZER, *All the Shah's Men: An American Coup and the Roots of Middle East Terror*
It's too great a responsibility.

E. L. KONIGSBURG, *The Mysterious Edge of the Heroic World*
Definitely.

ANNE LAMOTT, *Grace (Eventually): Thoughts on Faith*
I went outside and sat on the front step with my coffee and looked at the wild orange blossoms of the ginger plants in my garden until it was time to go.

MARGO LANAGAN, *Red Spikes*
Better to stay silent, better always to stay silent, to sit on my bottom among the Clay and fill my mouth with fish.

ED LIN, *This Is a Bust*
Then I hoisted the box onto my shoulder and went upstairs to see if I had gotten something good.

NORMAN MAILER, *The Castle in the Forest*
There may be no answer to this, but good questions still vibrate with honor within.

IAN McEWAN, *On Chesil Beach*
Instead, he stood in cold and righteous silence in the summer's dusk, watching her hurry along the shore, the sound of her difficult progress lost to the breaking of small waves, until she was a blurred, receding point against the immense straight road of shingle gleaming in the pallid light.

BILL McKIBBEN, *Deep Economy*
We have much to fear, and also much to desire, and together our fear and our desire can set us on a new, more promising course.

LARRY McMURTRY, *When the Light Goes*
Then, stopping for gas, he drove back to Arizona, to await the return of his lithe and lovely wife.

MARY B. MORRISON, *Sweeter Than Honey*
Another door was shut in my face.

PAT MURPHY, *The Wild Girls*
That, Verla says, is what writers do.

WALTER DEAN MYERS, *What They Found/Love on 145th Street*
Or what they found.

BARACK OBAMA, *The Audacity of Hope*
My heart is filled with love for this country.

CARL OGLESBY, *Ravens in the Storm: A Personal History of the 1960s Antiwar Movement*
When we crashed, it was from an enormous height.

ANN PATCHETT, *Run*
Maybe he never fully realized how fast she was until he had seen her at a distance, and so the one who was awake went to get the others up so that they could all stand at the window together and watch her run.

STEFAN PETRUCHA, *Teen Inc.*
I doubt that's actually an option, but I'm going to ask just the same.

MICHAEL POLLAN, *In Defense of Food: An Eater's Manifesto*
The cook in the kitchen preparing a meal from plants and animals at the end of this shortest of food chains has a great many things to worry about, but "health" is simply not of one of them, because it is given.

OLIVER SACKS, *Musicophilia*
Music is no luxury to them, but a necessity, and can have a power beyond anything else to restore them to themselves, and to others, at least for a while.

GEORGE SAUNDERS, *The Braindead Megaphone*
Resistance is futile.

MICHAEL SCHEUER, *Marching Toward Hell: America and Islam After Iraq*
Are we? We clearly are not.

STUART SCHUFFMAN, *Guide to Living Cheaply in San Francisco*
I don't really care, but it's here if you want it.

ALICE SEBOLD, *The Almost Moon*
"She's not here!" I heard a policeman yell. "There's no sign of her."

RUSSELL SIMMONS, *Do You*
We believe that we must continue to tell the truth about the street if that is what we know and we must continue to tell the truth about God if that is who we have found.

SUSAN SONTAG, *At the Same Time*
Long live the novelist's task.

WILLIAM T. VOLLMANN, *Riding Toward Everywhere*
The dark windowed locomotive is sinister, the train seemingly about to explode off the wall, leap through the air, and shatter into a shower of red-hot shrapnel.

REBECCA WALKER, *Baby Love: Choosing Motherhood After a Lifetime of Ambivalence*
I have no regrets.

ALAN WEISMAN, *The World Without Us*
Or even that one day — long after we're gone, unbearably lonely for the beautiful world from which we so foolishly banished ourselves — we, or our memories, might surf home abroad a cosmic electromagnetic wave to haunt our beloved Earth.

ZHU WEN, *I Love Dollars: And Other Stories of China*
I was starving — weak with it.

GARRY WILLS, *What the Gospels Meant*
As a whole, with the reverence they derive from the address, yet with the intelligence God gave us to help us find him.

NAOMI WOLF, *The End of America*
Or else we can stop going down this road: We can stand our ground, and fight for our nation, and take up the banner the Founders asked us to carry.

BIL WRIGHT, *When the Black Girl Sings*
And all I can do, I guess, is hope the answer will still be yes.

LLOYD ZIMPEL, *A Season of Fire & Ice*
Smell them oats, thought the boy.

Best American Names of Champion Show Dogs of 2007

FROM *www.akc.org*

The following are all names of American show dogs who competed in dog shows sponsored by the American Kennel Club (AKC) in 2007. Show dogs' names consist of two parts: the first is the name of the kennel at which they were bred, and the second is whatever string of words the owner chooses to add.

Dawnglow Legally Blonde
Riverwatch Frozen Assets
Z'Bee Che Bellina Dante
Gemstone Arachibutyrophobia CD Rae
Kenswith Tiny Planets
Tailwind Papaw Ride 'Em Cowboy
Moongaze Jomyr Some Splainin Ta Do
Nazirs I'm Ya Chunky Monkey
Briarbrooks Copyright
Ma Pat Ma Geoffrey Chaucer
Yumei's Sugar n Spice 4 Xlntoys
B-Mac N Lil People Ragin Cajun
Buff Cap Creslane Arcticmist
Tallyrand Our Daily Bread
Redawg Christofel O'Copprrdg
Dal Mars Moment Like This
Carowynd Creed Bois Du Portugal
Tacara's Down'n'Dirty Escapade
Solo's Drag Queen
Lonestar's Ava Ava Bo Bava
Whispern' Ln' I Shaved My Legs for This
S-K Danson's with the Stars
FC-AFC It's All Over Now Baby Blue
FC Jazztime's Hanging Chad
FC-AFC World Famous Telepath
Nanuke's Snoklassic No Boundaries
Elan Sebring's The Matrix
Whydom Brandywine Monte Q.
DC Shertom's Hardcore
DC/AFC Up N'Adams Super Sioux
Avater's Crusader of Bayshore
Kaleef's Geneva Aeval Achtung
Freedom's Five Star General by Tigris

Best American New Band Names

The following is a list compiled of newly performing and recording bands that to the best of the editors' knowledge were new in 2007.

Angels of Bedlym, Apostle of Hustle, Ashes Divide, The Band of Heathens, Beach House, The Besnard Lakes, Birds and Batteries, Blind Dog Aussie, Blood Orgy, Boxelder, Castles in Spain, Chowder Monkey, Crystle Castles, D'Zo Nutz, Dethklok, Dirty Little Rabbits, Dodobird, Dr. Dog, Dragging an Ox Through Water, Evil Army, The Famous Polka Squad, Foxboro Hottubs, The Fucking Buckaroos, The Great Bloomers, Great Lake Swimmers, Handsome Furs, Harry and the Potters, Health, Hercules and Love Affair, Hey Lover, Horse Feathers, Hossier Daddy, Hydrosonic, Infamous Stringdusters, J.U.S.T.I.C.E., Japanther, Junior Boys, The Knights of Gnarnia, L3-16, Land of Talk, Lights Down Low, The Luyas, The Mighty Quinn, Moska Project, Mouthful of Bees, The Muslims, The Naked Truth, Neon Horse, New Bloods, Ninjasonik, Perfect Citizen, Plants and Animals, Polkadot Cadaver, Rodentina, The Sadies, The Shaky Hands, Shanghai Surprise, The Shareholders, Sikth, Skuff'd Shoes, Sons of Sisters, The Spoon Benders, Stonehigh, Teenwolf, Telefiction, Tinkture, Tokyo Police Club, Truckstop Coffee, Two Girls, One Cup, Two Hours Traffic, Vampire Weekend, The Velvet Bombers, We Be the Echo, Woodhands, The Zoobomba

Best American Ron Paul Facts

FROM *www.ronpaulfacts.com*

Ron Paul, a Republican candidate for president during the 2008 primary, did not manage to win the nomination but did gain a large Internet following. His online disciples, called "Paulites" or, occasionally, "Paultards," raised money for Paul, spread his anti-government, pro-life message, and created a website of "Ron Paul Facts" in the vein of "Chuck Norris Facts."

Ron Paul invented Chuck Norris.

Ron Paul lost his virginity to Susan B. Anthony.

Ron Paul has no alarm clock, but instead wakes every morning to the call of freedom.

Ron Paul doesn't cut taxes. He kills them with his bare hands.

Jesus wears a wrist band that says "What Would Ron Paul Do?"

Ron Paul doesn't go the gym. He stays fit by exercising his civil rights.

Ron Paul delivers babies without his hands. He simply reads them the Bill of Rights and they crawl out in anticipation of freedom.

Ron Paul declared war on the war on drugs.

Ron Paul uses tax returns of U.S. citizens as toilet paper.

Ron Paul is an element on the periodic table.

Ron Paul has so many morals, he has to pay for two seats on a plane.

Ron Paul reproduces asexually.

Ron Paul doesn't pee. He liberates urine.

Ron Paul could lead a horse to water AND convince it to drink, but he doesn't believe the government has the right to so he refuses.

Ron Paul emerged from the womb wrapped in a flag of no more than thirteen stars and stripes.

Ron Paul can turn water into the American flag.

When applied directly to the brain, Ron Paul instantly cures socialism.

Ron Paul doesn't act like a patriot, a patriot acts like Ron Paul.

Ron Paul's tears can shrink government. Too bad he never cries.

Ron Paul let the dogs out. They were being held without due process.

It was going to be called the Paul of Rights.

Ron Paul can believe it's not butter.

When fascism goes to sleep at night, it checks under the bed for Ron Paul.

Ron Paul delivered over 4,000 babies. What is remarkable is that they were all on time, as promised, and under budget.

Best American Kurt Vonnegut Writings

Kurt Vonnegut was born on Armistice Day 1922. He would become one of the most beloved writers of this century, creating countless modern classics and reminding us of what it means to be an American, to be living a life of uninterrupted absurdity, and to speak the truth at a time when it's not popular. This year we mourn his death, looking back at his expansive literary contributions by gathering some of our favorite Vonnegut passages from his fiction and nonfiction.

Player Piano (1952)

If you can do a half-assed job of anything, you're a one-eyed man in the kingdom of the blind.

The Sirens of Titan (1959)

These unhappy agents found what had already been found in abundance on Earth — a nightmare of meaninglessness without end.

The bounties of space, of infinite outwardness, were three: empty heroics, low comedy, and pointless death.

The skeleton was one of Mrs. Rumsford's many bitter and obscure comments on the nasty tricks time and her husband had played on her.

Almost any brief explanation of chrono-synclastic infundibula is certain to be offensive to specialists in the field.

Sometimes I think it is a great mistake to have matter that can think and feel. It complains so. By the same token, though, I suppose that boulders and mountains and moons could be accused of being a little too phlegmatic.

A purpose of human life, no matter who is controlling it, is to love whoever is around to be loved.

The big trouble with dumb bastards is that they are too dumb to believe there is such a thing as being smart.

"Son — they say there isn't any royalty in this country, but do you want me to tell you how to be king of the United States? Just fall through the hole in a privy and come out smelling like a rose."

Unk was at war with his environment. He had come to regard his environment as being either malevolent or cruelly mismanaged. His response was to fight it with the only weapons at hand — passive resistance and open displays of contempt.

You go up to a man, and you say, "How are things going, Joe?" and he says, "Oh fine, fine — couldn't be better." And you look into his eyes, and you see things really couldn't be much worse. When you get right down to it, everybody's having a perfectly lousy time of it, and I mean everybody. And the hell of it is, nothing seems to help much.

Mother Night (1961)

And one thing she did to me was make me deaf to all success stories, the people she saw as succeeding in a brave new world were, after all, being rewarded as specialists in slavery, destruction, and death. I don't consider people who work in those fields successful.

As the war drew to a close, Heinz and I couldn't drink in our pillbox anymore. An eighty-eight was set up in it, and the gun was manned by boys about fifteen or sixteen years old. There was a success story for Heinz's late wife — boys that young, and yet with men's uniforms and a fully-armed death trap all their own.

Say what you will about the sweet miracle of unquestioning faith, I consider a capacity for it terrifying and absolutely vile.

I doubt if there has ever been a society that has been without strong and young people eager to experiment with homicide, provided no very awful penalties are attached to it.

I've always been able to live with what I did. How? Through that simple and widespread boon to mankind — schizophrenia.

"The only chance of my doing something really violent in favor of truth or justice or what have you," I said to my Blue Fairy Godmother, "would lie in my going homicidally insane."

We crossed the deserted parade ground together, dust devils spinning here and there. It was my fancy to think of the dust devils as the spooks of former cadets at the school, killed in the war, returning now to whirl and dance on the parade ground alone, to dance in as unmilitary a fashion as they damn well pleased.

Even my most cherished memories have now been converted into cat-food, glue and liverwurst.

Plagiarism is the silliest of misdemeanors. What harm is there in writing that's already been written? Real originality is a capital crime, often calling for cruel and unusual punishment in advance of the coup de grace.

I confess a ghostly lack in myself. Anything I see or hear or feel or taste or smell is real to me. I am so much a credulous plaything of my senses that nothing is unreal to me.

I have never seen a more sublime demonstration of the totalitarian mind, a mind which might be likened unto a system of years whose teeth have been filed off at random. Such a snaggle-toothed thought machine, driven by a standard or even a substandard libido, whirls with the jerky, noisy, gaudy pointlessness of a cuckoo in hell.

The dismaying thing about the classic totalitarian mind is that any given gear, though mutilated, will have its circumference unbroken sequences of teeth that are immaculately maintained, that are exquisitely machined.

I froze. It was not guilt that froze me. I had taught myself never to feel guilt. It was not a ghastly sense of loss that froze me. I had taught myself to covet nothing. It was not loathing of death that froze me. I had taught myself to think of death as a friend. It was not heartbroken rage against injustice that froze me. I had taught myself that a human being might as well look for diamond tiaras in the gutter as for rewards and punishments that were fair. It was not the thought that God was cruel that froze me. I had taught myself never to expect anything from Him. What froze me was the fact that I had absolutely no reason to move in any direction. What had made me move through so many dead and pointless years was curiosity.

I always know when I tell a lie, am capable of imagining the cruel consequences of anybody's believing my lies, know cruelty is wrong. I could no more lie without noticing it than I could unknowingly pass a kidney stone.

We are what we pretend to be, so we must be careful what we pretend to be.

"There are plenty of good reasons for fighting," I said, "but no good reason ever to hate without reservation, to imagine that God Almighty Himself hates with you, too. Where's evil? It's that large part of every man that wants to hate without limit, that wants to hate with God on its side."

"You hate America, don't you?" she said. "That would be as silly as loving it," I said. "It's impossible for me to get emotional about it, because real estate doesn't interest me. It's no doubt a great flaw in my personality, but I can't think in terms of boundaries. Those imaginary lines are as unreal to me as elves and pixies. I can't believe that they mark the end or the beginning of anything of real concern to the human soul. Virtues and vices, pleasures and pains cross boundaries at will."

Cat's Cradle (1963)

Call me Jonah. My parents did, or nearly did. They called me John.

"If you find your life tangled up with somebody else's life for no very logical reasons," writes Bokonon, "that person may be a member of your *karass*."

Anyone unable to understand how a useful religion can be founded on lies will not understand this book either.

Midget, Midget, Midget, how he struts and winks for he knows a man's as big as what he hopes and what he thinks.

There is love enough in this world for everybody, if people will just look. I am proof of that.

We talked about phonies. We talked about truth. We talked about gangsters; we talked about business. We talked about the nice poor people who went to the electric chair; and we talked about the rich bastards who didn't. We talked about religious people who had perversions. We talked about a lot of things.

She hated people who thought too much. At that moment, she struck me as an appropriate representative for almost all mankind.

New knowledge is the most valuable commodity on earth. The more truth we have to work with, the richer we become.

Sometimes I wonder if he wasn't born dead. I never met a man who was less interested in the living. Sometimes I think that's the trouble with the world: too many people in high places who are stone-cold dead.

"No wonder kids grow up crazy. A cat's cradle is nothing but a bunch of X's between somebody's hands, and little kids look and look and look at all those X's . . . " "And?" "No damn cat, and no damn cradle."

"Maturity," Bokonon tells us, "is a bitter disappointment for which no remedy exists, unless laughter can be said to remedy anything."

I remembered The Fourteenth Book of Bokonon, which I had read in its entirety the night before. The Fourteenth Book is entitled, "What Can a Thoughtful Man Hope for Mankind on Earth, Given the Experience of the Past Million Years?" It doesn't take long to read The Fourteenth Book. It consists of one word and a period. This is it: "Nothing."

I do not say that children at war do not die like men, if they have to die. To their everlasting honor and our everlasting shame, they do die like men, thus making possible the manly jubilation of patriotic holidays. But they are murdered children all same.

"Beware of the man who works hard to learn something, learns it, and finds himself no wiser than before," Bokonon tells us. "He is full of murderous resentment of people who are ignorant without having come by their ignorance the hard way."

Let us start our Republic with a chain of drug stores, a chain of grocery stores, a chain of gas chambers, and a national game. After that, we can write our Constitution.

God Bless You, Mr. Rosewater (1965)

Pretend to be good always, and even God will be fooled.

Hello, babies. Welcome to Earth. It's hot in the summer and cold in the winter. It's round and wet and crowded. At the outside, babies, you've got about a hundred years here. There's only one rule that I know of, babies — "God damn it, you've got to be kind."

Slaughterhouse-Five (1969)

All time is all time. It does not change. It does not lend itself to warnings or explanations. It simply is. Take it moment by moment, and you will find that we are all, as I've said before, bugs in amber.

How nice — to feel nothing, and still get full credit for being alive.

So it goes.

The most important thing I learned on Tralfamadore was that when a person dies he only appears to die. He is still very much alive in the past, so it is very silly for people to cry at his funeral. All moments, past, present and future, always have existed, always will exist. The Tralfamadorians can look at all the different moments just that way we can look at a stretch of the Rocky Mountains, for instance. They can see how permanent all the moments are, and they can look at any moment that interests them. It is just an illusion we have here on Earth that one moment follows another one, like beads on a string, and that once a moment is gone it is gone forever.

Breakfast of Champions (1973)

Teachers of children in the United States of America wrote this date on blackboards again and again, and asked the children to memorize it with pride and joy: 1492. The teachers told the children that this was when their continent was discovered by human beings. Actually, millions of human beings were already living full and imaginative lives on the continent in 1492. That was simply the year in which sea pirates began to cheat and rob and kill them.

New knowledge is the most valuable commodity on earth. The more truth we have to work with, the richer we become.

What is time? It is a serpent which eats its tail.

"We are healthy only to the extent that our ideas are humane."

Slapstick (1976)

History is merely a list of surprises. . . . It can only prepare us to be surprised yet again. Please write that down.

If you can do no good, at least do no harm.

Love is where you find it. I think it is foolish to go looking for it, and I think it can often be poisonous.

I wish that people who are conventionally supposed to love each other would say to each other, when they fight, "Please — a little less love, and a little more common decency."

Jailbird (1979)

I still believe that peace and plenty and happiness can be worked out some way. I am a fool.

"That was the strength of the Nazis," she said. "They understood God better than anyone. They knew how to make him stay away."

Deadeye Dick (1982)

This is my principal objection to life, I think: It is too easy, when alive, to make perfectly horrible mistakes.

My wife has been killed by a machine which should never have come into the hands of any human being. It is called a firearm. It makes the blackest of all human wishes come true at once, at a distance: that something die. There is evil for you. We cannot get rid of mankind's fleetingly evil wishes. We can get rid of the machines that make them come true. I give you a holy word: DISARM.

Galápagos (1985)

Mere opinions, in fact, were as likely to govern people's actions as hard evidence, and were subject to sudden reversals as hard evidence could never be. So the Galápagos Islands could be hell in one moment and heaven in the next, and Julius Caesar could be a statesman in one moment and a butcher in the next, and Ecuadorian paper money could be traded for food, shelter, and clothing in one moment and line the bottom of a birdcage in the next, and the universe could be created by God Almighty in one moment and by a big explosion in the next — and on and on.

Bluebeard (1987)

I've got news for Mr. Santayana: we're doomed to repeat the past no matter what. That's what it is to be alive.

Time is liquid. One moment is no more important than any other and all moments quickly run away.

Hocus Pocus (1990)

During my three years in Vietnam, I certainly heard plenty of last words by dying American footsoldiers. Not one of them, however, had illusions that he had somehow accomplished something worthwhile in the process of making the Supreme Sacrifice.

Another flaw in the human character is that everybody wants to build and nobody wants to do maintenance.

[Freedom of speech] isn't something somebody else gives you. That's something you give to yourself.

Just because some of us can read and write and do a little math, that doesn't mean we deserve to conquer the Universe.

Timequake (1997)

It appears to me that the most highly evolved earthling creatures find being alive embarrassing or much worse.

Let us be perfectly frank for a change. For practically everybody, the end of the world can't come soon enough.

I heard the poet Robert Pinsky give a reading this summer, in which he apologized didactically for having had a much nicer life than normal. I should do that, too.

I still think up short stories from time to time, as though there were money in it. The habit dies hard.

They say the first thing to go when you're old is your legs or your eyesight. It isn't true. The first thing to go is parallel parking.

He commented unfavorably on the camouflage suits our own generals wear nowadays on TV, when they describe our blasting the bejesus out of some Third World country because of petroleum. "I can't imagine," he said, "any part of the world where such garish pajamas would make a soldier less rather than more visible."

I say in lectures in 1996 that fifty percent or more of American marriages go bust because most of us no longer have extended families. When you marry somebody now, all you get is one person. I say that when couples fight, it isn't about money or sex or power. What they're saying is, "You're not enough people!"

In the third edition of *The Oxford Dictionary of Quotations*, the English poet Samuel Taylor Coleridge (1772–1834) speaks of "that willing suspension of disbelief for the moment, which consumes poetic faith." This acceptance of balderdash is essential to the enjoyment of poems, and of novels and short stories, and dramas, too. Some assertions by writers, however, are simply too preposterous to be believed.

A ballerina, dancing on her toes, went deedly-deedly-deedly into the wings as she was supposed to do. But then there was a sound backstage as though she had put her foot into a bucket and then gone down an iron stairway with her foot still in the bucket.

I instantly laughed like hell.

I was the only person to do so.

I would have accepted it. I would have recognized the opportunity for a world-class joke, but would never allow myself to be funny at the cost of making somebody else look like something the cat drug in.

Let that be my epitaph.

No matter what a young person thinks he or she is really hot stuff at doing, he or she is sooner or later going to run into somebody in the same field who will cut him or her a new asshole, so to speak.

Listen: We are here on Earth to fart around. Don't let anybody tell you any different.

I feel and think much as you do, care about many of the things you care about, although most people don't care about them. You are not alone.

Guess what? TV is an eraser.

That there are devices such as firearms, as easy to operate as cigarette lighters and as cheap as toasters, capable at anybody's whim of killing Father or Fats or Abraham Lincoln or John Lennon or Martin Luther King, Jr., or a woman pushing a baby carriage, should be proof enough for anybody that, to quote the old science fiction writer Kilgore Trout, "being alive is a crock of shit."

I say in speeches that a plausible mission of artists is to make people appreciate being alive at least a little bit. I am then asked if I know of any artists who pulled that off. I reply, "The Beatles did."

I am eternally grateful . . . for my knack of finding in great books, some of them very funny books, reason enough to feel honored to be alive, no matter what else might be going on.

A Man Without a Country (2005)

I saw the destruction of Dresden. I saw the city before and then came out of an air-raid shelter and saw it afterward, and certainly one response was laughter. God knows, that's the soul seeking some relief.

I think that novels that leave out technology misrepresent life as badly as Victorians misrepresented life by leaving out sex.

I wanted all things to seem to make some sense, so we could all be happy, yes, instead of tense. And I made up lies, so they all fit nice, and I made this sad world a paradise.

Do realize that all great literature — *Moby-Dick, Huckleberry Finn, A Farewell to Arms, The Scarlet Letter, The Red Badge of Courage, The Iliad* and *The Odyssey, Crime and Punishment, The Bible,* and "The Charge of the Light Brigade" — are all about what a bummer it is to be a human being? (Isn't it such a relief to have somebody say that?)

First rule: Do not use semicolons. There are transvestite hermaphrodites representing absolutely nothing. All they do is show you've been to college.

If you want to really hurt your parents, and you don't have the nerve to be gay, the least you can do is go into the arts. I'm not kidding. The arts are not a way to make a living. They are a very human way of making life more bearable. Practicing an art, no matter how well or badly, is a way to make your soul grow, for heaven's sake. Sing in the shower. Dance to the radio. Tell stories. Write a poem to a friend, even a lousy poem. Do it as well as you possibly can. You will get an enormous reward. You will have created something.

That specific remedy for the worldwide epidemic of depression is a gift called the blues.

My last words? "Life is no way to treat an animal, not even a mouse."

I was once asked if I had any ideas for a really scary reality TV show. I have one reality show that would really make your hair stand on end: "C-Students from Yale."

What you respond to in any work of art is the artist's struggle against his or her limitations.

Our daily news sources, newspapers and TV, are now so craven, so unvigilant on behalf of the American people, so uninformative, that only in books do we learn what's really going on.

All I really wanted to do was give people the relief of laughing. Humor can be a relief, like an aspirin tablet. If a hundred years from now people are still laughing, I'd certainly be pleased.

Can I tell you the truth? I mean this isn't the TV news is it? Here's what I think the truth is: We are all addicts of fossil fuels in a state of denial. And like so many addicts about to face cold turkey, our leaders are now committing violent crimes to get what little is left of what we're hooked on.

My father said, "When in doubt, castle."

Best American Diary of a Young Girl (aka My Massive Feelings)

LAURIE WEEKS

FROM *Vice Magazine*

The diary below comes from the second annual fiction issue of Vice *Magazine. Although inspired by some real-life events, it is fictional.*

Dear Sylvia Plath:
  Hi I am fourteen and I know you're dead but it's 1 A.M. and my dad is swearing and falling around in the pool like a drunken pork sausage, what a fucking asshole, I was standing in the kitchen two seconds ago with a butcher knife to go kill him before he shoots us to death, but I chickened out, which I know your dad was a problem too so I could totally relate to your poems about how he's a Nazi who kept you living in his boot even though I basically hated poetry until this minute, so I'm just writing this fake letter because NOW HE'S GETTING OUT OF THE POOL LIKE A MONSTER AND SAYING FUCK, Jesus Christ Sylvia, if you could hear him, it's like he's not even human. Now he just massively fell back in, Achtung you Nazi motherfucker, just drown and get it over with so I can RELAX. Listen, Sylvia, I can't believe you stuck your head in that oven, you crazy nut! I'm completely terrified to die, even though vastly depressed. There is so little time in this life to do what you want, more on that later.

I had to look out the window because it got all quiet but he's just slumped over in the grass like an ape. It's sad but fuck him. Anyway, Sylvia, I've been tortured about dying for years, ever since reading *Little Women* made me realize we're all doomed and ruined my life. But, one day however, I opened your book *The Bell Jar* and literally died of shock. For the first time I saw someone in a book portraying emotions that were exactly mine, I never even knew it was okay to write about them! I never would have figured it out by myself. Like when you said how the tulips were breathing I realized I always saw them breathing too but I was in denial. Oh my god I fucking HATE feeling bad for him after he just scared the shit out of me all night, I try not to but I can't handle him being all lonely in the grass like that, he seems so ashamed and confused, like he doesn't know what's happening and no one can help. I don't want him to slip and die for real, just knock himself out a little so I can sleep. Even though then I'll dream he's chasing us with the gun but whatever. I always want to tell him don't worry, it's not your fault, everyone loves you, we'll figure out how to make it stop. But I CAN'T, being insane and not human when he's like this you can't get him to make sense, plus no way am I going out there alone, he's like a bear who never learned English and seems sweet and nice when you pet him, but all of a sudden you feel a fang in your brain and a massive cracking sound blasts your eyes out, as slowly you realize your head is being crushed to death in his rampaging jaws!

Sylvia, there's so much to express but it's a school night, I will tell you more later. IF I am still alive tomorrow. How perfect would it be if my dad killed me tonight and they found this letter under my body, all smeared with blood!!

Dear Sylvia Plath,

Like you, I have been sensitive and depressed all my life. Ever since Beth went out with the tide in *Little Women*, my mind has been a dark chamber full of death. But did or does anyone hear my choking sobs of entrapment? Answer, No. My debate teacher Mr. Walker ("Greg") is this amazing person, age twenty-four. His hands express gently and he really likes your poems, which the only other guy I know who does is my friend Russ Marcus, he smokes pot in his car.

We hang out in the parking lot every day during social studies and even though he's totally hilarious and nice to me he's still popular. Well, there's this depressed older girl Marla in the other debate class. Greg's always saying in his caring way how sensitive and brilliant she is because she's depressed and writes poems for the literary magazine. I've only read one poem by her, about a spider. I didn't really get it. And even though she's in Debate I barely know her because she's too sensitive to compete. Greg says she's too shy and can't handle very much except reading Emily Dickinson. This is just so frustrating because I'm unbelievably shy too on the inside, but he doesn't understand. We talk about your poems and everything but I don't know what to say that's intelligent. I've been trying to show my depression more so he will see I'm smart but basically all I do is joke around with him like one of the guys, he's hilarious plus I get a little hyper from boys shooting me with spitballs during Rebuttal. I wish I looked more tiny and delicate, why am I always laughing even though worried about being murdered? (By my dad mostly, but basically anyone.)

Well I have been giving a lot of thought to this one poem where you go, *Love, love, my season.* A man such as Greg has not run across my path before and now that I am in my Season of Love you have helped me a lot. When the Season first started I was overwhelmed by torture. Yet Sylvia, you made me see how suffering is beautiful, instead of getting down on myself. Fuck Emily Dickinson. Even though I've never read her I'm at least as depressed as Marla. Also, not to be mean, I know how the spider is a metaphoric bug of sadness etc., but whatever. It still seems like poetry is mostly for assholes, no offense, but I'm trying to get past that.

I think Greg will see the pain behind my laughing façade if I can write like you. But not LOOK like you, ha!! I'm sorry, you can't help it that you were in the '50s with those hairstyles or whatever. I picture you like Jacqueline Bisset, except with glasses. Does that sound shallow? I guess that sounds shallow. Don't worry, I don't need to be attracted to you to like your writing. But it would help. Not that I'm a lesbian. I just need these visual aids to get into it or something. What am I talking about, I'm grossing myself out. I don't think anything about anything. You're dead and this fake piece of shit is over.

Dear Ms. Plath:

Please forgive me for troubling you when you have no idea whom I am, and of course you mustn't feel the need to answer as this is doubtlessly one amongst thousands of letters from your admirers. But, anyway I recently had the pleasure of being introduced #1 to *The Bell Jar*, #2 to *your poems*, respectively. I found myself quite moved, to my surprise, I never knew there was a poet as superior and perceptive as yourself. I am unfortunate to be trapped in a small farming town in the middle of NOWHERE much like *Jane Eyre* where we only get four channels with nothing edifying. I deeply adore and write poems thanks to you which Mrs. Gunn my French teacher says are quite interesting, but please don't think me immodest for I know they suck. I am surrounded by oafs who are nice to me unless I act like I like or love them for example *Mr. Jim Tedeschi* but fuck him he's simple country folk, forgive my language, often I am swept by tantrums, being tempestuous.

To get to the one worthless bookstore, Mother must drive me to the mall on the freeway that stretches like a flat black tongue through the hellish corn. The people rise from the dead to drive their glittering cars like shattered cries speeding into the throat of madness. Like you I am masticated in the grinding jaws of endless thoughts of death. One example is I couldn't drink out of a glass when I was seven because I thought glass would come off and slide down my throat, bleeding to death. If anyone is reading this in the future because they are writing my biography or snooping in my room as usual, looking for fake reasons to punish me, this part of my journal is private and not for publication. I am just thinking out loud because unfortunately I am surrounded by zombies who care nothing for inspiration and passion, just pheasant hunting and vacuuming. Saying how negative I am every time I say something true like how commercials on TV are total lies and people are sheep. And speaking of lies this is not being written because I am smoking pot as I am constantly accused of by a person or persons who say they can smell it on my personage when I come home, which is a total paranoid falsehood. It just so happens that my pot smoking is for purely personal reasons ONLY, being totally unrelated to my diaries or other creativity ventures.

So my point AS A STRAIGHT A STUDENT with many extra-curricular activities such as Marching Band and Jazz Band is that I smoke pot in my usual responsible way and not as the lazy criminal who feeds off of society, nor also for some meaningless high, but rather as a positive thing that INCREASES MY PRODUCTIVENESS by slowing my brain down enough to sit still without being carpet bombed by a herd of worrying about tumors and where is Dad.

> Blood is spurting like a seizure
> Do you not hear the tulips
> screaming in the vortex?
> The carefree child became a monster
> No more shall the small bee merrily prance

> *Or . . .*
> The carefree child became a monster
> Porcine bees come blasting
> from a shotgun
> Pierced by knives of cruelty
> Like a voodoo doll that everyone is stabbing
>   with pins for no reason

> *Is this one better?*
> Carefree child you are a monster
>   Or so the zombies say
> Whom once was an innocent baby
>   Explodes in the screaming vortex
> Stabbed by the prancing nightmares
>   Of a voodoo doll in a bloody seizure

> *Maybe this??*
> See the bloody Voodoo child of seizures
> Laugh at her hanging naked
> from your inscrutable rope
> Do you not hear her stygian screams
> Above the malodorous vortex?

That is filled with the
snapping bones of Madness?

Snapping Madness
Of Bones?

Madness of snapping
Bones?

God, poetry is HARD. Trying to find the perfect way to express the visions trapped inside me is like being a tiny bird pecking against the stone mountain of eternity. How can I be a madly brilliant artist with burning eyes and arms like sticks if I can't even have a nervous breakdown! If someone would think to take me to a psychiatrist like Sylvia Plath, the truth of my invisible SOS would be revealed by an EXPERT, PROVING this hellhouse. But no. Being so burnt out from planning the vacuuming schedule, the only thing you see is pot. Making up excuses to punish me for no reason WHAT-EVER, it never occurs to you that a girl with massive feelings about this magic life might stay in her bedroom all the time because like all serious artists she is depressed, for example by all the sadness and death in the world, starting with CERTAIN THINGS IN THIS HOUSE!!!!!

Also I wonder why this person or persons thinks they know what pot smells like because there is no way certain parties have ever been within walking distance of a joint. I'm too stupid to know you obviously hate me because I know all your friends stay drunk so they don't have to face the fact that their lives are meaningless even though they have a pool.

As I write this, Sylvia, my parents hurtle toward death in their sleep, strangled by the scarves of apathy wrapping their nose. I sit on my bed surrounded by the accoutrements of my lost childhood, looking out my window.

The moon is weeping in the window
of my prison cell

Where I am swinging naked
                              (in a noose)
    above the
            Bones
                  of
                      Snapping
                                Madness

                                              Where
                                              is
                                              the
                            ghostly lover
                who
                will
                be
                my
                        phantom teacher
Do you not see me BURN?!

Your initials are enigmatic
                          Your first name rhymes with Egg . . .

Yes I am haunted!
            Yes! How I yearn
                          for you to get this rope off of my
                                                    Neck
so I can suffocate
            in your lugubrious
                                caress

Best American Diary of the Living Dead or: Are You There God? It's Me. Also, a Bunch of Zombies

JAKE SWEARINGEN

FROM *www.pindeldyboz.com*

The diary below comes from the online literary journal Pindeldyboz. *It is fictional.*

DAY 1: Turns out all those reports about a riot at the cemetery were kinda right. Zombies pretty much everywhere now. Holed up in my office building with some other survivors. Temping is the fucking worst. The one day I leave my iPod at home, too. Bored. Cute girl trapped in here with us — apparently her fiancé got bit and she had to smash his head in with her car door. Want to comfort her, or at least share my ration of Cheez-Its with her. Too soon?

DAY 2: We've got about forty people in here with us now. My coworkers have claimed the cubicles, but I was a temp. I spent the first night sleeping in the lobby with the custodial staff and a UPS guy. One of the janitors has night terrors, and the UPS guy is kind of a grabber, so I'm thinking of moving into the supply closet. A zombie somehow got in last night, we had to chase it down. Daryl, he's our leader now I guess, cut off its head with the blade from one of those paper cutters. I smashed the head with a microwave from the break room, but everyone still thought Daryl was the big hero. What the hell? That head still could have bitten someone. Cute girl's name is Mary.

DAY 3: Split my bag of Sour Cream and Onion Lay's with Mary today. She's a nurse. I talked about how I think helping people is important. She sat next to me while Daryl gave a speech about needing to work together and precautions we should take to keep zombies from getting in. Speech sounded pretty rehearsed to me. Mary volunteered her services if anyone was hurt. She's so sweet.

DAY 4: Big invasion of zombies kept us pretty busy. We think they're getting smarter, because they managed to figure out how to open the front door. Four people ended up getting bit, which, you know, bummer. I used Daryl's paper-cutter blade to cut off the head of one of them before they became a zombie, and now I'm the bad guy or something. It's like people wanted to wait for the guy to become a zombie before we killed him. I thought we were all in agreement: we don't want zombies inside the office complex, period. Whatever. Also, why is it Daryl's paper-cutter blade? Shouldn't it be for everyone to use? Mary refuses to talk to me now.

DAY 5: Pretty quiet today. Vending machine ran out of everything except gum today, and there was a pretty severe fistfight over the gum. There's another office building across the parking lot, and I volunteered to try to make it over there and stock up on food. I was disappointed that no one tried to stop me, or even come along. Mary and Daryl seem to have spent last night together. Sometimes I look out at all the walking corpses outside the window and envy them.

DAY 6: After arguing with Daryl for thirty minutes that a staple gun would not be "pretty much the same thing" as the paper-cutter blade, I finally just grabbed it from him and went out the front door. Nearly got bit a few times, but the zombies are pretty slow and stupid. But then it turns out there's a separate band of survivors in the other building. They, understandably, didn't want to give up the food they had. Seeing that there was only about five of them, and that they didn't seem like big assholes like *some* survivors I could name, I decided to cast my lot in with them.

DAY 7: Well the other office building is pretty steamed I guess. They're hanging a sign out the window that says BRING US FOOD YOU SAID YOU WOULD and then underneath it says "and the paper cutter too you theif [*sic*]." And it's just like, you know, whatever. I'm thinking of maybe getting like one packet of Gardetto's and throwing it outside their door, just to see if they'll risk it. To celebrate me being a part of the new office building, we all split one of those fruit pies. It was apple. Pretty tasty.

DAY 8: More signs out the window, more conciliatory in nature. VERY HUNGRY PLEASE BRING US PROVISONS [again, *sic*]. Tom, who's the leader over here, wants to negotiate with them. I argued against. Those other guys are pricks.

DAY 9: No signs from the other office building today. We've been talking. Linda thinks the zombies will starve to death. I pointed out that they're already dead. I think that if, God forbid, one of the zombies bit Linda it would take about three seconds for her to become brain dead. Tom thinks we have enough food to last another two weeks. We found an old radio and some batteries today. Most of the stations are off the air, but one is playing "Time of the Season" over and over. Y'know, by the Zombies? Hilarious. I hope they ate the fuck out that DJ's brains. Wonder what's happening in the other office building?

DAY 10: All quiet on the western front. Tom, for some goddamned reason, has a guitar with him. Turns out he was the leader of his church's youth group before all this went down, and he knows some hymns. Like, a lot of hymns. Really missing that iPod.

DAY 12: Long time, no write. So, basically we're at war, I guess? Daryl and those homos in the other office building tried to storm our building two days ago. It would have worked except for 1) we locked the front doors and barricaded them with desks and 2) all the FUCKING ZOMBIES WANTING TO EAT YOUR BRAINS YOU BRAINDEAD MORON DARYL. I'd say about half of them got bit during the first assault and then they had to retreat and also keep out those who got bit. It was all pretty interesting to watch from the rooftop. The second time, though, they had the desk from reception and used it to sort of do like a flying wedge maneuver through the zombies, and that worked pretty well, and then they managed to break the glass and actually get inside the building. At this point it was about seventeen of them, and only six of us, and things weren't looking good. But Tom had the pretty sweet idea to do these, like, counter-weight swinging things with some of the copiers, with trip ropes and stuff like that. I guess it was for the zombies, but they worked against people too. So we barricaded them down in the lobby basically, and that's where they're at right now. I can hear Daryl still talking big talk right now. I bet if I threw down his precious paper cutter, it would be about, oh, five seconds before one of the others grabbed it and thunked it into his skull. Lunch: four pieces of beef jerky with a half can of Tab (they still make it!).

Day 13: Trouble at the homestead. Tom wants to offer amnesty to the people trapped below, work out some system and maybe try to make a plan for how to get more food or something. Basically work together, share, all that shit. Me, I guess I'd be for it, but only if they toss Daryl first. I explained to Tom that Daryl would just try to run everything anyways, and I think he was receptive to my input. If nothing else we need to figure out something for sanitation down there, at least give them a bucket to go in or something.

Day 14: Whelp, I fucked up. Tom and Daryl got to talking and reached some sort of agreement last night. They want to mount an expedition using Linda's minivan to a grocery store, get supplies, medicine, all that kind of stuff. So the others took down the barricade, over my objections. And I guess I would have learned to deal with it, except that when Daryl came up, Mary was hanging off his arm and he held out his hand for the paper cutter with this fucking smirk on his face, and I saw this red mist come down over my eyes and the next thing I know Daryl is holding his face and he's real pissed and Mary and everyone else is yelling and there's blood everywhere. Just everywhere. Long story short, I was able to hold everyone off until I made it out the door, and now I'm back where I started, in the original office complex, by myself. Luckily I had a thing of Combos in my pocket, so I've got a little food, but it won't last long. I dunno. Still have the paper cutter, but I think it's one of those hollow victories. Wish I had a television or something.

DAY 15: The minivan left and came back, so guess it was Mission Accomplished or whatever. I can hear them across the way. Saw Daryl, big bandage on his face, but seems to be okay. I thought I saw them unload a case of Busch Lite too. They turned up the radio and I can hear "Time of the Season" floating over from the other building. Bastards. Hungry.

DAY 16: Still hungry. Playing trashcan basketball. My record right now is 782 for 1,567. Found a pint of gin someone stashed in a desk drawer. Gonna get wasted.

DAY 17: Turns out hangovers when you haven't eaten in two days are a real bear. Went through break room systematically, found the seasoning packet for ramen noodles. Put it on some steamed printer paper. Tasted pretty much like ramen noodles, honestly.

DAY 18: Guess what? I'm out. Spent most of last night watching the zombies shuffle around and the people move around across the way. I suppose I could probably go back over, beg and whine and grovel and all that happy horseshit and maybe they'd let me back in, but look: the zombies aren't going away. This survivor thing is gonna last, maximum, one or two months. And then it's starvation or suicide or becoming a zombie. So here's what I'm gonna do: I'm gonna drink the rest of this gin, and then I'm gonna go outside and get bit, and then me and the zombies, we're just gonna chill. We're gonna wait. Sooner or later, they're gonna come outside. Or we'll get inside. After that, we'll go storm a church or something. I dunno. We've got time.

MARJORIE CELONA

∎

Y

FROM *Indiana Review*

THAT PERFECT LETTER. THE wishbone, fork in the road, empty wineglass. The question we ask over and over. Why? Me with my arms outstretched, feet in first position. The chromosome half of us don't have. Second to last in the alphabet: almost there. Coupled with an *L*, let's make an adverb. A modest X, legs closed. *Y* or *N*? Yes, of course. Peace sign reversed. Mercedes Benz without the *O*.

Y, a Greek letter, joined the Latin alphabet after the Romans conquered Greece in the first century — a double agent: consonant and vowel. No one used adverbs before then, and no one was happy.

My life begins at the Y. I am born and left in front of the glass doors, and even though the sign is flipped closed, a man is waiting in the parking lot and he sees my mother hunch and kiss my cheek — a furtive peck like a small bird — and when I grab for her hair, she stands and scoots away. She doesn't look back so the man watches her turn the corner onto Quadra Street and disappear into the cemetery beside the cathedral. It's 4:45 A.M. She's dead to me, all at once. The man wishes so badly I weren't there that he could scream it — he's always the one who notices the handkerchief drop from an old woman's purse and has to chase her halfway down the block, waving it like a flag. Every twitch of his eye shows him something he doesn't want to see: a forgotten lunch bag, the daily soup spelled dialy, a patent shoe about to step in shit. *Wait! Watch out, buster!* All this sloppiness, unfinished business. Me. I'm so small he thinks "minute" when he squats and cocks his head. My young mother has wrapped me in her favorite sweatshirt because it's cold this time of day and I'm naked, just a few hours old and jaundiced: a small, yellow thing.

The man unfolds the sweatshirt a bit, searching for a note or signs of damage. He's trying to form the sentences he'll have to say when he pounds the door and calls for help. "Hey, there's a baby here! A baby left by her mother — I think — I was waiting for the doors to open, she put the baby here and walked away, young girl, not good with ages, late teens I guess? There's a baby here, right here. Oh, I didn't look." He looks. "It's a girl."

There's a small search. The police mill around and take a description from the man, who tells them his name is Vaughn and that he likes to be the first in the door at the Y in the morning, that it's like a little game with him.

"Gotta be first at something, guy," he says to the cop.

They sketch my mother but don't quite get it: Vaughn thinks her hair was short, but she had it in a small bun at the nape of her neck. When she takes it out, it falls to her collarbone. He says she was wearing a pair of navy coveralls — he gets that part right — and she didn't look homeless, just scared and young. He wants to know if I'm okay, but the cop can't answer. Some lady pushes through the crowd of officers and people in sweatpants; she swirls her arms like a windmill and her mouth opens like a cave.

"Ma baby!" She shrieks and sets her grocery bags in a lump at her feet. "Ma little *bambina! Non ce la facciamo più!*" Her body hiccups and her head jerks. The cops roll their eyes and so does Vaughn. She's the quarter lady — the one who descends when you plug the meter: "Eh *amico*, got a quarta'?" Her red hair's like those wigs at Safeway when you forget it's Halloween. If she had wings, she'd look ethereal.

What she said to me: *we can't stand it any longer; we can't go on like this.*

I am adopted immediately, but my new parents don't baptize me because they aren't religious. They name me Shandi and we live in a brown apartment on Harrison Street. They've been told I passed the tests okay, but that they should watch for signs of distress, so they do. My new mother, Raquelle, searches my face and body for abnormality. I don't cry much and my new father, Par, discovers that I fall asleep if he sings the national anthem, which is all he can think of when Raquelle suggests he sing me lullabies.

"Ohhh, Caa-nada," he croons. He's Turkish, moved here to start a restaurant. He thinks true patriot love is all one word. He sings it fast and doesn't know what it means.

"She's going to be a model," Raquelle decides because I'm a thin baby and a bit longer than average. "Top model. Superstar!"

"Nah," says Par. "I would like for her to work in trades. This is where money's at. Plumber, 'lectrician." He won't let Raquelle dress me in pink. "You see that? How good is she with her rattle? Maybe an athlete, full of sport."

Raquelle sniffs. "A dancer. I want her to take ballet. I never got to."

I like to think that if I stayed with them, I would have become a ballerina with a pipe-fitting business on the side, but after a year Par lost his job and they couldn't make ends meet.

"We don't bring baby to Turkey."

Raquelle doesn't go to Turkey, either, but she tells Par she'll be there soon. She starts waiting tables at Scott's downtown. Everyone's on coke so that's where her paycheck goes, too.

"I'm real sorry, superstar Shandi," Raquelle says and taps her nails on the social worker's desk. "But your new parents'll have lots more money than me."

They do. Julian and Moira have me baptized and change my name to Shannon. I'm eighteen months old. We live on Oswego Street in a periwinkle house and they are lawyers. Julian plays the piano at night with one hand; in the other, he holds me on his lap. Moira makes molasses cookies and applesauce from a recipe her mother gave her. She dresses me in her old baby clothes, which are hand-sewn and maybe expensive. There are pictures of me in little velvet vests with soft white moons, corduroy tunics, and wide-striped sweaters. They buy a rocking horse, a nightlight made of cool marble, and the complete set of Beatrix Potter books. Julian begins teaching me to read after Moira goes back to work.

"But I can't," he begins when she comes home at eleven, "I can't have her crying all the time."

Moira ties her apron round her waist and warms the soup. "Clint says I can have the long weekend off." She scratches the back of her calf with her big toe. Julian winces — he hates it when she does that.

She takes me in her arms and I press my body into the crook of her hip. It's soft-lit here. They like the lights off. Moira bends to smell the steam and her face glows blue from the gas flame. She puts her nose to mine. "Aye-bee-cee-dee-eee-eff-gee. Now what?"

Julian has trouble holding me. He says he fears I'll wiggle out of his arms and drop like a stone. He prays for me to be still. When he was a boy, his father hit his legs with an iron poker until they buckled and bled. In bed with Moira, Julian shakes off the memory. He shudders when I cry.

"Will she ever stop?" he pleads.

Another year goes by and the family doctor finds purple thumb prints on my limbs and tells them to make sure they're gentle with me. He sends a nurse over a few times but Moira tells her it's the staircase and my wobbly legs.

"She's a bit of a Jell-O jiggler," Moira laughs and the nurse does, too. When I break my arm the second time, the doctor makes a phone call and I am taken away.

The longest word in the *Oxford English Dictionary* is floccinaucinihil-ipilification. It means "the action or habit of estimating something as worthless." This is the last thing Julian teaches me as I'm rushed out the door in the arms of a lady who works for Child Services. One of my fingernails tears on the zipper of her coat and leaves a bloody trail. In the back seat of her car, she has an old video game: Pac-Man. I play it with another boy who is older than me and he says if I get the keys sticky he'll sock me in the gut.

I'm afraid of the dark. We are led by the hand down a carpeted staircase and I can't tell if we're in a church or somebody's house. Little wooden crosses dot the walls and everywhere I look, there's a Styrofoam cup with a lipstick smear. It smells like Hamburger Helper. The man who's holding my hand looks like Raffi, but he speaks in a gruff voice and has dirt under his nails. There are fifteen cots in rows of five and we each get a blanket and a small pillow. When he lets go my hand, I ask him to stay, but my voice is too quiet and the room sucks the sound. *Lights out,* someone says and someone else says, *I don't wanna be next to this stinky fucker,* and someone else says, *shut it,* and that's that. The boy is in the cot next to mine. When my eyes adjust, I can see the whites of his. We watch each other and when I reach out my hand, he whispers, *baby,* but takes it nonetheless.

I am placed in a home the next day, the sixth child in a four-bed house. I share the bottom bunk with a smelly girl who wets the bed. None of us belongs to anyone. The woman who owns the house calls me Samantha and for a while I think that's my name.

On my third birthday, I am placed with a woman with two kids of her own. We live on Mason Street in a beige townhouse. There is the usual squabbling, but I stay there until my sixteenth birthday, mostly happily. Miranda, my foster mom, is a cinnamon-colored woman from Nepal who works as a Molly Maid and was once married to a man named Dell. Her eldest girl, Keela, is my age minus a few months and a tall, startling girl who teaches me to recycle and compost. I hate the fruit flies and I find it impossible to peel labels off soup cans, but she says I must persevere. The other girl, Rhea, is more my type. We catch sucker fish and try to make them mate and she is always up for putting salt in Miranda's wineglass when her back is turned. Rhea is spanked or sent to her room and I am lectured about maturity and sentenced to dish duty for a week.

I am a noisy child. At dinner, I babble in every direction. Even the salt shaker sets me off. I ask where salt comes from. Then I want to know who built the ocean and if French children think in English and who invented Cheerios. I won't eat peas unless there's sugar on top and I get angry if Miranda's outfits aren't color coordinated. She tells me I'm oversensitive. She says I need to learn the art of conversation.

"Conversation," she says, "is when we all talk about the same thing. Pick a topic, Shannon." A rule is invented: I have to leave the table if I ask too many questions. Miranda says that if she wanted to be interviewed, it would be by Mike Wallace, not me. I discover that if I pick the skin on the back of my knee I can stop myself from blurting out. Kicking my ankles together works, too, but then I get my ears boxed and I don't do it again. My nails dig in; I scab and bleed.

*

By sixteen, it is clear what I am and what I am not. I'm not going to be a supermodel — Vaughn hadn't noticed that my mother stood barely five foot two and that her shoulders were twice as wide as her hips, giving her the build of a miniature linebacker. This becomes my build. It also becomes clear that I am blind in my left eye, though no one knows what or who to attribute that to, and that I unabashedly adore the color pink. Miranda agrees to let me paint my room pale rose and when I insist that I want a neon pink bedspread, she buys dye and throws my white one in the washing machine. Her own kids are not afforded such luxuries, but they are fair children and I hear Miranda whisper to them that "at least they are not blind nor rattled by such a stark beginning."

Late one night, Miranda crawls into my bed and tells me that people with a sense disability sometimes make up for it by having another, heightened sense. She says she has a blind friend who can play anything on the accordion or the piano. I ask if this person is some kind of prodigy and Miranda says, no, not really, but that she *really* is a good player. I don't have any such heightened sense to make up for my bad eye, though I've got a nose as strong as a bloodhound's. But no one's going to celebrate that: the little blind girl with a snout so keen she can tell what you had for breakfast. Big deal.

Some of the kids at school get cars for their birthdays. Miranda gives me a bus pass and a five-dollar bill. She says if I fold it a certain way I can make Sir Wilfrid Laurier's head look like a mushroom, but I've got other plans.

"Ticket to Tssssshhwassen," I say, my right eye focused hard on the queer spelling under the destinations. "That's Vancouver, right?"

"Yah. Well, almost. You get the bus, little missus. Traveling alone?" He pushes the ticket under the glass but keeps it under his thumb. "Nine dollars."

I start counting.

Here's a trick: mind over matter. When you're counting five bucks in change but it's got to add up to nine, say "twenty-five" instead of "five" when you throw down a nickel. They're almost the same size.

"Safe trip."

"Yup. Thanks." I've got on my pink backpack, pink shorts, and a red V-neck. Red flip-flops. Toenails done French-manicure style with Wite-Out. I'm the shortest person waiting for the ferry and probably the weirdest looking person, too. My dad must have had really curly hair because I've got blond ringlets so tight they could hold a pop can. My bum eye is usually off to the side, sleeping in the corner by my temple, so people don't know where to look when they talk to me. They stand there, bounce back and forth between my eyes, and try to figure out which is the good one. And I don't know who I inherited it from but I've got a turned-up nose like a cartoon pig. My best feature is my mouth: a perfect puffy pout. I'm not hideous, but I'm a cross between Shirley Temple and a pug.

The ferry's engine rumbles to a start and so does my stomach. I stand on the deck and watch the water move in big white sprays. Most people have cameras. Someone behind me says, "Let's get a hot dog," and I dig in my pocket for more change but find a paperclip instead.

The inside of the ferry is warm and smells like vinegar. When one safety announcement ends, another begins. I wonder what everyone's so scared about.

Here's another trick: walk up to the vending machine, slide in a paper clip, press A5, B6, or whatever.

"What? Hey! Hey! This thing ate my loonie! Give me my chips! Aw, c'mon, I don't have another loonie —"

"'Scuse me? Honey? Here's a loonie." It's a nice mom or a nice grandma and I hope she buys me a pop, too. "What's your name, sweetie?"

"Shannon."

"You traveling by yourself?"

"Yah. I have to take the bus into town. I'm pretty hungry, too."

"Maybe we could give you a ride. Why don't you come over to where we're sitting and we'll see if we can work something out."

I'm not trying to be a user, but people are curious about me. They stare and try to figure out if I'm mentally slow or what it is exactly that makes me so odd looking — I pique their interest. I'm saying that they're very happy to give up a seat in their car or a dollar to find out what's wrong with me.

"Hugh, this is Shannon. I met her over by the vending machine and she's having to take the bus all the way into town and I just thought that we —"

"Sure we could! Hi, Shannon. I see you've met my wife —"

"My name's Belle, dear. I forgot to tell you my name."

"We've got plenty of room in the car, Shan. Our kids grew up years ago — where are you going to by yourself?"

I have to stop and think about this because I don't know the answer. "Vancouver."

"Yes, dear, but where do you want us to drop you? Are you meeting someone at the bus station? I hope they won't find us odd to be giving you a ride. Will they find that odd?"

"No, I don't think so. The bus station is fine, thank you so much."

"Our pleasure. Belle, why don't you offer the girl a piece of your Toblerone."

By the time we've rounded Active Pass, Belle and Hugh have bought me a tuna sandwich and another bag of potato chips. It's my sixteenth birthday, but I've told them I'm twelve, and Hugh says when he was twelve he was independent also.

"Had a job at the shoe store," he says. I can tell he's a nice man, that he's been good to Belle. I guess they're in their sixties, but I can't really tell. Neither of their children has married and that makes them sad. They want grandchildren. Belle, I bet, is wishing she had a granddaughter like me, only not so funny looking.

"What do you want to be when you grow up?" she asks.

"A firefighter. Or dog trainer."

Yeah, my vacation didn't work out. The police find me at a homeless shelter on Burrard Street, just around the corner from the Y. Vancouver has a bigger Y than Victoria; I think, actually, it has more than one. Miranda called the police after I'd been missing five hours and my description got faxed to every station in B.C. I'm hard to miss.

I had an okay time. Vancouver smelled of rain and pizza. The SkyTrain was like this big white snake that darted all over and into parts of town where no one spoke English. Everywhere I went, someone wanted my money for drugs. It's a gray city, mostly because the buildings are made of glass and the sky is gray. Someone should have thought this through a bit.

I met lots of people in fur coats. Some were homeless; some were rich. Everyone gave me a dollar or two. One lady paid me three bucks to hold her poodle while she went for lunch and I met a guy who hadn't slept or eaten in six days. He said it was the crystal meth. He told me about the shelter and we walked together and talked about hot dogs. You can get six dogs for a dollar at the Mustard Seed and they throw out perfectly good bread at the bakery on Robson, he told me. The dumpster's got a lock, but a small hand can fit inside. We passed an electronics store and the guy wanted to go in. Everything flickered and for the first time I felt scared of film and television and all things visual. I've felt scared before, but not very often. When I do, I pretend I exist in the alphabet. I squeeze in where I'd fit so nicely. Feet up on the *J*. Back curved in the nook of the *F*, the awning keeping me dry from the rain. I could be so many words.

After we were in the store for a bit, the guy tried to sell his watch to the clerk, but it was a fake and the clerk knew it. He asked us to leave. We walked up Burrard and it started to hail so we walked faster. There were cops outside the shelter, and when the guy saw them, he bolted.

"You're Shannon, I bet," one of the officers said and held my arm tight.

I took the ferry back in a police car, and they bought me things, too. French fries with gravy and one of those pens where the whale moves when you tilt it the right way. The ferry ride lasted a year. Everyone looked at the cops and then looked away real fast. When the cruiser turned onto Mason, Miranda and the girls were waiting in front of the townhouse, hands on hips.

"I think," Miranda said, "it's time we found alternate living arrangements."

"But —"

"We're at a real fork in the road here, Shannon," she said.

What I know about my real mother: her name is Yula. Her father is Filipino and her mother is Irish. She has thin, coffee-brown hair past her shoulders — it's so fine she can gather it in a knot the size of an apricot. Yula hadn't realized she was pregnant until it was too late and the abortion clinic turned her away. She'd always had a weak, pudgy stomach and figured the morning dry heaving was from last night's two-four of beer. Not that she was an alcoholic, just a sixteen-year-old girl living in a basement suite with a punk rock band. Free rent if she put out and kept the kitchen clean. My father, I guess, was one of the musicians. I wonder: bass, lead guitar, or drums? Maybe something unusual like saxophone or electronic keyboard. I have no ear for music — the notes clink around in my head when I listen to it and I can't tell what's good or bad. He must have been blond.

From hospital records, I find out Yula was born in Duncan and was missing her left pinky finger. It doesn't say why. On her right ankle she has a tattoo of a peace sign and was treated for infection from the dirty needle. She turned seventeen the day after I was born and there's no record of her after that. In pettier moments I like to imagine she walked into the ocean or disappeared in the woods to be eaten by the elements, so racked with guilt from leaving me. I met a woman in Duncan who knew her; she told me things like Yula liked chocolate donuts and had it rough growing up.

When I was fourteen, I found the basement suite she lived in with the punks. A skinny boy with glasses and an Iron Maiden T-shirt answered the door and told me to skip off.

"Yula? Who-la?" He laughed and offered me a toke of his joint, then slammed the door before I could decline. It looked dark in the apartment, peeling linoleum and beer bottles on the floor. Maybe a cat meowed in the back.

I'm blind because of amblyopia. Lazy eye. My right eye got so good at seeing, it told the other to give up. It takes too much energy to look after a sick thing. The world is flatter; I see in a dimension just under third. Rembrandt had this problem and some scientists think he was a better painter because of it. I think it makes me trip. Where's that stair? How far from my foot? I can't tell. It's all by feel. It's not my mother's fault. We're born blind. Amblyopia comes later, when one eye fails to thrive. I wore a patch for a while, but why kick a dead horse. In the doctor's office, the eye chart starts with *E*. For eye, for easy. Everyone can see the *E*.

Miranda says I'm grounded and Rhea takes possession of my new whale pen. I stuff my backpack with baked beans and Mr. Noodle and tell Miranda I'll get by on my own. She yelps when I run out the door, but she doesn't chase me. She shouts, "You'll be back," and "For Christ's sake, Shannon," and I don't stop hearing her voice until I'm five blocks away.

People are accommodating to someone so small. The police station is a pink building and I like it immediately. After some yackety-yak, a nice officer provides Vaughn's address and a sticker that says THIS IS A DRUG-FREE ZONE. I press it to my backpack.

I stand for a long time on Vaughn's doorstep before I knock. Hillside Avenue, just up from the mall. There's a few blocks where every house is one story and has lots of crap lying around in the yard — they look like the houses along the highway long after you've left the city behind. Yellow lawns like hay fields. Paint cracked, homemade FOR SALE signs on the cars, spider plants in the window. Vaughn's kept his house a little neater I'm pleased to see. He's put down shale stepping stones in the middle of the yard and his front door is freshly painted burgundy. The curtains are drawn and the eaves are full of twigs and dead leaves. The traffic on Hillside makes a constant buzz. A couple of weird looking guys walk by and give me the eye, but I don't have anything to worry about. I've never gotten a period. I don't radiate sexual. I could be standing in a nightie and spike heels and they'd still walk on. Miranda said I'd get my period soon, but I just don't think I have it in me.

Some more scruffy characters wander past and there's a guy on the corner who looks like he's waiting to make a buck. Something about him reminds me of Julian, my father from age eighteen months to just under three. Shifty eyes.

Julian used to watch me in the playground after Miranda dropped Rhea and me off to play. The first time I saw him, we were playing "Hunter/Gatherer," a game we'd made up about being cave people. I was busy strangling a pudgy three-year-old underneath the monkey bars. I was almost five and had been living at Miranda's for just under two years.

"Bad antelope! Bad antelope," I kept saying to the kid. "Gonna feed my wife and kids with you." I dragged the kid by the ankle and set him down in front of Rhea. "Eat! Eat! Eat!"

Rhea got busy fake-eating the kid's foot, and I looked up.

"Hey, Shannon." He said it like he'd been saying it for years. "You probably don't remember me. Brought ya some gummy bears."

Julian wasn't a handsome man. He was soft in the stomach but real skinny everywhere else — my least favorite body type. His hair stuck up like a hedgehog and he looked a bit hedgehoggish, too: mean little eyes and a sharp snout. Full cheeked. He was in a suit, maybe on his lunch break.

I took the gummy bears from his hand, gave half to Rhea, and watched him wave good-bye.

"Who that?" asked Rhea.

"My old dad." The words sounded funny in my mouth.

He came again a week later. Always gummy bears, sometimes wine gums, too, but I thought they had wine in them so I declined.

"I don't drink," I said one time when we were sitting in his Mercedes Benz.

"I don't drink either." The radio was on. A husky voiced woman talking about the prairies. Something about jazz. His car seats were black leather and hot from the sun. He had a lot of hair on his arms. "There are things I shouldn't have done," he said.

I reached for a gummy bear and squished it between my fingers.

He laughed and squished one too. "You were my daughter for a while."

"I remember."

"I played Chopin for you at night." He hummed a few bars but I didn't know what to say. "I taught you the alphabet."

"Moira."

"*Me.*"

I stuck my toe in the air vent and swiveled it around to blow the air conditioning this way and that. Julian asked me not to. He asked me again.

But I couldn't stop. "Who invented air?"

"No one invented air."

"Can I have an ice cream?"

"Just — please, Shannon, take your toe out of the vent. It's getting dirt all over the —"

"Miranda doesn't let me have ice cream."

"Okay — your toe, Shannon, *now.*" He made a sound like a whinny and gripped the steering wheel. "Stop it. Fucking stop it now." Big vein popped out in his forehead, hands taut.

That's when I remembered. Just a little. Just a nudge at first — small flash in my brain — after all, I'd only been two. A hand, a fist? Smack of skin on skin, grip too tight, a lazy kick meant for no one to see, crunchy crack of bone. The whir of the X-ray machine. White bones on film. My hand dipped in the boiling pot of soup to see if I could be taught that way. An eye-patch, a cast. His voice thick and weary: What comes after *G?* Say it backwards, faster now. Define palindrome, spell naive. Jell-O jiggler. Wiggly worm. Did I fall or did he drop me? Thin skull on hard linoleum. Dull thud. Then: no sound.

After ten minutes Vaughn comes to the door. "I can see you through the curtains. You want something or what?" He looks past me at the guy on the corner and tries to gauge the odds of us being some kind of criminal operation.

I don't give him a minute to think. I've rehearsed this my whole life. "You might be the reason I'm alive, sir. I'd just like ten minutes of your time."

By now Vaughn is used to the way his life works: he is the seer. When the cars collide, he knows it two minutes before it happens. He doesn't think he has special powers and he doesn't believe in psychics. But his eyes are wide, wide open — they always have been — and he sees everything. And he takes in the whole world at once.

"If you stand back a bit, that leaf won't hit your face when it falls." The little stuff, too, is important.

"Oh, thanks," I say. We watch it tip off the edge of the eave and fall between us.

"I'm just starting dinner, so come on in." He steps back and rests his weight on the doorframe. I had hoped for a nice, grandfatherly type, or a handsome man in a suit, but Vaughn is neither. His shirt says DON'T MESS WITH THIS TEXAN. He's a red-haired guy with a week-old beard and a deep, oily tan. Every muscle in his body is ready; his calves look like they've been stuffed with rocks. Pale jean shorts and bare feet. But he wears square, stylish glasses and behind them, his eyes are soft. "So come on in," he says again. "Mind the step up and when you take your shoes off, put them to the left of mine on the floor — if you put them on the right side, we won't be able to open the door again without moving them."

I slide my flip-flops next to his runners and he shuts the door behind me. His house smells like fried chicken and salt and vinegar potato chips.

"Forgive me if I don't know who you are immediately, but I've done quite a few things in my life that might prompt a person to knock on my door and thank me for saving them, so maybe if we sit down and have a soda first you can tell me the story again until I remember."

So I tell him what I know while he pours ginger ale into two tall mugs: cold morning, 5 A.M., the glass doors of the Y on Courtney Street, a young woman. A small, fresh version of myself wrapped in a sweatshirt with thumb holes.

"Well, you wouldn't have died, Shannon. The doors were just about to open — yer mom woulda known that. She was leaving you there so that they would see you. I just happened to see you first."

"Was she crying or anything?"

Vaughn considers this and motions to the kitchen table. He sets the soda down and pulls out a chair for me. His kitchen is tidy except for one stretch of counter stacked high with newspapers. A few photographs of him and a white border collie are stuck to the fridge with wooden magnets. "That was sixteen years ago — sheesh — you don't look a day over — yah, she bent down and kissed your cheek, I think," he says. "I'm pretty sure she was crying real hard."

"Was I hurt at all?"

"Nah." He blinks. "You a chicken-eater? I'm making a roast; there's plenty for both of us."

"I would love to stay."

He puts his hands together and makes a face like he's being squeezed. "I really don't remember anything other than that. It was real early and the whole thing happened pretty fast. I was more interested in you than I was in her, if you know what I mean."

Vaughn takes out a stack of napkins and folds them into triangles and I wish I could fold napkins the way they do in restaurants but it never works out. I can tell he wants to ask me questions, but he's not sure what's appropriate. He doesn't want me to cry.

"My brother Blaze might pop over," he says. "Teaches tango at this little joint on Herald Street. Nice guy. Won't stay long."

"Sure." I watch him heat up a cup of butter in the microwave and tip it over the chicken. He crushes rock salt between his fingers and stuffs the cavity with whole lemons and thyme. Every time his hand moves from salt to chicken to lemon to thyme, he wipes it with a paper towel. No contamination. I peel potatoes and carrots and slice them thin, then halve the onions. Vaughn says he does Shake and Bake when it's just him.

"But this is more of a special occasion," he says. We watch the timer on the stove and he tells me bits of his life: a retired decathlete, a brief marriage to a kayak instructor, his days now filled teaching weight training at the Y. "I'm there every morning anyway," he says and picks at his beard. "You know, it's still weird. Every morning I pull up, I think of you being there."

I watch him break pieces of iceberg lettuce into a plastic bowl. He slices a tomato and sets a bottle of ranch dressing on the table.

"When I was sixteen, I thought I'd like to play in the pro leagues. You a sports fan?"

"My eye's not so good."

"Well then," he starts. He scans the counter top. "I swear I put that oven mitt down a second ago and I'll be darned if I can't find it."

I think after dinner I'm going to ask Vaughn if I can stay with him awhile. I'll clean his house and mow the lawn. I could probably get a job at the mall. I took a food safety course at school so I could work at the souvlaki place or Mrs. Vanelli's pizza, I guess. There's so much fast food around. This would be a good neighborhood if it weren't for this one stretch of houses. What happened here? There's a good Chinese place around the corner, too. Wonder if Vaughn likes Chinese. I bet he does. There's gas stations and the Thrifty Foods and a Zellers store and it's a little noisy being right here on Hillside but I can buy some earplugs tomorrow and I'll buy some for Vaughn as well. His brother can teach us the tango.

"I always wished I could be a dancer, Vaughn," I say.

"Nothin' to it."

I press my foot into the floor and Vaughn starts to talk real fast.

"Now I didn't really see your mom's face, but I do remember she had some kind of work pants on — overalls or something — gray or black, too big for 'er. Dark hair. Little woman I think, not too little — our eyes have the hardest time at dawn or twilight, you know — it's the hardest light for our eyes to process . . ."

He talks until the timer beeps and the whole room fills with the smell of chicken and thyme when he opens the stove and the steam rushes out. I let him go on. I can tell he doesn't have kids. If he did he'd say a lot of nonsense about love and hardship and the troubled girls of the world.

He tells me all kinds of things while we eat: the detective's side part, how the van smelled like diesel fuel that morning and he thought he might have a leak, that my mom took short steps not long strides when she walked away. He offers no hypothesis. In the last sixteen years, he says, it was the one day he didn't get a proper workout. The night before he watched *Uncle Buck*.

Vaughn's happy with the way the chicken turned out and we both like the burnt carrots best. He tries to put more salad on my plate, but I'm filled to the brim with food. And then it's Vaughn's favorite part of a chicken dinner: the moment of silence when we sit back in our chairs, plates pushed back. He plucks the wishbone from what's left of the chicken and holds it out for me to reach. It's the one thing in life he can't predict: who will get the lucky break.

J. MALCOLM GARCIA

■

The White Train

FROM *The Virginia Quarterly Review*

THE WHITE TRAIN CARRIES US.

We racket from side to side on warped steel tracks, our nostrils burning with the odor of aged brakes and wearied engines in winter's brittle, fog-laced air. Above us cars hurtle along a freeway in the last minutes of rush hour, golden in the glare of sunset glinting off the glass high-rises of downtown Buenos Aires, and we — *cartoneros*, collectors of cardboard, black as chimney sweeps striped in pink light and motes of dust — stare out broken windows covered with grilled steel plates that chime from rocks thrown at us by fleeting figures on the ground.

Puto! one of us shouts at them and laughs.

Only minutes ago, we sat amid the ruined decadence of Victoria station, its colonial archways cracked and mildewed from decades of neglect. We smoked cigarettes between our carts that held the jumbled, leaning masses of flattened cardboard and heaps of nylon strips and sacks of newspaper and every other piled-high bit of scrap we had collected. Hunched and bristling, dogs rushed beneath our towers of discard, so fearful were they of collapse. There in the exposed dirt we waited for the White Train; what little warmth we had came from small fires over which we rubbed our hands, shared mugs of *maté*, and the hot breath of our worried conversation awash in blowing ash.

They want to take us out of circulation.

When I was a truck driver, I didn't like the cartoneros. I didn't think much of them. Now look at me. Perhaps this is justice for my previous life.

Last Friday, a train went off the rails and we couldn't get transporta-

tion for the day. Imagine if they take the train away and it's like that all the time.

The White Train, blue and white and wet with dew, pulled in just when we had nearly lost all hope. Cats scattered and we hefted our loads. Cardboard scratched the pavement.

I don't like this, a woman said, *but it's the only way to make ends meet.*

Drinking from bottles of soda mixed with wine, we set about loading the train. Dust swirled around us and stuck to our wet lips. We shuffled past car batteries, refrigerator grilles, abandoned TVs, and always cardboard and paper — the echoing clatter of our boarding consumed finally by the slow rising grind of the train's wheels as it pushed forward once more and now, lulled into sleep, we dream dreams of ceaseless motion.

Most people in downtown Buenos Aires avert their eyes when the White Train rattles past. They pretend not to see it and its trash-scavenging passengers. They may want to believe it doesn't exist. After all, it has no official timetable, no windowpanes, no doors in the frames, and no seats.

And soon those people who dread its appearance will no longer have to lie to themselves about its existence. No longer will they have to wish it away. The government will remove it for them. This year, Buenos Aires officials intend to eliminate the White Train, one of the most visible signs of the poverty afflicting a city still known as the Paris of South America.

Cartoneros began appearing during the recession of the mid-1990s, when factory workers, maintenance workers, domestic workers, and other marginally employed people began losing their jobs. They found they could make a meager living by collecting recyclable materials, and many resorted to this trash scavenging as a means of temporary support. But in December 2001, Argentina went bankrupt. Mass riots toppled President Fernando de la Rúa, and a 70 percent devaluation of the currency left more than half the population below the poverty line. The new government devalued the currency, with the unintended effect of driving up the price of paper and copper.

They became too expensive to import and soon more cartoneros were on the streets looking for anything of recycling value.

Now people who once told themselves that they would do this only long enough to ride out the recession pay welders thirty-five dollars to attach car wheels to a steel frame, creating contraptions that allow a single person to push up to five hundred pounds of scrap down the street, and it seems unlikely that they will find other work any time soon. Argentina's unemployment rate stands close to 25 percent. Nearly 60 percent of the nation's 36 million people are poor, and 10 million live in extreme poverty. It will take years to rebuild an economy crushed by mismanagement and a mountain of debt.

The city of Buenos Aires made its own concessions to this reality when it legalized garbage picking and gave commuting cartoneros a train of their own — so they wouldn't bother "respectable" passengers with their carts of scrap paper, cardboard, cans, and salvaged food. The first train was white, hence its name — but others called it the Ghost Train because of its unofficial status and skeletal appearance. The seats were ripped out to make room for carts. The guts of the cars were recycled along with everything else. Additional cars for the cartoneros were added onto passenger trains until a total of sixteen train cars were devoted to them.

The city also launched a campaign encouraging residents to separate recyclables in green bags so that cartoneros would not have to rifle through rotten food; the city started offering vaccinations to protect against tetanus. The government also established new garbage contracts to include cartoneros, who were accused of "stealing" garbage from the waste-management companies paid by volume for the amount of rubbish they bury. Under the new rules, companies were paid according to how clean they keep their areas — a task for which the cartoneros proved helpful. Indeed, the cartoneros have reduced the amount of solid waste going into landfills by 25 percent, and they have proved a boon to the economy as well.

They only earn about forty-five centavos per kilo for white paper, seventeen to twenty centavos for cardboard, twelve centavos for newsprint, twenty-five to thirty for plastic bottles, and seven to ten centavos for glass — which is to say pennies to the pound. But the materials they gather feed Argentina's recycling industry. Neighborhood bosses add 20 percent to the price paid the cartoneros before they sell the bulk to larger recycling collectors, who add another 100 percent before they sell it to mills as raw material, who themselves sextuple the price when they turn it into finished products that they sell into the public market.

All of Argentina, it seemed, was benefiting.

That changed, however, this June when Mauricio Macri was elected mayor of Buenos Aires. He belongs to one the wealthiest business families in the country and is the president of one of the biggest football clubs, Boca Juniors. Given the city's budget of some three billion dollars and a population of nearly three million, the post of Buenos Aires mayor is seen as the third most important political office in Argentina, after the country's president and the governor of the province of Buenos Aires. Macri's election as mayor has now turned him into one of the main political figures in the country, and many believe this is a step in his bid to become president of Argentina.

Macri, whose family has a city sanitation contract, has vowed to find "a definitive solution to the problem of the cartoneros." He has renewed the accusation of stealing. He accuses them of not paying taxes and ruining the city landscape. Since the train does not officially exist, the new city government can say what it wants, do with it as it pleases. He reminds everyone that the White Train was never a service officially sanctioned by city government or transportation officials. It was meant as a temporary remedy for the employment crisis. The White Train never existed on company records — and Macri does not believe in ghosts.

From beneath the freeway we watch Buenos Aires rush past us in blurs of sagging clotheslines, tin roofs weighted with rocks, grazing horses . . .

Macri puts us all under the same label: thief, homeless — that's not the case, Cora says. *You know what it feels like to wake up with a fever, to know you have to collect cardboard anyway? If you don't work, you have no money. That's what happened two days ago. It was raining and I had to go out and work anyway.*

. . . families huddled under bridges, dirt roads, crumbling brick buildings, pools of stagnant water, boys playing soccer and the dust rising around their feet until they too disappear from the gaping hole where once doors opened and closed and from which we stare out . . .

I have done this for seven years, Cora continues. I worked at a supermarket. It ended and I started doing this. Motherfuckers. This week, I already made forty pesos. I work every day but Saturday. My cart is the one I used in the garden of my house when times were better.

. . . past faded yellow campaign posters of a smiling Macri, all through the barred windows.

In the beginning, I felt bad, Cora's husband, Omar, tells us. Like a huge bird, when it is ashamed, it puts its head in the ground. I never thought I'd be doing this. For eighteen years I was a truck driver before the company was sold and I lost my job. Maybe things will get better. The last thing you lose is your faith.

We slow to a stop at Garín station, unload in a confusion of rolling bale-size bundles of cardboard and scrap metal and metal tubing and grubby toddlers being passed overhead hand to outstretched hand . . .

Over here! This way! Lift, lift!

. . . until we fill the station platform with our carts and the discard we have collected. We wait for trucks from the *depósito* where fourteen-year-old Franco has already delivered his load except for a stuffed toy chicken he found in the garbage. He gives it now to his younger sister.

It looks like you, she tells him, holding the filthy toy close to her chest.

They live with their mother in a squat one-story brick house only a block away, cold with winter dampness, the thin rugs beneath their feet having already absorbed all the moisture possible from the mud floors. Two dogs and a cat run in and out of the house. Broken radios and televisions collected by Franco add to the clutter atop a chest of drawers also found on the street. As if these abandoned possessions, the attainment of others, lend respectability to this sorry hovel. Franco has been a cartonero since he was seven.

I live only in the present, not the future, he says. I just push myself so I have the energy to do this. If they stop the trains, there will be blood.

*

Few in the government will take seriously the warnings of a boy. Franco may have revolutionary fervor, but no one has yet emerged from the ranks of the cartoneros to spark a proletarian revolt.

"With a few exceptions, they are not organized," says Pablo J. Schamber, professor of anthropology and social research at the Universidad Nacional de Lanús in Buenos Aires Province. He has studied the cartoneros since 1999. "Maybe when the decision to stop the train occurs, that will be the time an organization becomes established."

We shall see. Shortly after Macri's election, Trenes de Buenos Aires (TBA) and Comisión Nacional de Regulación del Transporte (CNRT) confirmed that the White Train would be eliminated by the end of 2007. The train cars in use by the cartoneros will be reconverted to add to the normal passenger trains; in exchange, some trucks will be assigned to transport the cartoneros' carts to recycling centers.

The trucks would travel parallel to the tracks — the cartoneros would ride the train like any other passenger while the trucks drive alongside. When the train stops, the trucks will also stop. That way, the thinking goes, the cartonero and his cart will reach every destination at the same time. Another plan calls for the city to provide warehouses where the cartoneros could store what they collect, so they wouldn't have to transport it to dump sites outside Buenos Aires. Whatever the final plan, officials agree that the White Train can be replaced.

"It's just another train," says Gonzalo Covatto, train station operator at Retiro station in downtown Buenos Aires. "It's a train of workers, like a regular train but for people who don't have money."

Few here believe, however, that simply substituting trucks for trains will work. They question whether enough trucks will be allocated for the task. More importantly, they doubt the government's motives.

"Even if they create more dump sites I doubt the cartoneros will go, because there would be no trust," says Gonzalo Rodríguez, manager of a recycling center used by the cartoneros. "They are used to dealing with one person now, and that person respects them even though they might be ignorant or idiots. The cartoneros are like animals. They don't trust."

Does Macri want to create a more efficient and humane system for the cartoneros or is he instead protecting the interests of companies with sanitation contracts — companies such as his own? So far, no cartonero — or anyone else for that matter — has demanded answers to this and a much larger question: Is it Macri's hope to eliminate the cartoneros all together?

"I don't think my job will be affected one way or the other because garbage will exist forever," Rodríguez says. "But it's going to be a problem for the cartoneros. The problem is that if [the politicians] want to get rid of the train, they will want to get rid of the trucks another day. I think it's more of a political problem than anything else. Garbage is a real good business."

Every day new rumors spread.

The train will be shut down in two months.

No, no, two weeks.

No, no, two days.

I heard next week.

Estelle Maris Gómez lurches within the jolting rush of a White Train and listens to the worried gossip. She has been a cartonera since 1995, when she lost her maintenance job. She works 4 P.M. to 4 A.M. every day. When Estelle first started collecting cardboard, she was surprised at the amount of good clothing she found. She washed the pants, dresses, and shirts and clothed her twelve children.

Since 2002, she has been trying to organize her fellow scavengers. She calls herself the president of Friends of the Train, *a fifteen-hundred-member union,* she asserts, before conceding that only a few, if any, attend irregularly scheduled membership meetings.

Today, no one seems interested in the union. Only the future of the White Train concerns them.

There was an accident at another station.

The train is not shut down, just delayed.

Accident?

Yesterday it was really late.

Estelle, bundled in a corduroy coat and a wool cap that conceals her short black hair, carries a clipboard with petitions to save the White Trains. She tells the cartoneros their concerns should energize them to act. She urges them to sign the petitions.

Together we can do things, she says. *One alone cannot.*

What are we going to do if they take the train in two weeks?

We're going to fight.

Every one of us will be damaged by this.

Fight until the last moment.

We should burn the trains.

But then what would be left for us to use? Estelle asks.

The train stops at Lisandro de la Torre station where several cartoneros get off. They push out their carts sagging with the accumulation of a night's work. Estelle follows them, clipboard in hand, and works the platform. Most of the cartoneros ignore her. Instead, they continue their idle conversations.

Is it cold in the United States?

No. Our winters are their summers.

Let's go to the United States so we don't have to live with this piece-of-shit government.

In a park behind the station, police handcuff a cartonero. Around them, families lounge in the grass and watch, temporarily distracted from whatever had previously held their attention. *Crostas,* they call the cartoneros. Scrap. Bottom of the barrel.

Go back home, puto, a cartonero near Estelle shouts at the police.

No, no, Estelle cautions him. *Don't say that.*

She boards another White Train headed back toward Victoria station and continues pushing her petition. Estelle has collected one hundred twenty signatures. She does not know how much money she has lost recruiting signatures instead of collecting cardboard herself. But if she doesn't do this and the trains stop running, she'll be screwed just like everyone else. Someone, she reasons, must collect the signatures. What good they will do, she can't say, but she feels a sense of accomplishment looking at the filled sheets of paper, the names scrawled on thin blue lines. We are nothing if not the names our fathers have given us, she reasons. She decides she enjoys doing this because it is necessary.

Estelle stands next to an old man who sits, beside his cart, in a cracked plastic chair. *You are smart,* she tells him, *to bring your own chair.* He smiles wearily. He injured his left leg. A woman beside him listens to his woes. He rolls up his pants leg and reveals a bruised and swollen thigh. The woman makes a face. She has children in school, and she became a cartonera when she lost her job at a pizzeria. It's not a fortune, she says, but what she earns as a cartonera is enough to feed them.

We've got to organize, Estelle tells them both.

If we lose, we've got nothing, the old man agrees.

At Victoria station, young men step out of another White Train bound in the opposite direction from Estelle's train. She watches them saunter on the platform collecting their carts with belligerent self-assurance. Rebels. Young kids. They don't want to organize. They think only of themselves. Like dogs, they will move on to something else if Macri stops the trains. They think only of today. Do they not understand that she fights for their rights too? She offers her clipboard to a woman and asks if she has signed the petition.

I am hearing the train will stop in two weeks, the woman tells Estelle. *We don't know this.*

So all these people telling me this, they are liars?

No, says Estelle.

We need the train to keep running so we can keep working.

Yes. They start pressuring us, we respond with protests. If they continue, there will be a national protest with the support of ten thousand people!

The woman signs the clipboard, energized for the seconds her pen scratches across the paper. Estelle watches her, feeling the undertow of exhaustion in her outstretched arm, the weight of the woman's hand pressing down on the clipboard she holds. Tomorrow, Estelle must put aside the petition drive and go out with her cart. If she had as many pesos as signatures she would not be standing here now.

Far from Victoria station in the posh Palermo District, María Cristína Lescano stands in a warehouse, surrounded by bundles of cardboard, and sympathizes with the efforts of women such as Estelle. She knows how difficult it is to organize the cartoneros. She was one herself.

For seven years, burning with shame, she picked through trash. Then she and several other cartoneros realized they made more money when they pooled everything they had collected and sold it as one large parcel, rather than cart by cart. They started a recycling cooperative, El Ceibo, named after a local tree. Today Maria employs fifty-three people. The have an established clientele and walk door-to-door collecting recyclable garbage.

It's going to be hard to get rid of the cartoneros, she says. Now she's seated at a desk in the cool shadows cast by ceiling beams. *Poor people have always existed.*

Julia Navarro, one of her staff and a former cartonero, interrupts, speaking excitedly.

We have government contracts, Julia explains. *Before this we also broke into trash bags. But now we are more important than the cartoneros.*

Maria glances outside at a swirl of old money that has been discarded and shredded and now waltzes in the clear air, a multicolored flurry spilling from black plastic garbage bags in a bizarre, celebratory tornado.

When we started this, the neighborhoods didn't want us. Imagine the way we looked at the time, Maria says. She pulls her pink sweatshirt closer to her chest and blows on her cold hands. Her glasses steam and she wipes them. *The neighborhoods were scared of us. We went from working at night, when no one saw us, to working in the day. We had to teach our employees how to speak to people. We identified ourselves with uniforms.*

From a drawer she withdraws pink invoices, unfurling them like a deck of cards on her desk, a sign of her legitimacy as a businesswoman. Maria sells cardboard and other recyclable goods to eight local companies.

The cartoneros have to organize themselves, she says. *The White Train offers them unity. I feel sorry for them because there is no overall big movement. it's a constant struggle. At El Ceibo we still feel marginalized as workers, but one gets used to being marginalized. One gets used to anything.*

Under a bright sun, men and women in long winter coats wait for their train at the Martínez station downtown. Shoppers fill the sidewalks, pausing at window displays or ducking into coffee shops. A TBA official paces the platform, notices the light of an incoming train. He watches it approach and then turns to the waiting men and women and urges them to step back. The sound of the train grows louder, the tracks vibrating with the weight of its passage, and it emerges fully into view. A White Train smeared with graffiti LOS CARTONE-ROS, ÉSTE ES LO NUESTRO hurtles past. Disjointed faces stare out through the barred windows and a blasting backdraft stirs the station into a swirl of paper loosened from overstuffed trash cans. Everyone turns against the sting of biting dust and the train roars otherworldly until it vanishes and the dust settles and the papers fall and the commuters look at their watches, brush their coats clean of the grit of this upheaval.

A passenger train approaches Victoria station, stops, and then thrusts faster and faster into reverse.

Word spreads among the commuters.

The cartoneros have blocked the tracks!

Men and women disembark and rush down a street toward a bus stop. Shoe heels clipping against the sidewalk. Wrapped in coats, ties blown over their shoulders. Scarves wrapped furiously around red cheeks. Their breath, puffs of clouds in the winter wind.

This fucking government has no shame, an old man mutters, his sliver hair unruffled. Despite all the commotion everything about him pristine, smooth. A briefcase firmly in hand. Only his commute disrupted.

Terrorists stop the train and they do nothing! he says and curses again.

The old man and dozens of others stand in lines for buses. The train remains motionless, powerless to go forward. A desolate object. Beneath its still wheels, the tracks vibrate with the sound of distant voices rising and rising until the shouts of an angry knot of cartoneros burst onto the tracks.

We're fighting to save the train!

We are here to block the road so the train won't get out!

We all have the same right to work. We're all fighting same thing!

We want train to keep going!

We need more cars!

Estelle stands to one side, away from the protesters. She does not know who called the demonstration. She appears intimidated by the arrival of TBA officials. Journalists ask her to comment, and she tells them she will in a minute, in a minute. She has to think.

First she wanted to turn in the petitions. Then she planned to organize demonstrations if necessary. Fearful the protest will antagonize the Macri government further, she watches in amazement. She does not understand what is happening. Her fear infects others.

The police will come and take us, a woman warns the protesters.

Our kids should leave right now, another woman shouts.

Estelle shrinks from the faces looking toward her for guidance, dwarfed by the anger rising around her. Another woman, Coronel Elsa Mabel, instead exhorts the crowd.

We must fight for each other! she calls out.

Yes, a man complains, *but since last week I can't work. I don't have carts like you to come and work. Do you think that's right?*

Why doesn't she stay inside? a commuter complains of Coronel.

Why is she fighting? another commuter says. *I have a job to get to.*

A TBA official in a blue uniform approaches Coronel. Estelle moves farther away. Coronel faces him, pushed by the crowd until they stand nose to nose.

You cannot stay here any longer, the TBA man says. *It has already been twenty to thirty minutes.*

Can you give us a solution? Coronel asks.

That's what we're trying to talk about, but you have to get away from the rails first.

The problem with the trains is they don't have enough cars, a man shouts.

The TBA man gestures and talks. The crowd shifts to give his roving hands space. He steps forward and they move back. A few people break away as if he had somehow loosed them from orbit. He gestures again and once more steps forward. Additional men and women drop off from the glut of protesters. In this way, through the quiet ruthlessness of his calm manner, he herds the crowd farther and farther away from the tracks.

Please get off the rails, he says gently. *Let the train pass.*

He asks Coronel for her name. He promises to add more train cars for the cartoneros. But he needs names so their complaints can be properly heard. He gestures, steps forward, gestures, steps forward. Behind him, some cartoneros move their carts from blocking the tracks. The space where Estelle stood has absorbed her until she stands there no more. Nothing now inhibits the station.

Coronel stands alone with the TBA man. Then she, too, leaves wondering what, if anything, was gained.

Does the TBA man know what he is talking about? Can he really provide the extra cars? Is it all just lies? Coronel rubs her face. *The cartoneros have to wake up. This is everyone's fight.* Too many of them, she worries, believe the trains won't be shut down. She doesn't know why anyone would want to get in their way. The government has to let them work.

The TBA man joins commuters on the platform. He watches buses crossing the tracks, vendors selling phone cards: the day again resumes its irresistible rhythm, the unstoppable tide of routine that makes no space for delays.

In the evening, Coronel readies her three carts for the night's work. When she first started working as a cartonera, in 2001, she did not own a cart. Just plastic bags that she filled with cardboard. At night, she camped in a park by the side of a school.

Coronel shakes her head — her long black hair brushing the small of her back — and rubs her face. Those days, a long time past. And still she scavenges.

Inside her green clapboard house, she fills a bucket with water, and bathes. After she dries herself, she puts on a brown sweater and dark pants. It will be cold.

Clothes for the next two days — sweatshirts and blue jeans and socks — drape the back of a wood chair. Also set aside are three heavy comforters. She moves about the house drying her hair. Everything she owns, a chest of drawers, bunk bed, pots and pans, the kitchen stove, she found in garbage. It surprises her, the things people discard. A washing machine, see? It still works. Some of what she finds her husband, a painter, restores and sells.

She collects cardboard Friday night through Sunday morning, allotting just five hours for sleep. Before the economic crisis, she used to clean houses and sell tortillas, but after 2001 her family needed more. Her husband has a painting job tonight and won't be home. Coronel will pay a neighbor twenty pesos to watch their daughter.

Be good, she tells the girl and kisses her forehead. She puts a ribbon in the girl's hair.

You take a shower?

Yes.

Did you perfume your body? Even your butt?

Yes.

Coronel kisses her again. The humiliation of picking through trash means little compared to the pain of leaving her daughter.

People don't know the sacrifices we make, she says. *They don't know we have less. The train has a soul. It's everything to the cartoneros. We have a soul. Human beings ride the train, not ghosts.*

An hour after dropping off her daughter, Coronel drags her three carts off a White Train at the Núñez station, and slips on a reflective orange band. She attaches two carts with a belt and pulls them behind her as she pushes the third cart with her free hand.

Apartment buildings line the sidewalk. The glow of streetlights reflects off her band. Flower-decorated patios jut out overhead, and music drifts without direction, dissipates within the rumble of buses and trucks and cars and the chatter of café couples arm in arm outside, smoking cigarettes. Coronel leaves two of her carts at a DVD store. A sympathetic manager whom she has known for years agrees to watch them for her. When she fills one cart, she will hide it at her campsite and return for the remaining two and continue working.

She walks down the street. A car horn blares. She ignores it as couples on the sidewalk ignore her, though she walks a little closer to the curb. The lights of an intersection change and break her stride. With her hair concealed in a long stocking cap, she has the appearance of an elf out-of-season, dwarfed in the skewed multicolored glaze of billboard lights and commotion.

La Faustina Bar.

Tucson Steak House.

Victoria Babalonia DVD Store.

Coronel stops, feels a garbage bag propped against a lamppost. Some people mix paper with trash. Through the plastic, her fingertips sort out what might be recyclable.

Nothing.

When she first started scavenging, she was a mess. She didn't know what to take, so she took everything. She would see paper, grab it, and find that it was filled with dog shit.

Trabaja sucio, she says. *This is dirty work.*

Coronel empties a box of paperback books and paper sacks and throws it all in her cart. She continues down the street.

Aceituna Pizzería.

Keira Café.

Plaza de Juegos.

Coronel finds a bag of fresh bread, which she leaves for other cartoneros because she brought food with her. A case of bottled orange juice, however, she keeps. The juice expired four days ago but the bottles weren't opened. In another trash pile, outside a Chinese restaurant, she discovers a pane of glass. She will use it for her night table.

La Parfumerie.

Disco Salsa.

Maidenform Bras, Panties, Shapewear.

A pizza deliveryman parks outside a gated apartment complex and rings the buzzer. He leans on his motor scooter and watches Coronel pushing her cart.

You are the worst of us, he says.

She stops and faces him.

I'm not the worst. How much do you make?

One hundred fifty pesos a day.

I make more.

A woman crosses the street walking a miniature pinscher. The click of her heels on the pavement. People gather in a courtyard behind the apartment gate. Their voices low. Music. Perhaps a party.

Everyone here has a right to work, Coronel insists.

Lick my dick, the deliveryman says. *People like you don't want to work.*

Coronel walks away. She must fill her cart. He is less than her. This is hard work. She would not want to deliver pizzas. She won't be a cartonera forever. She does this for her daughter. She won't work near construction sites because of guys like him. Motherfuckers! He must have been burned by a woman for what he said to her. Maybe he is a drug addict. She doesn't know. Fuck him! She pushes her carts. She doesn't get lonely. She focuses on the work. She feels lonely only when she thinks of her daughter, and when small men mock her.

*

One A.M.

Coronel sleeps. She camps in El Barrio Rojo near Núñez station beneath a billboard for a new apartment complex with a pool and an exercise room.

Weights. Yoga. Treadmill. Medicine balls.

For a Better Life.

Two transvestite prostitutes hustle a street corner nearby. They watch out for Coronel between tricks. Her comforters hold the aromas of home, and she snuggles beneath them and dreams of her daughter.

In the darkness of this hour, boys paste cinema advertisements on the sides of vacant buildings, around frayed campaign posters promoting Macri. He smiles beside his smiling vice-mayoral candidate Gabriela Michetti and promises VA A ESTAR BUENO BUENOS AIRES. *It's Going to Be a Good Buenos Aires.* A catchy slogan. A play on the city's optimistic name. Like promising "It's Going to Be a Newer New York." Such pitches are aimed at voters who don't work nights picking trash or pasting up posters. His campaign was for those who believe Argentina has risen above its past economic woes and into prosperous times again.

The cartoneros remind everyone that those times, should they return at all, won't include opportunities for everyone. That some will be left behind and be forced to cope on their own as they do now. The pocked and mottled White Trains run like a daily gash across Buenos Aires, the dividing line between people with means and people without.

If the trains remain, Macri faces more than just an annoying symbol of poverty. The cartoneros are a captive audience ripe for anyone with the drive to organize them. They spend hours on the train fretting about their fate, eager for a leader. Perhaps Estelle will rise to the occasion. Perhaps Coronel. Perhaps Cora and her husband, Omar. Perhaps young Franco. Perhaps one of their listeners. A leader who would represent not just the cartoneros but all of the people left behind by the economic chaos of 2001.

It seems that Macri won't wait for that day. No, the train must go; the cartoneros must be controlled. Controlled before they understand the threat they pose. Soon they will ride passenger trains like anyone else. What does it matter if there are not enough trucks to carry their carts? That is not the point. Neutralize the threat. The cartoneros must blend in with other passengers sitting stop after stop, numbed by the sheer numbers of other people, dormant, faceless in the docile trap of a new order. The last thing Buenos Aires needs is a socialist boom sweeping South America. Let Juan Evo Morales Ayma stay in Bolivia. Let Hugo Rafael Chávez Frías stay in Venezuela. Let Macri be mayor so as to pursue the Argentine presidency one day.

Coronel sleeps. She has potential to be an organizer but it is hard to lead when she must work such exhausting hours. But one day Coronel or someone like her may not need sleep. Macri knows this — as strong men before him have known.

No, of course Macri cannot wait. Not another moment. The train must disappear and with it the cartoneros. He smiles forever on his campaign posters.

It's going to be a good Buenos Aires.

Coronel sleeps.

Sometime after midnight, Sunday morning, Coronel wakes beneath the cardboard cave she had made for herself between two carts. She rises and cleans her campsite. When she finishes, she hides her broom in a tree. Washing with a bottle of water, she changes clothes. She has filled her three carts with cardboard, paper, a fan, some carpet and nylon wrapping strips.

She sips *maté*. When she gets home, she will send her daughter to school. Then she will sleep. She sips the *maté*, feels the drawn tautness in her tired face. When she gets this hungry, when she thinks her ribs are about to cave in, *maté* gives her strength.

Coronel needs to be strong. Last night, a man stopped, circled around, and stared at her.

Do you like men or women? he asked.

Coronel chased him with piece of metal. She knows she was not wrong about his intentions.

She joins other cartoneros at Núñez station. A man she has known for years helps her push the carts up a ramp to the platform. She calls him King Kong. *Two heads think better than one even if they don't have a lot of brains between them,* she says.

You look like the Grinch, she tells Kong.

You look like Olive Oyl, Kong says.

You really think you're smart!

Skinny girl, he says. *You're taking up the whole platform with your three carts.*

They stop teasing each other long enough to help the half-dozen cartoneros gathering at this nomadic hour pull their overloaded carts onto the platform. A hodgepodge of plastic stools, heaters, faucet handles, countless pieces of cardboard, all of it swaying above them in absurd disjointed stacks that somehow never fall but shift at odd angles and cut the pavement with unsteady shadows. The cartoneros pause in the labors, frozen like figures in fading daguerreotypes — still, solemn, the lines of generations etched on their faces.

Streetlights snap off.

Gray light spreads into day, revealing empty streets and closed shutters against the dawn . . .

Cartoneros! Coronel shouts. *Ready!*

. . . and the hue of an approaching White Train.

Two hours later, Coronel hauls her carts off at Savio station. The train had hit a truck parked alongside the tracks. No one was hurt but the accident caused delays.

What's going on with the train? asks a cartonero who arrived before her.

There was an accident, Coronel explains.

I thought they were going to add cars.

I don't know.

But Estelle said . . .

She can't speak for us, Coronel insists. *We have to speak for ourselves. We've got to unite and say what we want.*

At the *depósito* three blocks away, Coronel unloads her carts onto a scale. A bare bulb hangs over her and the damp stink of mildewed cardboard presses in on her. A man reads the weight and writes it down. For thirty-six hours of work, she has earned one hundred sixty-six pesos, about fifty-five dollars.

I'm happy, Coronel says. *I'm going to be able to pay for the shoes I'm using for work. I'm going to be able to pay for the jacket I got last week because of the cold. And I'm going to be able to buy a few things I need at home for the house. So yes, I'm happy. For two days it's a good salary. A lot of sacrifices, but it's worth it.*

The White Train carries us.

Into the night, holding the walls for balance. Our cell phones provide blinking light to see by, and we stand pale-faced and temporary in the brief light before the dark and the movement of the train consume us again. We pass cups of *maté*. Always *maté* to fill us and keep us warm. The wires from broken ceiling lights remind us that the train, like ourselves, has been recycled into something new. To that we drink, and to good finds on the street tonight.

Throughout Buenos Aires the lights are out. Soccer stadiums stand empty. Bus stops offer spaces with none to occupy them. The streets lie beyond us with no one upon them, in a profound silence not broken even by the rush of the train.

Cartoneros! Ready!

The train passes Savio station. Garín station. Victoria station. Núñez station. And all the stations in between. Mile upon desolate mile, the hoarse sorrows of its engines burrow into the night. Then it stops downtown and lets us off. We stand on the platform with our carts and watch the fading light of the train, until it disappears and what we have left is ourselves and our need, alone in the silence.

But we are here. We exist.

Let us work.

DAVID GESSNER

■

The Dreamer Did Not Exist

A boy's obsession with nonexistence.

FROM *Oxford American*

1

THE PIG SIZZLES ON the spit, its eyes not so much blank as boiled. I am forty-two years old and it is the middle of my first term as an academic, a professor, though right now, intent on tearing apart my prey, I bear more resemblance to Cro-Magnon man.

I rip skin from the pig's body and delight in its taste on my tongue. I am drunk, by the way. I especially like the skin.

My new job is to teach people how to write, and I am surrounded by fellow members of my tribe, writers all, who tear along with me at the porcine carcass. But if what we have in common is wielding words, at the moment our communication is decidedly nonverbal. Though we say little, there must be something happily primal in standing around a kill. It just *feels* right. We grunt with pleasure at the food.

2

Artists, writers, and poets all have pat answers when they are asked why they do what they do, and I'm no different. Usually my reply is a soft one peppered with the word *love* (as in "I love what I do" or "labor of love"), and sometimes if I'm feeling fancy and literary I throw in a Robert Frost quote about "uniting my avocation and my vocation." When less inspired, I resort to some well-worn variant of "I write because I *have* to write." Whatever. These are nice answers, all of them, but the truth is I haven't thought too deeply about it, and, if I did, I suspect the real answers would be significantly darker and less verbal. A series of angry but self-asserting grunts, maybe. A howl or a pounding on my chest.

In fact, as I turn toward rooting out a truer answer, I can't help but suspect that my current obsession with words is entangled with my first obsession, the one that plagued my late childhood and early puberty. I was a fairly normal kid, if there is such a thing, good at sports and not ugly, and though my brain teemed with the usual childhood insecurities, many adults seemed to be fooled into thinking that I was a confident and relatively healthy-minded young man. They were wrong. Below my ready laugh and not unpleasant exterior lurked a grim and nearly constant fear of nonexistence.

I think I was around ten when I had my first crisis of being. This was not a Sartre-like intellectual consideration of nothingness that provoked mild nausea, but a visceral sensation that induced something close to real madness. A sudden and overpowering sense that there was nothing in the world: that the world and, more importantly, that *I* didn't exist. This sensation provoked something wild and strange in me, panic attacks so severe that the child psychiatrist who later observed me described them as being like "an LSD user on a bad trip." Not the kind of thing young parents want to hear about their ten-year-old.

It all started when my dog Macker died. Macker had been my life-long companion, brought home from the pound the same month I was born. His death was a terrible one: He ate some of the salt that was used to melt the ice on the roads in Worcester, Massachusetts. My mother found him frozen dead in a snowbank in our backyard. But neither she nor my father told me anything about his death for almost a week. They waited because they were worried about my reaction, and as it turned out they had good reason to worry. I fell apart when I finally heard. I couldn't believe that this thing — this horrible cold ending — had happened to my best friend. Even more appalling, as the days passed, was the notion that something similar might one day happen to me. Lots of kids start to worry about death around this age, I understand, but not many to the point of pathology. Lying in bed at night, a thought — or, more accurately, a series of thoughts

— would grip hold of my mind. It was these thoughts that would constitute my first full-blown obsession.

I called it "the feeling," and though it began with thought, it ended in outright panic. It was a little like walking up a mental staircase where each step was more frightening. It all began with the fact of death, but that was just the first step. Next, I'd imagine how it felt not to exist at all, and it felt like nothing, as well as nothing I could imagine. But with some effort I would manage to put myself in this state of not-being, and with that I would begin to sweat and grow nervous. At that point, I wasn't quite terrified. Not yet. Terror was the next step and with it I left logic behind. In my solipsistic manner, I reasoned that if I didn't exist then nothing else did either. It was about then that "the feeling" usually took over.

It is impossible to exaggerate the sensation of terror that came over me as I ascended the next step. Suddenly, I was certain at that moment that *I did not exist* and, equally if not more terrifying, *the world did not exist*. I was nothing — not even something that might have ever existed. I hit my own chest to remind myself that I was solid, but it did no good. I told myself that I had to exist because I could *think*, but that didn't help either. I felt like an imaginary wisp, a fleck of nothingness, a passing notion in someone else's mind. Worse, it was as if I were merely a fleeting second in someone's dream, but I was even less than that: the dreamer did not exist.

While my logic might have been faulty, the power of what I felt was undeniable. I had a room on the attic floor, and when "the feeling" hit I would sprint down the stairs screaming. I ran through the house at top speed, eyes wild. Once I picked up a painting and almost smashed it over a chair — after all, it was *nothing* — only holding back at the last second.

Usually the first person I encountered was Heidi, my sister. Heidi knew me well and had seen this behavior before, but it still surprised her when her lunatic brother came charging down the hall and hugged her tightly in his arms. But even squeezing Heidi like a boa constrictor, I couldn't make her real to me. I would sprint off to find my mother, then clamp onto her, trying to find something *real*. But it didn't work, it never worked. Though she was substantial enough, I knew the truth, knew that she was just another illusion.

I tried desperately to explain how I felt as if that would somehow reduce the horror.

"Nothing is nothing!" I yelled at first, getting my words mixed up in my panic. "Nothing is nothing!"

"Of course nothing is nothing," my mother said with a gentle smile.

Couldn't she see? Why was she smiling? Was she *insane?*

"But don't you understand: nothing is nothing!"

She smiled again and suddenly I realized my mistake.

"Everything is nothing!" I screamed.

I wanted these words to strike her with the force of revelation, just as they'd struck me. But I couldn't make her see, no matter how I tried. She would pat me on the shoulder and assure me that it would be all right. But it *wouldn't:* nothing would ever be all right again.

One time I had the doubly unpleasant experience of having "the feeling" strike when my father was home. While usually intimidated by him, that day, overwhelmed by my obsession, his presence hardly mattered. He was just another whiff of "nothing" (though, granted, a more substantial whiff). I charged around, throwing things, yelling, *"Everything is nothing!"* (I'd gotten the words down by then.) At first he yelled back, angry, until it finally dawned on him that I was, at that moment, almost completely out of my mind.

He looked at the frothing maniac who was his firstborn.

"Calm down, David," he said. "Just calm down."

He rapped his knuckles on the coffee table to show me how hard it was.

"This isn't nothing," he said. He touched his own burly chest. "I'm not nothing."

He had the right idea, I'll give him that. But it didn't help. I stared for one intense second at his puzzled apelike face. Then I sprinted off down the hallway, screaming and yelling.

"David!" he called after me. "David Marshall Gessner, you come back here this instant!"

I didn't come. He found me cowering in the garage.

"Look, David, just try and calm down —"

"You don't understand!" I yelled.

He'd had enough.

"I understand one thing, my friend. I understand you don't see how lucky you are. Lucky to live in this house, to have food on the table, to have two parents. Do you realize there are millions of children starving and dying of disease?"

I looked up at him as if he were the crazy one.

"I'd like to be starving or dying right now!" I yelled.

And I believed it! Believed that I alone was cursed with this awful understanding, an understanding that made starvation and disease look mild.

I ran away from him, down the street into the neighborhood. I couldn't listen to him and his logic. Didn't he understand? *Everything was nothing!* I did not exist!

Of course, "the feeling" didn't happen every day, but it happened often enough to cause my parents serious worry. I imagine them suddenly contemplating turning in my Pop Warner uniform for a straightjacket. Though I tried to convince my mother it would do no good, she finally dragged me off to see a psychiatrist. With the first one, I got nowhere, but the second was different. I was twelve or thirteen by then and I folded my arms as I sat up on the couch, convinced that mere words couldn't change "the feeling."

"I won't try to 'cure' you," he said. "All I'd like to do is teach you how to relax yourself. So that when you have your 'feeling' you can use these techniques."

He was a bearded black man who smoked a pipe and seemed calm and wise, but deep down I knew mere "techniques" didn't have a chance in hell against "the feeling." Still, when he asked me to, I stared at the spot on the wall.

"I'm going to hypnotize you, David, but it's not like in the movies. Anytime you want you can come out."

I nodded and counted backward. The plan was that, while under hypnosis, he would teach me self-hypnosis. Then, when "the feeling" came, I would simply calm down. I went along with him, knowing full well that I wasn't about to close my eyes and count backwards when the real thing returned.

And, just as I guessed, it did return. But then, slowly, mysteriously, it faded. Maybe I was just getting older, growing out of childhood's illogical logic, or simply getting used to the idea that I was "nothing."

By the time I got to high school, I was only experiencing "the feeling" about once a year, then not at all. I never believed I was cured (and I still don't, I suppose), but, on the other hand, it stopped. Whatever the reason, "the feeling" finally faded away.

3

The dead pig tastes wonderful and I nod and smile at the other writers. But then, just as I am losing myself in this mindless pleasure, a grad student of mine begins to talk about God. Which makes me shift uneasily. I'd rather stay focused on pig. One thing I've learned about this new place where I find myself is that the air is thick not just with humidity but with religion. There is much talk of the Lord. Just this morning I drove to get my coffee behind a pickup with a bumper sticker that read LIVE HARD, PRAY HARD. There are signs like this everywhere (as well as countless flags, both American and Confederate). I am not sure if people are actually any more religious here, in a deep sense, but they are quicker to bring up religion, to display it, to drop Jesus' name. Of course, it's as easy to be a regionalist as any other kind of bigot, so I need to watch myself.

The boy keeps talking and I find myself backing away. I mumble a full-mouthed apology and shuffle off to the woods to piss. On the way back I make a detour by the keg. Then, when I see that the God-talker has moved on, I sneak back for another go at the pig. I am thinking that spiritual topics aren't entirely out of place here. There is something naturally religious about the sacrifice on the spit, but maybe with more of a pagan flavor. The hog has given us the greatest gift. The wordless one has died for the word-makers. I take a long pull on my beer and once again partake of the body.

4

The word *nothing*, which had so terrorized me as a ten-year-old, lost its power in my teens. My family very occasionally attended a Unitarian church, with a minister who was less like a preacher than a good humanities lecturer in college, a man only slightly this side of an atheist. Fittingly, for a Unitarian in central Massachusetts, I spent my high school years worshipping at the church of Thoreau and Emerson. If I had a religion it was a kind of paganism, and one of its few rituals was woods-walking (sometimes aided by the sacramental smoking of a joint). God had never taken a firm hold on my mind when I was a child, and by now had faded entirely. More surprising, my fear of annihilation also atrophied, or at least was buried below more pressing preoccupations like girls and drinking. And something else rushed in to fill the void. Not writing, not quite yet, though I filled my journals with profound thoughts about the color of maple leaves. No, what had begun to preoccupy me was less putting words down on the page than the idea of becoming — or, better yet, *being* — a writer. A *great* writer, it goes without saying. A writer whose name others would think about, who would fill their minds. And a writer who — why not, since I was just daydreaming anyway? — would be immortal.

5

Now I see that while I thought of myself as burningly unique back then, many of my concerns were in fact socioeconomic and, moreover, regional. My family was sufficiently well off that I did not have to concern myself with helping to put food on the table, which freed my mind for other terrors. The regionalism came out in my Unitarianism, my overriding love of the Concord nature writers (though certainly dreamy-eyed adolescents all over the country shared this one), and my community's easy acceptance of my off-handed atheism. When I was shipped away to prep school in western Mass, I found myself with many like-minded members of the same tribe. We wore tie-dye, listened to Pink Floyd and the Dead, smoked pot, and drank wine.

Then my family endured a great and cataclysmic event. My father took a job in the South and transplanted our family from Worcester, Massachusetts, to Charlotte, North Carolina. The move, which later assumed a mythic quality in family history, stunned my mother and three siblings. I, already safely tucked away at school, was the only member of my family who was spared and stayed behind in New England, the only one who would continue to say "you all" instead of taking the sensible verbal shortcut.

6

We eat our pig deep in the woods. Earlier my wife, my two-year-old daughter, and I took the bridge over the Cape Fear River and then north on a road more like a path. The land here is full of live oaks and long leaf pines, as well as a few abandoned refrigerators and washers. The smell is of pine smoked with pig. I talk for a while with Elton, the old man who is letting us borrow his woods, and he gives us a tour of the one-room cabin where his grandmother grew up. When he shows us his stuffed bobcat and raccoon, my daughter points and makes monkey noises. We take a buggy ride through the woods in the dark, which seems quaint at first, until the horse balks at some tree roots and then rushes forward, nearly throwing my daughter and me from the buggy. Suddenly it is not play, and I clutch her tight during the last few hundred yards as the horse trots through the dark woods, pulling us bumpily along. We survive, and settle down around the fire. I help myself to yet another plate of pork, which is still succulent. We all stare at the fire and drink while some of the students play guitars.

I note thankfully that the God-talker has left. I sing along with my fellow writers, my fellow pagans, my fellow pig-eaters.

7

If I sometimes stereotype the Southerners around me, then they stereotype me right back. Since I come from the North — from Massachusetts no less, that land of liberals and bloodless intellectuals — I must know nothing about the traditions of hog-eating. My Southern students relish the role reversal and, assuming I am ignorant of local custom, tell me all about pig etiquette. They chatter like excited anthropologists explaining a new culture. But they are wrong. I know pig. I have traveled to the Gessner ancestral home in the former Eastern German town of Aue, where all my father and I ate for a week was some form of pork or another. And this is not my first pig pickin', far from it. Though I am polite and nod, I am willing to bet the cold beer my hand is wrapped around that I have ingested as much meat straight from a hog's side as any of them.

I was eighteen when my family first moved to North Carolina.

Though I stayed at school in the North, I often came down to visit. Later on, family members would speak of the move to the South the way the early Jews must have spoken of Egypt, a time of massive up-rooting and exile. But the fact is that my family is filled with gregarious sorts and they make friends easily, so after a few months in the South, we decided to celebrate with our new friends by throwing a party and barn dance in the country outside of Charlotte. Following the local tradition, that party would be a pig pickin'.

School was just out and I was visiting my family at the time. My father and I and some other men got out to the barn at the crack of dawn to start roasting the pig on a spit. No matter what you choose to baste the hog with, booze is the true lubricant at any celebration of pig. The men all drank heavily, and before long we were savages around the fire, a Southern version of *Lord of the Flies*. And if we were acting out that book, there was little doubt who was playing the part of Ralph. My father downed a six-pack of Schlitz before noon and got that glimmer in his eye, the one he always got when he drank. He took the pig's head and put a baseball cap on it and jammed a Lucky Strike in its mouth and hooked a Schlitz around its ear using the plastic six-pack loop. He then somehow managed to hang the head over the barn door so that it greeted people when they arrived.

Of course, the guests didn't start to trickle in until late in the after-noon, giving us long hours to achieve almost complete inebriation. When my sister Heidi's new Southern friends arrived, they imme-diately got me stoned. This was a bad combination of intoxicants in-side the teenage me: the pot made me paranoid, the alcohol violent. The next thing I knew I was alone in the back of someone's car and that someone, a real Southern boy, was in front flirting with Heidi. They passed me a bowl and I lit it and pulled the smoke deeply into my lungs. Some time went by, and, apparently, though I'd passed the bowl up front, I'd forgotten to pass the lighter. The Southern boy asked me to pass it, but in doing so he made a grave mistake. He mispronounced my last name.

"Gezz-ner," he said. "Pass the lighter."

I tightened.

"My name's not Gezz-ner. It's Gess-ner."

It was then that my sister's new friend made another fateful error, one he would soon regret. *He laughed at me.* I can't remember exactly what he said after laughing, but through the haze of pot and alcohol this is what I heard:

"Gezz-ner, Gess-ner. Gessner is a nothing."

What the poor kid was probably trying to say was, "Hey, it's nothing. Don't worry about it." But what I heard was something closer to: *"You are nothing."*

In a flash, I was over the seat and on him. We toppled out of the car and rolled on the dirt, fists flying. I punched and punched, a savage attack that he could in no way have anticipated. My family's new friends all gathered around to watch the fight. As was the custom, as is the custom everywhere apparently, a primal chant began, one word over and over: "Fight! Fight!"

Somehow, later, it was all right. I apologized profusely, the way I always did back then. Later we shook hands, though the boy was still understandably confused about what he had done wrong. As it turned out, I'd picked the right kid to attack: many of my sister's friends came up to me to say that they'd often wanted to beat the crap out of old what's-his-name. I was forgiven and the night turned wild. The music cranked and we all danced like dervishes in the barn. My father spun my mother across the floor; my little sister Jenny leapt and whirled; Heidi and I danced in a mad flight of self-forgetfulness.

We were the Gessners. No one could say we were nothing.

8

Tonight is not quite as wild, though with the guitar strumming, and the fire flickering, and the good, bloated feeling in my belly, it's not bad. When my wife says it's time to bring my daughter home, I decide to stay and get a ride with one of my students. Now I can really drink and I begin to tilt the beer cans more aggressively vertical when I lift them above my mouth. By midnight, only a small band of us remain and when we are not singing we stare into the fire as if looking for the answer to something vexing. Really, we just like the way all that flickering looks, like a great animated painting, the whips of orange and blue and white, the ash rising as if bobbing in an anti-gravity chamber. The fire tightens our faces so that we feel like skiers in the lodge after a day in the cold. We have done nothing more than eat pork and drink beer, but we experience the healthy glow you get after a hard workout. The woods are dark around us.

Ambition lured my father to the South. A chance to run his own company, a larger company, a chance to be the king of a wider realm. At forty-two, I am the exact age he was when he moved. My siblings always thought me the lucky one, not having to uproot, but now fate has added this nice little twist. Like my father before me, I pulled up stakes in Massachusetts and landed in North Carolina. Like him, I am ambitious, though not for this teaching job. My ambitions focus more on my continued attempts to put words on the page, though I certainly no longer believe those words will live forever. While it still grips me, I have come more and more to recognize ambition as phantasmagoric, no more substantial than the ash rising from the fire. In fact, it is the same airy stuff that "the feeling" was made of. It is interesting that my father's instinct, in the midst of his ten-year-old son's panic attack, was to rap his knuckles on something solid, like the living-room table. This wood, he seemed to want to say, is the world. Not the insubstantial ideas in your head.

But my father was susceptible to phantoms, too. Sometimes I wonder how much our German heritage affected my family's melodramatic, if not operatic, concept of ambition. During the last years of his life my father indulged himself in what amounted to a Teutonic version of *Roots*. By that time, the Berlin Wall had come down and he had begun to seriously explore the possibility of extending his kingdom beyond the borders of North Carolina by buying his great-great-grandfather's textile company back in Aue, in what had been East Germany. He had made several visits to Aue, had traced the Gessners back hundreds of years to the goat herders in the surrounding hills, had walked along the town's central square, which had just recently been returned to its original name, Gessner Platz (after forty years as Karl Marx Platz), and had essentially been greeted as the great American savior by the nearly bankrupt company and its employees. At that point, many, if not most, East German companies were going under and thousands of employees were losing their jobs. Perhaps the most telling moment of his several trips came when he closed the deal on his grandfather's company, Gessner Textilmachen. He was

walking on a balcony above the factory floor when dozens of machin-
ists and press rollers stopped working and looked up at him. Then
they started chanting his name. "Gessner! Gessner! Gessner!" over
and over, louder and louder. My father just stood there above them
waving like Eva Perón and, knowing him, basking in the adulation.

9

The three students left are all in a class I teach called "Creative Nonfiction." One of them pulls out and lights a cigar, which at this moment
seems an inspired act. We pass it around, sharing saliva and pig juice,
all of us growing stupid with smoke and beer. This stupidity manifests itself when one of the students asks me how I feel about "memoir," which many critics have deemed a sure sign that our civilization
is crumbling. I am only slightly less interested in this topic than I was
in talking about God. "God, this cigar is good," I say in response.

I find myself briefly thinking about a fine piece of memoir I read
called *Whole Hog* by a writer named Tenaya Darlington. She wrote of
the joys of "big meat," of "something slow-roasted that leads to an un-
leashing of energies." A pig pickin', according to Darlington, is a celebration of "joyous crudeness" and at its center are the central facts
of fire and smoke: "The whole affair is testament to the power of fire,
our innate attraction to it, the strange sense of community it awak-
ens." I want to articulate thoughts like these to my students, to make
our meat-eating seem literary, but I find my tongue and brain will not
obey. Instead I point my beer at the fire as if to say "Look," and take
another puff. Soon I am bogarting the cigar, suckling it, ignoring all
those warnings to not inhale, and pulling in the sacred smoke.

10

What is the craze for memoir all about? Doesn't a lot of it come down
to just this: Here is my life. I *lived*. I made my mark. Don't forget me,
please.

But does anyone really believe that that mark — that any literary
mark — is even mildly indelible? There is a reason, of course, that
few people these days talk smirklessly about "immortality." Science
has extended our perspective so that the time between us and Shake-

speare becomes a mere speck in contrast to geological time, a speck that can only seem significant, if not large, in comparison with the planet itself, which is the tiniest wisp of nothingness in the vastness of millions of galaxies. Hard to believe anyone is reading *King Lear* in the Omega galaxy. Hard to believe the words of Shakespeare would survive a supernova.

In his brilliant book *The Denial of Death,* Ernest Becker argues that much of our energy, much of our creativity, much of our *life,* comes from our attempt to deny the essential fact of our existence: that that existence will end. Whether we consider ourselves life-affirmers, who claim the fear of death has no hold on us, or "realists," who admit to living in death's shadow, we are all, according to Becker, both terrified and propelled by our not-so-happy ending. We throw ourselves into frenzied attempts to fill up the nothingness with "something," hurling our objects of work or art — our creations — into the void. At the same time we try to make a *name for ourselves,* knowing that the worst thing we can be is a "nothing." Speaking not just of artists but of human beings in general, Becker says that in our realization that we are nothing, we fight to stand out, to be *something,* trying to build a narcissistic shield around ourselves that keeps death out. We see this need to win, to be first, most obviously in the competition between children as siblings, but it is also obvious enough in adults. Becker writes:

> But it [narcissism] is too all-absorbing and relentless to be an aberration, it expresses the heart of the creature: the desire to stand out, to be *the* one in creation. When you combine natural narcissism with the basic need for self-esteem, you create a creature who has to feel himself an object of primary value: first in the universe, representing in himself all of life.

The next step is finding obsessions that embody ourselves and our shining narcissism. For artists, obsession obviously comes in handy. It not only gives us the energy and power to create the artistic object, but it fills up our minds in a way few other things could. But can obsession fill the death hole? Of course not, though maybe it is out of nothingness that we all begin to create. If the world doesn't exist, then we will make our own world.

In the end, Becker acknowledges, death always wins. The least hardheaded moments in Becker's book are when he reasons that since everything man does is an illusion, why not pick the best, the highest, illusion? This is Becker's somewhat convoluted path back to the spiritual, to God. But there is another path to take, another choice. What if we acknowledge that all our dear passions — ambitions for fame or love or spirituality — are illusions, and then go trudging ahead without them? Of course, illusions will still tug at us, most of us do not have the discipline of a Zen master emptying his mind, but even if we sometimes go where they tug, we at least give up on the idea that these obsessions offer us any real protection against The Big D. What then? What are we left with?

Well, nothing really, but, on the other hand, everything — all that is solid, the world.

11

My father, that master pig cooker, feared death his whole life. But when it actually came, he responded well.

I stayed with him during his last days. His death took over the book I was writing. I typed and scribbled straight through those final hours, taking few breaks except to care for him and write his obituary. Once, near the very end, he looked over at me in the corner of the room, where I sat scribbling notes about his end. Because of the morphine, he hadn't said anything coherent in over a day. But suddenly he snapped alert and looked directly at me.

"Make sure you get the facts down!" he barked.

My father was only fifty-six when he died. Two years after his death I faced another one. I hadn't gotten close, really close, to any dog since Macker, but as I was falling in love with my wife, I also fell for Zeke, her dog. Zeke was a curmudgeon who bit many and loved few. Part Saint Bernard, part collie, he took his last watery breaths in the garden behind our house. Zeke's death has stayed with me, in no small part because of how startlingly it resembled the death of his fellow curmudgeon, my father. Both animals drew long, labored breaths as they closed in on death, then shallower gasps at wider intervals as the moment approached. Both, Zeke in the unplanted mud of the garden and my father in his hospice bed, seemed ready to let go before hanging on and fighting back. Their eyes looked off beyond us, but they were clearly aware that we were holding onto them. The sheer physicality of the moment was like none other, the only thing comparable for me being the final moments of my daughter's birth.

Another way that the two deaths were alike: Neither Zeke nor my father took solace in religion.

My father was a nonbeliever and remained one to the end. This didn't surprise me. I would have been shocked if he made a cowardly retreat in his last hours.

I am full of admiration for the man of faith who stays faithful in the face of this sternest test. That is every bit as admirable as my father's death. But what is not so admirable is, having lived one way, trying to suddenly fudge things with the end near. "I'm sticking to my guns," my father said in his usual businessman vernacular. And he did.

I, like my father, am a nonbeliever. So what does that leave me with?

Again, I say, quite a lot. For one, this world — its smells, its tastes, its feel, and, of course, its people. One thing I have learned in the years since "the feeling" is that the world exists quite separate from me, thank you very much. But what nonbelief doesn't leave me with, in the end, is the self. When I die, I am gone. *Kaput. Poooof.* I can't imagine that I will turn to prayer. As for ambition, what will that get me? Perhaps a slightly longer obituary.

But this is too glib an answer. Even if my work is not remembered, it gives me much. It fills me up while I am here. But it is more than that. In the end, my work is the something I make out of the nothingness, even if the work does not help me escape oblivion. My work is my sacrifice made at an empty altar.

12

The night is fading, the pig is picked. Our pagan rituals are done and soon all that will remain will be bones and bellyaches and hangovers. Only Elton and one other student, my ride home, still sit with me around the dying fire. Not much stands out from the black except for two similar sights: the fire's red embers and the taillights of a car exiting through the woods. I feel beery and deeply tired. I stand up and thank Elton, then tell my ride that I am finally ready. Together we stumble off into the dark night.

■

Darkness

FROM *Zoetrope: All-Story*

WHAT WERE THEY LIKE THE FIRST DAY?
The way we all were.

WHAT WAS THE FIRST THING THEY DID?
What we all did: opened the window. Helen opened it, the bedroom window; the lace curtain fluttered out into the cold air like a waving handkerchief and they saw it.

WHAT DID THEY THINK IT WAS?
A mistake of their clock; a power outage in the night; the work of Louise's diabolical sleeping pills (that felled her nightly like an axe to a tree), making her into a sleepwalking clock-changer; a cloud. They spent half an hour trying to figure out if they had lost their minds; they were old women, so it was not impossible; each of them had lost things before, had spent a secret hour in a hotel room searching for keys, only to discover them right in her pocket. But very soon the radio told them they had not gone insane. The sky had.

"How could particles in the air do this?" Louise wanted to know. She sat on the sofa, perhaps too frightened to look outside again. Every light in the house was on, a parody of morning.

Helen sat bravely by the window. "They say it happened after Krakatoa, all those years ago," she said. "The ash was so thick that for three whole days it was utter darkness."

"But nothing's happened. They don't say anything's happened."

"They said it isn't dangerous. The sun just isn't out."

"Are you going to school?"

"I don't think so. Were you going to work today?"

"I don't know."

Helen stared out at the gloom, shivering. All down the street the young people wandered beneath the still-unlit streetlights, some with flashlights or lanterns, laughing. No old people out on the street at all, not in this kind of confusion, not with sidewalk as loud as a carnival and the crash of police lights everywhere. In the apartment across the street, Helen could make out a couple sitting down to a candlelit breakfast. And below, in front of the building, stood an old Russian woman and her son, hand in hand, nearly indistinguishable in fur hats, looking straight up at the sky.

It was nine o'clock in the morning and as dark as the inside of an eye.

"It's not-hing, I'm sure of it," Helen said. "It isn't time to worry yet."

But she looked over at Louise on the sofa, her dear Louise, her sweet white-haired girl, rubbing a spot out of the coffee table; and though it was not time to worry yet, she began to cry, because there was no helping it.

WHAT DID THEY DO THE SECOND DAY?

Called friends. They could not be alone — Helen said it felt like her grandmother's house in the war, with blackout curtains and the roar of jets along the California coast and the threat of something happening — and so they invited friends over for lunch and made what they could from the pantry; for some nameless reason they did not dare go outside, though the city had put the streetlights on and the throngs of young people had lessened with the dimming novelty of it all. Louise made pasta by dropping eggs into the crater of a flour volcano. She did this in silence, flour puffing into the air as if she had burst the seeds of a milkweed. Helen thawed and roasted a chicken. Then, her hostess's instinct intact, she thawed and roasted another.

At noon, she heard a rattle from the living room, which was Louise drawing the curtains. She understood; they were not Aleuts; they could not bear constant night. Then she heard — like an exhalation of relief — the sound of a match. Candles.

Only two people came: an elderly colleague of Helen's at the college and a kindly, nervous painter Louise had met at an artists' colony. They were good, intelligent talkers at a party; neither was suitable that day. They had clearly come out of loneliness. Helen and Louise found themselves smiling and dutifully filling wineglasses and listening for a doorbell that never rang. What was meant as an afternoon of solace had become one of duty.

"I hear they are turning to rations," said the colleague, a professor of Victorian realism with a waxed gray mustache.

Louise wanted to know what kinds of rations.

"Gas," he said. "And fresh food and meat. Like in the war." He meant World War II. "Who knows? Maybe nylons, Helen."

Helen would not have it; "Ridiculous," she said, regretting the company of this pompous man. The curtains blew open to reveal the unearthly blackness, like the Roman servants who marched beside victorious generals and periodically reminded them of death.

Louise said she could not remember the war.

The painter spoke up, and what she said chilled them: "I think they've done something."

Helen quickly said, "Who? Done what?" Louise gave her a look.

The painter winced at her own thoughts, and her jewelry clanked on her wrists. "They've done something and they haven't told us."

The old man salted his chicken. The optimistic second chicken still sat in the kitchen, glistening and uncarved. "You mean a bomb?"

"An experiment or a bomb or I don't know. I'm sure I'm wrong, I'm sure —"

"An experiment?" Louise said.

Just then, they heard a roar. Instinctively, they went to the window, where in her haste to open it, Helen knocked a little terra-cotta pot over the sill and into the afternoon air, which was as red-dark as ever, but they could not hear its little crash above the din: the streetlights had gone out and now the city was alive with cries.

WHY DID THE STREETLIGHTS GO OUT?

It's unclear. Perhaps a strain on the system; perhaps a wrong switch thrown at the station. But it was a fright to people. That was when the blackouts began, the rolling blackouts, meant to conserve electric-ity. Two hours a day — on Louise and Helen's block it was at noon-time, though it made little difference — with no lamps, no clocks, just flashlights and candles melting to nubs. It was terrifying the first few days, but then it was something you got used to. You knew not to open the refrigerator and waste the cold; you knew not to open the window and waste the heat. "Temporarily," the mayor said. "Until we can determine the duration." Of the darkness, he meant, of the sunless sky.

When he said this over the radio, Helen glanced at Louise and was startled. As a child, she had noticed how sometimes, in old-fashioned books, full-color illustrations of the action would appear — through some constraint at the bindery — dozens of pages before the moments they meant to depict. Not déjà vu, not something already-seen, but something not-yet-seen, and that was what was before her: a woman in profile, immobile, her hair modern and glacially white-blue, her face old-fashioned as a Puritan's in its fury; her eyes blazing briefly with the demonic retinas of a snapshot; her hand clutching the arm of the chair in a fist; her lips open to speak to someone not in the room. A picture out of sequence.

"Louise?" she said.

Then it was gone. Her girl turned to her, blinked, saying, "What on earth does he mean by 'duration'?"

WHY DID THEIR GOOD FRIENDS NEVER COME?
They were afraid. They were all waiting for someone to come to them. They sat alone in the darkness, reading by candlelight, panicked as pigeons, waiting for someone to come, and yet they would not stir an inch. Young people will never understand this.

WHEN DID THEY DECIDE TO LEAVE?
After the riots, about two weeks later. Louise and Helen were out to dinner that night, Midtown, only the second time they had gone out to eat since the first day of the darkness, and they were still unsure if they were right to do it — if it was frivolous to be seen in a room with chandeliers and mirrors and poor people fussing over wealthier people. Louise felt everyone should be in mourning.

"The mirrors should be covered," she said to their dinner companions, who were Louise's agent, her husband, and their friend Peter. "Our garments should be rent. Don't you think? Shouldn't there be wailing somewhere?"

"If you covered the mirrors we'd have nothing," Peter said. He was an antique sort of comic-type still seen only in old movies: the amusing bachelor. Despite his fastidiousness and absolutely secret private life, he seemed convincingly heterosexual; and despite the gray in his conical Victorian beard, and the lines now permanently tooled across his forehead, he appeared all the more boyish, as an adolescent actor appears all the more innocent costumed as an old man.

The agent shook her head. Light gleamed off her glasses. Light gleamed everywhere: off cutlery and plates and crystal, sequins and earrings and pearls; it was indescribably beautiful. Perhaps like the aviary of some rare bird, the last of its kind.

"We have a blind friend," the husband said. He was a scientist, a physicist working with lasers.

Helen found herself laughing. "Oh I hadn't thought about the blind! Aren't they lucky?" She absently drank from Louise's wineglass and Louise gave her a look.

The husband went on seriously; he was a very serious, very emotional man. "She says she can't help it but it's satisfying. She says she hates herself for feeling it, but it amuses her that the rest of us think the world is going to end. Because it's the same world for her."

"It can't be," Louise said. "She can tell there's no sun, and the plants —"

"For her, it's the same world."

Peter raised an eyebrow.

"That's stupid." Louise said. "I'm sorry, Frank. But it is."

Her agent put her hand on Louise's wrist. "Louise, don't be a bore."

Louise turned to her lover. "Helen?"

A moment later there was glass all around them in great shards and a hundred, much more than a hundred young men running down the street, and . . . it seemed like torches, and lanterns, and certainly things were already set on fire in the street before the awestruck diners had the sense to stand up and run to the back of the restaurant. It happened all at once and yet took an extraordinarily long time; there was no way to remember it right. All that Louise knew was that, when she awoke from the scurry of action, she found herself against the wall with Helen and all of them, her napkin in one hand and her fork in the other. Like the net and triton of Neptune, she would later say to others. *I am a useless woman,* she told herself. They spent the night at her agent's place on an inflatable bed. Peter slept on the living-room couch. Outside, they could hear the low moan of the rioting streets as if a monster were being tamed. "It feels like intergalactic warfare," Helen whispered, kissing her lover.

"I've never felt so much like an old woman."

"Enough. You're five years younger than me."

"Do you know the Byron poem?"

"Get some sleep. We'll see how things are tomorrow. If they've suspended classes, we can drive out to Nathan's." This was Louise's son.

"'I had a dream,'" Louise said quietly, "'which was not all a dream. The bright sun was extinguish'd, and the stars . . .' Something. I can't remember."

"Hush now."

"'I had a dream, which was not all a dream . . .' Oh, what is it?"

"Hush."

In the morning, things were no better, and so they left.

How did they meet, Helen and Louise?
They met twice before they fell in love. The first time was when they were very young, in their twenties, and they both taught at an all-girls school in Connecticut; they had the brief kind of passion trapped young women have, kisses in a back room of the library, then it was forgotten. The second time was many years later, when Louise was married to Harold Foster, the composer, and they saw each other at a fundraiser for Helen's college; Helen wore a black spangled pantsuit and stared at the woman in the pink dress who, although clearly in the midst of an argument with a tall, sour-looking man, smiled merrily; Helen stared at this woman as if called upon to perform a feat of memorization, and at last Louise turned, startled, and met Helen's eyes for a breathless moment — it was almost, for Helen, as if she

held something bright and fantastic in her palm, a thimble of mercury — until the president began to speak. When it was over, Helen discovered that her former colleague had been taken home by her husband because she had not been feeling well. Only the sour old man remained.

The third time was on the street in New York City and it was winter, the air as cold and tense as the skin of an apple; the leaves had already brightened and browned and fallen, so the trees that had shaded the avenues in summer were now invisible — and this is how Helen thought of herself as she walked down Second Avenue, the kind of woman who could not seem to hail a taxi, was always leaping out of the way of trucks, getting knocked aside by young people racing down the street; this is how she thought of herself: an invisible old thing in a brown plaid coat.

The light changed; a car leapt right for her, and she braced herself. And then there was Louise.

She did not see Helen at first. Louise was standing on the corner in a long white wool jacket, with embellished little buttons, holding a bouquet of out-of-season irises and trying to hail a cab. Short little Louise, her tiny hand dangling from that great coat sleeve, like a butler ringing a dinner bell in a too-loud room, so hopeless.

Helen said her name.

Louise did not hear her or, more likely, didn't consider that anyone on Second Avenue could be talking to her.

More loudly: "Louise. I found you."

She turned. Astounding how life is, how it will shift ever so slightly and reveal something in the fold of its garment that you hadn't noticed before, something there all along, how it will turn just like a person turns and show you a face you once had memorized amid the chatter of a tedious party, memorized as if for a test, and here it comes, years after you expected it: the test.

"Helen," she said. With no surprise at all. A pale, polished face with the craquelure of age, that haughty upturned nose, the brightly-colored lips no longer full as a boarding-school teacher's, and all of her gone soft with a little fat, a trick photograph of the woman to whom Helen had made a promise so many years before. She would no longer have cared to meet that young woman, that foolish young woman who turned away from her in a snow-bright room, married an older man, and wore a pink dress to a formal party like a fool; Helen was too old to care about a woman like that. But of course that woman no longer existed. Only this woman existed, Louise, here on the sidewalk with a bouquet of flowers and no surprise in her face at all: "Helen."

"Who are the flowers for?"

"For me." She laughed. "No good reason."

A month later she moved into Helen's apartment. They did not explain themselves to anyone; when friends asked, in private, how they had met and joined their lives so suddenly, each acted as if it were something that had been decided long before.

And in these memories, of course, they would always later place one more object in the scene. Ridiculous to have thought of then, almost like remembering that your lungs filled and emptied themselves of air each moment, or that your heart dutifully pumped its ration of blood. Glowing dimly in every memory: the sun.

WHEN THEY LEFT, WHAT DID THEY LEAVE BEHIND?
Helen left her knitting, her records, her running shoes, her files, her research, her plants (already dying), her stones and shells picked up for no reason on foreign beaches and kept, lovingly, purposelessly, and every glittering necklace and earring and bauble anyone had ever given her. She could easily have taken these things, but the mood was rush-rush, and she was the kind of woman who prided herself on efficiency, fortitude, decisiveness; so many small, easily taken things were left behind in the too-proud spirit of the refugee.

If you asked Louise, years later, what she had left, she could have only stared at you angrily and said: "My books."

And the neat shoeboxes untidily crammed with photographs. And the nubbly, Ovaltine-colored couch that they had bought together before Louise had her teaching position and always meant to replace. And the jam in the fridge that a friend had made that summer: strawberry jam. And Louise's old wedding ring. And the art on the walls, made by friends in unfashionable artistic circles. And the mouse under the dishwasher. And the boy upstairs who had finally, loudly mastered "The Entertainer" on the piano. And the early morning shadow of the window falling across the bed, a neat cross with one broken pane, the first vision of every day, which they could have inked from memory on the coverlet. But of course shadows were already a thing of the past.

WHO DROVE?

Louise drove; it was her car, bought for a teaching stint at Yale that was accepted with fantasies of autumn drives during which she would make long speeches to her enemies, her parents, to people from her past who hadn't loved her; but the drives had been crowded and rainy; the stint lasted only a year; and the money, in the end, just barely paid for the car itself. It was German and plum-yellow and she loved it.

They left early in the morning, not that it would have made a difference. That same shade of dim red at all hours, like a flashlight held inside a mouth. Stepping out of their apartment house into the gloom: every time, it was like a deep-sea dive.

"Where are we going?" Helen said at the first wrong turn.

"I talked to Peter while you were in the shower. He's in a state. He's all alone."

"He's across town, Louise, it's going to take —"

"Hel, I said we'd take him. I'm sorry."

"Phone him now and say no. We can't. Phone him now and say no."

They both knew this was nonsense; cell service had stopped nearly a week before. Besides, they did not even own a cell phone.

It was an hour of traffic and police barricades until they reached Peter's building; his street itself had been a horror show of streetlights blinking in and out of sleep, shadowy crowds of young men smoking outside early-open bars — nightmare creatures to the no-longer-young — and, in the shifting spotlights of the lamps, things that looked like baseballs rolling along the road, which were simply rats with no daylight to fear.

It was all too much for Louise. She sat there with her face bruised by the dashboard light and said she couldn't get out of the car; Helen had to do it.

Helen said, "You goddamned old woman. You brought me here and now I've —"

"Oh Helen."

And of course she did; of course Helen kissed her dear Louise on the cheek and slammed the door and went inside, but Helen planned to remember this, to save it in her catalog of hurt.

It was only five minutes before she came down with Peter, who had not finished his packing. He insisted on bringing books, twenty of them, because he said the three of them were basically anchorites locking themselves in a holy room, taking vows, sealing the entrance, and they needed their bibles; and that took longer than Helen would have hoped. Still, it was only five minutes, yet so much was different. They could barely see Louise for all the broken glass.

WHAT HAD HAPPENED?
She wouldn't say. "Let's go!" she kept shouting, motioning them inside, huddled now in the passenger's seat, unharmed except for a small cut below her eye and a wild look. It was her window that was broken. "Go! Let's go!" Helen tried to touch her, tried to coax a story from her, some version to explain the glass, some of which still clung to her like ice, the animal flush in her face, but Louise would not answer. The lamplight shone in streaks through her thinning white hair, on her lips open in an unnamed fury, and it glowed in the bones of her face; she was like a painting, Helen thought later, a great beauty in a painting who will never tell, who will never reveal a thing. A brooch and a ring and a stark madness in her eye. Helen had loved this vain, private, exasperating creature for so long. They were wives, in their way. "Go!" Louise shrieked, "Go!"

So they went.

WHERE DID THEY GO?
Deep into Pennsylvania. I cannot describe how long it took to leave Manhattan, the eccentric streetlights, the stifled, bottled-up feeling of the traffic, the complete blackout of the Holland Tunnel as if they

were drilling (in slowest possible motion) into the diamond-hard center of the world — and Helen's eye was ever on the fuel gauge, a neon miniature pump, because it had already come over the radio that gasoline was to be rationed, along with firewood and vegetables, beginning the next day. And so that explained the crowds, the panic. Peter, smoking out the broken window, picking a piece of tobacco from his upper lip, said: "Oh it must be madness at the farmers' market." And on they went, mile after dark mile.

Three hours later they stopped at the brightest-lit restaurant they could find and ordered a gravy-soaked lunch, suffering the suspicious glances of a downy-mustached waitress who clicked her retractable pen like a switchblade. In the corner sat a silent family, dressed for church, and their teenage daughter (in flour-sack floral) with her eyes closed, wincing, as if recent events had happened just to ensure her personal humiliation.

Peter said, "You know what Gertrude Stein did?"

"What?" said Helen, dipping her fries into an impasto of ketchup. It was a relief not to care, not to pretend to care, about good food. Louise, on the other hand, looked childishly shocked at her sandwich.

Peter: "What she did in a time of disaster."

"I'm not sure I'd take Gertrude Stein's advice on disasters —"

"They lived in France when the Germans came in," he said, smiling at the waitress, who had brought his milkshake in a sundae glass, the leftover in a canister, in the old-fashioned pretense that she had made too much and was giving him the rest. The canister wore a shimmering chain mail of frost. "They would listen to the radio," Peter said, "and every Tuesday the announcer came on telling of some new city that had been taken, and it was horrible; she said it was so horrible that they laughed. Every Tuesday, it became comic. And what she did when the Germans did arrive, when she saw the planes, when the French boys all hid in the hills because they feared being taken into the German army and people left bread and cheese for them in secret places — when it was over, and they were occupied — what Gertrude Stein did was she trimmed her hedges."

Helen noticed Louise eating just the bacon from her sandwich. "Metaphorically?"

"No, it wasn't poetic, it wasn't metaphor. She was done with metaphor," he said. "And with news. She wouldn't listen to the wireless. I think it was . . . the truth was a gorgon, and she could see it only reflected in others' faces, in Alice's, or in the girls' from the village who gave her illegal butter; but if she looked directly at it she would turn to stone. So she trimmed her hedges."

Helen looked away, to the teenage girl in the vinyl booth, who now seemed mortified almost to the point of sainthood.

"Then she was a coward," Helen said.

"We never hear what Alice did," Louise said softly.

Peter smiled and pulled on his beard. "She trimmed her hedges and she thought when she had finished trimming, then the Germans would leave."

Louise started to say something, but Peter opened his hands ecclesiastically: "She was very superstitious. She and Alice thought their car would take them to places it wanted them to go, places they belonged."

Helen's laughter rose in shining rings around them, and it was the carelessness of her voice — just as when she had laughed about the blind — that made the people stare. The gray-featured family, the anxious daughter, the waitress whose hair glowed from the light behind her. It was too wrong and strange, with the sky outside, and the world the way it was. It was a luxury. She might as well have brought out a diamond tiara and worn it just to spite them.

Louise entered loudly into the conversation: "I've been learning French."

Helen said, "You have?"

Peter said, "Their car had a flat tire and so that's why they didn't leave France."

Louise sat up very straight. Her eyes were on Peter, and with one hand she clipped and unclipped her Turkish earring (her ears had never been pierced). She said, "I've decided that when I learn to speak French, really speak it, then this will all be over."

Peter spoke to no one in particular: "Gertrude also had a prophecy book."

Helen said quietly, "I didn't know you were learning French."

The family in the corner folded in together, listening to their daughter, who had begun to whisper with one eyebrow cocked. She glanced only once at Helen, bitterly, cleverly, before joining back into her family.

And Louise, too, looked at Helen as if to say: *Yes. I have a stupid, secret belief, a magic belief. Yes. Aren't we vain, ridiculous creatures?*

Tell me, what happened to Louise in the car, surrounded by broken glass?

She never did say whether it was young men out with crowbars, or a stone thrown by rioters, though these explanations were very possible; perhaps she could not remember what happened, but Helen and Peter both wondered silently why the glass was outside the car and not inside.

Did they spend the night in that town?

They could not imagine it — there was something hard and wary in the people's faces there, a look that Helen had seen only out West in desert towns — and the one motel sat uncomfortably far from the cluster of shops, two cars alone in its parking lot, its front office trembling with a purple glow that Peter identified as marijuana grow lamps. He also warned them that he was known to sleepwalk in strange places, ever since he was a boy. Any place would have been too strange, though, any motel or rooming house, with thin sheets and an amateur oil painting above the dresser, and brief-lived mayflies seeking the bathroom's incandescent sun, and the darkness poking in at every window like a burglar.

"I think," Louise offered once they were on the road again, with a plastic bag taped over the broken window, where it howled like a ghost, "I think we can make it to Nathan's."

Peter said, "I'm fine. I had too much coffee but I'm fine."

Louise said, "Maybe also we should — we should be careful."

"What do you mean?" Peter said.

She put up her hands to arrange her hair against the loud wind. "Maybe Helen and I shouldn't mention we're gay."

"Oh Louise," said Helen.

"You felt it. It's dangerous now, somehow. I don't know why. I don't know why just darkness would do that. But please."

"We'll get to Nathan's," Helen said. "We'll get to Nathan's in Pennsylvania and everything will be OK."

And no sooner had they crossed the state line, rounded a bend, than they came upon the incredible: a bright patch of day.

"Oh God!" Peter said. "Oh God!"

But not day — it had only the brightness, the clear ordinary delight of day, shifting and waving in the wind like a sheet pinned to a clothesline. What it was: it was a whole forest set on fire.

The cars moved in a sluggish row past this awesome thing, while helicopters busied themselves in the flames like bees in their flowers, and fire trucks sprayed long, gleaming fountains that turned, instantly, to smoke and to steam. Everything was bright and hot at last, and in some terrible way they were grateful; it was hard not to applaud whoever had done this. Peter was driving now, so slowly that he said, "Get out, you two, get out and look at it and I'll pick you up around the corner," and they did. They stood there with dozens of other people with their hands up in the air as if they were all ready to catch something, looking behind themselves and laughing at their shadows, which were back briefly from the dead and could wave at them; then the people looked at last on what their eyes could hardly bear to see: what Helen, smiling (while Louise groaned), called "the prodigal sun." It took a minute or two to make out, in that sublime light, hidden among the crackling pines, the cross-paned windows of a house.

You never told Louise's version of their meeting.
If everything were saved from life, nothing forgotten, then she would have with her still the scent of Helen's hair in 1968, when they were both in their twenties and teaching at St. Margaret's — Helen history, Louise the language arts — standing very still in the back room of the library (lit only by one window and its fluorescent snow-glow) as Louise announced her engagement to Harold Foster. They were leaving for Harvard. The blond scent of Helen's hair as they embraced. And of the room's airborne dust immobile in its web of static, and the odor of ancient, unread books and moldering maps of places that none of their students would ever visit and whose citizens would

one day, not understanding why, awaken to a sunless sky. The watch in Helen's breast pocket, pressing like a tumor between them. The shiver of passion in that nubile body — gone, all of it, gone or mis-remembered now. But how could even an old woman forget what Helen whispered to her in that time when they were very young? What she hushed into her ear before she walked out the door — that she would find her one day — and Louise was left alone in that un-used room, looking out at the snow's mounded brightness with the sensation of someone going blind?

And at the party: the feeling of someone tapping on her shoulder, and then a furious woman staring at her from across a room; it made her ill and she had to feign a migraine to get her husband to leave.

And on the street after his death: windblown leaves scratching along the sidewalk, the wet scent of the flowers, the light staring Cy-clops red, and, from behind her, a voice: "I found you."

Did they stay at the fire?

They had to get to Nathan's, though it was hard to pull themselves away, even after they saw the burning house among all the burning trees. "Well aren't we all mayflies?" Helen whispered, giggling. Back in the car, they described the fire to Peter, what it felt like to walk a lit-tle ways down the hill to where the grass was dry and crackly, to have the hot wind on your face like a day at the beach — "God I always hated the beach," Helen added — and he nodded and they drove like that, in silence, for a long time until even looking back they could not make out the blaze except as a shimmer in the clouds, and ahead of them were blank unburned forests and the fistfuls of light they knew to be houses.

"'I had a dream,'" Louise said softly after a while, "'which was not all a dream.'"

Peter made a pleased noise in the front seat. Helen said nothing, only watched the black-on-black of the trees against the sky, and what she took for bats flying above, or perhaps birds, because they must wake up at last, mustn't they?

"'The bright sun was extinguish'd, and the stars did wander dark-ling in the eternal space.'"

"I love that," Peter said. "'Wander darkling.'"

Helen said, "Go on."

"Something . . . oh," Louise said. "'Morn came and went — and came, and brought no day, and men forgot their passions in the dread of this their desolation; and all hearts were chill'd into a selfish prayer for light.'"

Helen said, "'Men forgot their passions.' I don't see how that could be." There was not a single light on the road, nor anywhere in the landscape. Then they passed a darkened farmhouse and Helen thought she saw a woman in a white apron walking in a field of fallen corn; it seemed like everyone was a ghost now. But it was not a woman; it was a lung-shaped patch of melting snow on a hillside, and then it was gone.

Louise said, "I don't remember the rest. Maybe Nathan will have a copy."

Peter rolled down the window a bit, letting in the cold smell of trees. "I've been wondering, what will they do in New York when they're out of wood?"

"In the fireplaces, you mean?" asked Louise.

"I can't see men ever forgetting their passions," Helen said. "And I don't know what dread is anymore."

"When they're out of candles," Peter explained. From the backseat, they could just see his eyes in the rearview mirror.

Helen told him: "They won't run out of candles. They don't run out of those things in New York."

"Eventually. They've run out of vegetables, haven't they? And gas."

She pulled her shawl around her. "I'm not worried about New York."

In that rectangle of mirror, they could see him blink in concern. "Do you think they'll set things on fire? Like the forest we saw?"

"I know what they'll do," Louise said quietly.

Helen took Louise's hand and shook her head, looking out at the shapes of things beyond the road, things unlit for days. "I'm not worried about that, New York can take care of itself. I'm not worried about dread, either. What did you say, honey?"

"I know what they'll do."

Louise took her hand away from Helen. She put it to her own

cheek as if she had been struck by something. She looked into the hatchback where their things lay, piled and gathered, and Peter's things, and then the fingers of her other hand began to curl around the armrest in a fist. Her eyes went forward. A rare passing car lit up the interior and her hair went white.

Louise said, "They'll burn the books."

"Lo . . ."

Louise had a frozen look on her face. "Before they burn their furniture, they'll burn the books. Before the curtains or the sheets or their old letters. They always do."

She sat very regal in the backseat with the headlights illuminating her glacial hair, her furious jagged profile, her parted lips. The look was in her eyes again, a brightness that was not a reflection but its own light, the way the snow on the hillside was its own light, a lunacy, as if this old white-haired poetess were capable of something terrible, in which case we all are.

"They always do," Louise said loudly. "They'll take down the *Moby-Dick* they've had since high school, and they always hated how it sat on the shelf and gloated at them, and they'll throw it in the fireplace, there'll be a kind of . . . relief, satisfaction! They'll light it and put the kids around it and it won't matter." Her left hand gripped the armrest as tightly as a broomstick, but she would not look at either of them. "We are truly cannibals. *Don Quixote.* Or just a whole pile of them. *Huckleberry Finn.* Why not? If there's no light to read by anyway —"

"Lo, don't —"

Peter said, "You said that when you spoke French at last —"

She shook her head, talking almost in a shout. "I'm never going to learn it. I'm too old, and of course that's ridiculous. I'm ridiculous. These are the Dark Ages now, and it's going to come to that. All the books! And why not?"

"Louise!"

Louise was shrieking now: "The books! All the books!"

The car rushed by them and they were thrown into darkness again, that old darkness, and Peter could now hear only a movement in the backseat, maybe a struggle of some kind, maybe someone crying, and then silence as his eyes strained to see the two old women in the rearview mirror.

WHAT DID HE SEE?

A memory from his boyhood: two objects in the darkness, fallen into a quiet embrace. Just as he used to come upon his mother's hairbrush at her vanity table, lying on its back, her silver comb nestled into its bristles. A still life to which he often awoke after his sleepwalking trips. An old woman and her lover, clutching one another, the sound of one of them weeping, he could not say which, and nothing behind them but a lightless window, a mirror, a reflection of his wide eyes within it, a memory. A comb in a brush. If he watched them, they would wait. They would wait, the silver things, perfectly still, until dawn.

TELL ME: DID THEY MAKE IT?
Somehow.

HELON HABILA

■

The Hotel Malogo

FROM *The Virginia Quarterly Review*

THE SUN WAS SETTING when I got off the bus and entered the empty hotel bar. Most of the space in the dim rectangular room was taken up by iron chairs arranged round iron tables, the white paint peeling off to reveal the rust, brown and streaky, underneath. The wooden windows were closed and a single light bulb in the ceiling illuminated the room faintly. A long counter with whiskey bottles on shelves along the wall behind it covered one side of the room. A door behind the counter stood ajar.

"Hello," I called, dropping my bag on the rough concrete floor. "Is anyone here?"

A man in a dirty yellow singlet came out wiping his hands on a towel. "Yes?"

"I want a room."

He looked me up and down with his sickly yellow eyes, and I could tell he was trying to determine my age.

"You get money?"

"Yes."

"A room na fifty naira for one night. You fit pay?"

I had four hundred naira in my pocket. He reached into a drawer and brought out an old register. On the tattered cover was handwritten in blue ink: Hotel Malogo. He opened a page and lifted his pen.

"Wetin be your name?"

I hesitated. "Diaz."

His pen hovered. "Diaz? Which kind name be dat?"

His anaemic eyes betrayed his confusion. "How you spell dat?"

I spelled it for him.

"How long you wan stay?"

"Three days." I'd get a job and move to a more permanent accommodation as soon as possible.

"You pay now, plus fifty naira deposit."

"But . . ."

He closed his register with a bang. I paid and followed him down a corridor and up a flight of concrete steps to the first floor. My room was the second to the last in a long row of rooms on one side of a dark, uncarpeted hallway whose walls gave off a musty, airless smell. He flicked the light switch on and off a couple of times to prove that the light was working, then he turned to the fan. We stood in the center of the room, looking up, waiting for the blades to start turning, when they did he looked at me and smiled.

"This one na correct room."

I threw my bag on the bed and sat in the only chair. Before he left he had said the bathroom was outside, and I had to share with the other occupants of the first floor, but I should be happy because at the moment there was only one other guest on the floor.

But even that did not diminish my optimism. I had come to Lagos to get a job, a new life. That was why I had chosen a new name. Diaz. I took the name from a popular Mexican soap opera my mother and sisters never missed. My mother once said a second name is like a charm, it protects one from evil, like a back door, a fire exit.

Night came suddenly: one moment I was unpacking my bag in the lazy twilight coming in through the window, and the next moment I was in darkness. I went outside and bought akara and bread from the roadside vendors. I sat before my window over a narrow backstreet and ate — below me, the cars and buses, the daredevil bikers who weaved between them at speeds almost too fast for the blinking eye, the hawkers who shoved their wares into the car windows while calling out prices. Eventually sleep overcame me, and I rolled into bed.

I woke up early. When I came downstairs the barman was cleaning the floor with a long-handled mop, reaching under tables and chairs to push out pieces of broken glass and bottle caps and cigarette stubs. Most of the floor was covered in camouflage patterns of spilled beer from last night. The room stank of it, and of stale smoke. He was still wearing his yellow singlet; around his waist was a print wrapper that reached all the way down to his ankles. Every once in a while he'd stop to take the chewing stick out of his mouth and spit the bits into the water bucket before resuming. He walked with a bowlegged gait that I hadn't noticed yesterday.

"Good morning."

He turned with a scowl on his face. His hairline began almost at his eyebrows. The stubble on his chin had formed ugly bumps, and some of them were oozing blood and pus.

"Yes?" he growled.

"Where can I have breakfast?"

"Outside," he said with a wave of his hand, impatient, as if I were some passerby whose frivolous gossip was keeping him from his cleaning. I was uncertain what to do next. I wanted to set out early to Victoria Island, where most of the newspapers had their offices, to start inquiring about job openings, but I had to eat first in case it turned out to be a long day.

"I can show you a good place to eat, if you want."

The voice came from a dark corner of the room, from which an old man emerged, an apologetic, ingratiating smile on his face. The barman paused and threw the man a contemptuous look before resuming his mopping. "Come, please," said the old man, already at the door.

The street was alive with hawkers and beggars, though it was just 7 A.M. The yellow danfo buses inched down the narrow road, stopping to pick up or drop off passengers. The sun was bright and steadily rising. The old man was ahead of me, weaving from one side of the narrow road to the other, occasionally turning to flash me a smile, one hand permanently pointing forward as if to shrink up the distance. His faded khaki trousers were too big for his waist and he kept pulling them up with his other hand. I could tell he was hungover. I had an uncle like that. His mind would most likely be scheming on how he might wheedle a drink off me.

We passed through warrenlike alleyways where families sat on verandas, eating their breakfasts of beans and bread sold door-to-door by women carrying huge basins on their heads; where garbage overflowed from roadside dump sites into open gutters and into the roads; where naked children ran in and out of doorways, young girls passed us returning from community taps with buckets of water on their heads, and fathers stood in groups chatting, occasionally pausing to take out their bamboo chewing sticks and spit long streams of saliva.

"It is not far, is it?" I called, my misgiving showing in my voice. He was quicksilver, moving faster whenever I tried to catch up with him, so that I remained the same distance behind. Then he turned a corner behind a house and when I followed I saw that he had stopped, the hand pointing to a tiny doorway, the smile lustrous on his face.

"Here it is. Not far at all."

A woman was standing in a narrow veranda, inclined over a huge pot of goat stew on a stone hearth, the heavy aluminum lid in her hand, the other hand stirring with a ladle.

"Munirat," the old man said to her eagerly, pointing at me, "I bring you customer. Na my friend, we stay for the same hotel."

The woman turned and looked at me briefly, disinterestedly, before turning back to her pot. I could see the old man was not highly regarded by her.

"Come inside." He led me to a window table. Used plates and cutleries littered the peeling Formica surface.

"Munirat, come and clean this table," he called, but without much conviction. He picked up the plates himself and took them outside, telling me as he went to sit. A few customers sat in the dim room, hunched over their plates of rice and beans.

"You stay at the hotel?" I asked when the elusive old man finally sat down opposite me.

"I stay there long, long time. In fact, na me be the oldest guest there."

"My name is . . ."

"Diaz," he said. "I know. Clement told me."

"Are there a lot of guests in the hotel?"

He shrugged. "People come and go." He leaned forward and dropped his voice to a whisper. "Mostly na married men with their girlfriends, that's all. Even now some of them will be coming with their secretaries from office, just for one hour," he ended the sentence with a wink. My face must have expressed my shock because he laughed and patted my hand, "You be young man, that's why you are surprised. But it is true. Every day I see them. How old are you?"

"Seventeen," I said, adding a year to my age.

"Ah," he said.

Munirat came in then and asked me what I'd have. She was a heavily built woman with powerful shoulders and a fat behind; her sweaty face echoed a distant, neglected beauty.

"I'll have rice," I said. She turned to go. I called after her, "But what of him?"

She looked the old man up and down and hissed. "No way. I no sell to am unless he pay me my hundred naira first."

The old man squirmed, and for an instant, before his ingratiating smile returned, he looked sad, embarrassed. "I will pay, as soon as I get my gratuity. This week. I promise."

"That's what you been de say for the past one year."

"True," he protested, "government go pay us this week. I swear."

"It is okay. I will pay for his meal."

"Give me *eba* and *egusi*," he said, a triumphant look on his lined face. "In fact," he advised me, growing ebullient, "you should eat *eba*, not rice. Munirat's *eba* is the best in this whole Lagos, and her soup, hey, I no fit describe that one."

"You this man," she said, pleased, shaking her head, injecting a slight sashay into her gait as she left. As we ate I noticed that beneath his rough exterior there was some refinement in his manners: in the way he listened without interrupting, and the way he thoroughly scrubbed his hands before eating. I could see how a woman such as Munirat might find his words flattering. He asked me what I came to do in Lagos; I told him I wanted to become a journalist. He listened with his encouraging smile, and then he told me he was sure I would get something, that Lagos was full of opportunities.

His words gave me courage as I set out for the island.

When I returned to the Hotel Malogo I found the old man waiting for me. His door, two doors down from mine, was ajar and he came out as soon as I stood before my door to take out my key.

"Diaz, my friend, you are back," he said. The job market had been

fiercer than I had anticipated. I had spent most of the day not in editors' offices but at the gates explaining to guards why I wanted to see
the editor even though I had no appointment; once I made it past the
guards to the secretary's office, but not once had I had the chance to
show my writing samples, which I carried in a waterproof folder under my arm.

"I am back," I said.

"This is my room. Come in and see my room. Please, please."

I was exhausted, I needed rest, but I was scared and I wanted reas-
surance that tomorrow things might be better. The room was exactly
like mine: the bed by the window that overlooked a nondescript backstreet with hawkers hawking and beggars begging; the only difference was that his room showed evidence of longer occupation. There
was an old radio on the table and a pile of old newspapers on the
floor by the bed, and I could see under his bed the side of a wooden
portmanteau. On the window ledge were his toilet tools: a comb, an
economy-size bottle of Vaseline, a toothbrush, a half-empty tube of
Close-Up, and a mirror — or rather, a broken piece from a larger
mirror. He asked me if I wanted a cup of water, and I said yes. He
brought out a big can from behind a chair and poured a cupful.

"This is good clean water. I boil it myself." He looked proud as if he
had made the water, then the pride disappeared and he grew fidgety,
moving too quickly whenever he had to pick up something, speaking
too fast. At last he blurted out what he really wanted, and when he did
he spoke in perfect English, "I wonder if I could borrow some money
from you? I will pay, later, tomorrow, when I get my gratuity."

I told him I didn't have money, that I had to get a job soon, otherwise I would be out on the streets. I lowered my face to my water
glass.

"I will pay, I swear. My gratuity will soon be here. I swear. See, see,
let me show you." He jumped off the bed and picked up a newspaper
from the table. It was already open at the page he wanted to show me,
a piece about the happy resolution of the long impasse between the
union of retired railway workers and the government, with the government finally agreeing to pay each retiree a sum of 100,000 naira.
He brought out further documents from his portmanteau; one was a
copy of his retirement letter.

"They will pay us, soon, tomorrow, this week. I swear. I just need fifty naira, or thirty."

I imagined how many people he must have shown these documents, including the barman, Clement, and the food woman, Munirat, and how convincing he must have sounded when he spoke in his good English. I was too tired to argue. I gave him thirty naira. A tear dropped out of one eye when he held the money in his hand.

"Come, let's go to the bar. I must buy you a drink," he said as he wiped away the tear.

"But I thought you wanted the money to eat."

"It doesn't matter. Tomorrow I will get my gratuity. I will be rich. Today, we will celebrate. Come, let's go to the bar. Leave your papers here. Let's go, now."

His name was Papa John. His story went like something out of a Bollywood tearjerker, unremitting tragedy after unremitting tragedy. His parents had died in 1967, just before the Nigerian civil war; and when the war broke out, his uncle, who was his guardian, encouraged him to enlist just so the uncle could be rid of him. After the war he married a woman he met in a war refugee camp, and she bore him a son, John. After ten years of marriage, his wife deserted him when he lost his job with the railway, and because of a burgeoning drinking habit. He didn't go to see his boy, John, till almost ten years after the divorce, and the son publicly denied him, calling him a useless old man and forbidding him from ever contacting him again.

Papa John was crying over his third bottle of beer as he narrated his story. I had bought him the third bottle because the thirty naira I loaned him was already gone. I drank a Fanta, which was warm because all day there had been a power outage. Our table was in the center of the barroom, which was crowded with drinkers; it was the end of month and pockets were bulging, hands were itching, camaraderie flowered, watered by alcohol, and once in a while someone would stand up and drag his rather reluctant girlfriend to the narrow space in front of the bar to dance to the tinny hi-life music issuing from a hidden speaker. From behind the counter I could feel Clement the barman's suspicious eyes on me; he followed the old man's every move. Once, when Papa John went to the bathroom, Clement came over and whispered into my ear: "Dem don pay him the gratuity?" His breath stank of fish and onion. I said no, I was the one buying the beer. He looked at me as if he didn't believe me, then he said, "You de waste your money for this useless man."

When I told the old man, he said, "I owe him five thousand, that's why. But what is five thousand? Common five thousand, when my money comes I will pay him, like this," he clicked his fingers. He looked around before whispering, "Listen, don't ever trust that Clement. He is a crook. He has dangerous friends who come at night. I've seen them. Be careful with your money. Always lock your door."

When I told him my name was not really Diaz, he smiled and said, "It doesn't matter. It is a good name. I know someone with a name like that once. He was our controller at the railway. A white man, with red hair. Once, when the workers were protesting because of the late payment of their salaries, and the police came and were about to shoot, he stood up in front of the people and said, 'Shoot me first before you shoot anyone of these honest workers.' Ah, Diaz, Diaz. A good man. A good name."

I listened attentively even though I sensed that he was making up the story. I wondered if he had ever worked for the railway, if the documents were genuine, if I would ever see my thirty naira again. But it didn't matter. For a moment he made me forget the harsh world waiting to crush me as soon as I set out again tomorrow.

I went to bed with hope.

I bought him breakfast in the morning, and after breakfast I lent him twenty naira for the bus because, he said, he was being paid his gratuity today. I left him in front of the hotel and I took a bus to the island, thinking I had to say no to him at some point soon, and the sooner the better because after tomorrow I wouldn't be able to afford a meal.

I came back around 4 P.M. and to my relief Papa John wasn't waiting for me. I lay down in bed trying to read, but it was too hot in the room to concentrate; there was a power cut and the static fan hung over me like the sword of Damocles. I kept drifting into a slumber and waking up again. Around 7 P.M. I jerked awake. Someone was hammering on my door.

"Diaz, my friend, are you in there?" It was Papa John. I didn't reply. He knocked again till finally the door retreated under the weight of his persistent pummeling, and I heard his steps coming in. How obnoxious, I thought, and just then the lights came back. We stared at each other and immediately I realized that something had changed. He stood taller. His stubble was gone, he was wearing a new dashiki with a matching hat, and even before he said it I knew. He had been paid.

"Come, come to my room. Tonight we will celebrate. Come, you are my only friend in this Lagos. Come and enjoy with me."

The food seller, Munirat, was with him. She was dressed up in aso oke with a tall scarf on her head, a tiny bag in her lap; the heavy makeup on her face almost disguised her features, making me look twice before I recognized her.

"Diaz, welcome," she said. She didn't look overly happy to see me. Today she wanted the old man all to herself. A bottle of Aromatic Schnapps stood on a side table, and next to the bottle were two plastic cups. The radio on the table played a soft juju tune and the old man twirled around to the beat, a big grin on his sweaty face. I stood by the door and watched him dance.

"I will leave you two now," I said, but he shook his head and danced toward me and took my hand and led me to the bed. "Sit. Have a drink."

"I don't drink," I said.

"Leave the boy alone, Papa John. He too small to be drinking," Munirat said, batting her eyes at the old man. He waltzed toward her and threw his arms round her clumsily, resting his head on her mountainous bosom; she pushed him away coquettishly, laughing.

"You this old man, you no get shame o."

When the song ended Papa John switched off the radio and said to Munirat, "Let's go to the bar. You go first. I have something to tell my friend Diaz before we join you."

He walked her to the door and stood there to make sure she had gone, and then he came back. He bent down and pulled out the heavy portmanteau from under the bed. He opened it and took out a medium-size red bag, and then he stood up and dramatically poured out its contents onto the bed. It was a lot of money, bundles and bundles of it in fifty naira notes.

"They paid me today, Diaz. Cash." He spoke in hushed tones, his eyes on my face, a sheen of sweat on his forehead under the hat. I could see that he was slightly drunk and I felt worried for him.

"You really shouldn't have so much cash lying around."

He raised his hand, stopping me. "You are right. Tomorrow I will take it to the bank. But first, here's your money." He took out fifty naira and handed it to me, then he began to return the rest into the red bag, but halfway he stopped suddenly and sat down; his shoulders began to shake. He was crying.

"I waited eight years for this money. Eight years. I suffered so much. Tomorrow I am getting out of here. I will get a nice room somewhere in Ikeja. Maybe Munirat will come with me. She is a nice woman."

"What of your son, John? Won't you get in touch with him?"

His shoulders suddenly stiffened. He turned back to the bed and resumed placing the money into the bag. "I have no son," he said gruffly. "I don't care. I have my money now. I don't need anyone."

When he finished putting the money into the bag he handed it to me. "I want you to keep this for me in your room. Now everyone knows I have been paid, my room is not safe. Keep it for me. I will get it back tomorrow."

"But," I began, "you don't even know me."

He patted me on the head. "But I do. When you get to my age you will know people. You are a good boy and one day you will be a great man. Go."

He started dancing the moment we entered the bar. People came over to our table to shake his hand and to congratulate him, and he handed out bottles of beer like a monarch handing out favors.

"Clement, give this my friend a bottle of beer. Don't worry, I will pay," he would say to the barman. Munirat kept pulling at his hand under the table, whispering, "You this man, you go finish all your money tonight." But the old man only laughed and told her, "Don't worry. Money no be problem. Trust me."

He had a thick wad in his dashiki pocket which he kept whipping out to pay for each order, and I saw the pain on Munirat's face increase as the wad's thickness decreased. I sipped my Coke, my mind anxious about the money upstairs under my bed. Clement was all smiles, so I assumed the old man had already paid him his money; he hovered around our table like a vulture waiting to pick up the gleanings, shaking the old man's hand at every opportunity. He rushed back to change the music when Papa John requested a special number by Rex Lawson. The whole room fell silent as the old man and Munirat stood up to dance to "Guitar Boy."

I bade them good night when the music ended and I went up to my room.

But I couldn't sleep. The money under the bed was like a layer of nails, pricking at me through the mattress, and twice I brought out the bag to check that its contents were still there. I had never seen so much money in my life, and even though it wasn't mine I could feel a rising excitement whenever I touched the thick bundles of notes. I turned off the light and went to sit by the window, staring out into the still-busy backstreet. The yellow danfo buses were even now dropping off and picking up passengers, and the call of the tired conductors assumed a plangent, wailing note. The buses' rear lights were iridescent, mobile, twinkling briefly, and then were swallowed up by the night.

At last I was able to drift into a restless slumber, but it didn't last long. I was awakened by voices just outside my door. It was Papa John's, and the other one was unmistakably Munirat's. They were parting. She was advising him to get some sleep. I went back to sleep myself. But almost immediately I came awake again.

This time it was a scream, clear and sharp at first, then it became muffled, as if someone had put his hand over the screamer's mouth. Then came sharp whispers, then silence. I stood up. The voices were coming from the direction of Papa John's room. I went to the door and quietly pulled back the bolt, then I opened the door a crack, but I couldn't see anything. There was a power outage and the corridor was pitch-black. The voices came again; someone at the door was urging someone inside the room to hurry up. Now I could see a dim, wavering light. I heard the muffled scream again. Robbers. The money. Under my bed.

How long would he last before he told them the money was with me? I quickly closed my door, but before I moved away from it I heard footsteps coming from the old man's room. I leaned my back against the door. Waiting. But the footsteps passed my door, toward the stairs, the voices talking angrily. But even in my fear I recognized one of the two voices: it was Clement's. My legs felt weak; I sat down on the floor, my back against the door.

Almost an hour later I opened my door slowly, and after making sure the corridor was deserted, I went to the old man's room; when I touched the door, it creaked open and in the silence the creak was amplified a million times. I went in, shutting the door behind me.

"Papa John, are you in there?" I whispered. I moved in, straining my eyes to see in the complete darkness, but at that moment the lights came back. He was lying on the bed, his back to me, and for a moment I thought he was sleeping, until I saw the blood. It was almost invisible on the blue bed sheets, but on the front of his white dashiki it was stark, startling, like a splash of cold water on the face in winter. His face was frozen in a grimace of pain; they had cut him on the fingers and on the face repeatedly before slitting his throat. I felt dizzy. For a moment I forgot where I was, then the dizziness passed and I bolted. I went back to my room and locked the door.

I sat on my bed, my mind a blank. Soon they would come for me, I was sure. Even if he hadn't told them, it wouldn't take them long to figure out that he might have left the money with me. But when the hours passed and they did not return, I began to relax a bit. I packed my bag in the dark and sat on the bed, waiting for morning. I tried to think what best course of action to take, but my mind was like a block of stone.

I ran all the way to Munirat's place. I found her in the small yard behind the buka, pounding yam in a mortar.

"Where's Papa John?" she asked.

"I . . . the . . . they killed the old man," I blurted. Her wide smile of welcome shriveled as I told her the events of last night. Tension and fear lent my words directness and sincerity that immediately arrested her. Her shock became terror when I told her we should go to the police.

"We ke? I no want police wahala! I no go any police o."

"But what should I do? They killed him."

"These people na bad people o. Just carry your bag and leave that Hotel Malogo now now. Go, a beg. I no wan any trouble o."

I left, thinking the best thing for me would be to walk away right now, without my bag, without the money. But like most sixteen-year-olds, I thought I could get in and out of the hotel without being seen. I was wrong. When I opened my room I saw that someone had been there when I was out, and they hadn't even made any effort to hide it; my bag on the bed lay open and my clothes were scattered on the floor, and when I looked into the bag I saw that the red bag was gone. Just then the door opened and Clement came in, another man was behind him, in the corridor. They must have been waiting in one of the rooms.

"Diaz."

I tried to act calm. I told myself that they mightn't know for sure that I had seen the dead body. "Clement. I was just coming to you. See, someone broke into my room. We have to tell your manager, and the police."

I saw them look at each other.

"Where you go?" Clement asked me. Now I had a good look at his friend. He was over six feet tall, with a clean-shaven head and red eyes that remained fixed on me. I was sweating. I said I had been to Munirat's to eat.

"Dem steal your thing?" He was trying to trap me, he was waiting to see if I'd mention the money or not. I made a show of hesitating before mentioning it.

"Well, there was some money, a lot of money."

"Ehh, money? How much?"

"It was a lot. It was Papa John's money. He gave me to keep and now I don't know how to tell him when he wakes up." I sat down on the bed acting distraught. "I don't know what to do."

"Wait," Clement said. They went outside to whisper. Through the door crack I could see the hefty man talking, one hand on Clement's shoulder. I looked toward the open window, telling myself it was just one floor down, and if I trusted in my legs . . . But they returned before my legs could obey.

"Let's go to the office." It was the first time the other man was speaking to me. His voice was low, gruff. "You can write a statement for me. I am the manager." There was an amused smile on his lips. I doubted if he was the manager, but he seemed to be the brains of the duo.

"Come," he said, his eyes still fixed on my face, his hands hidden in his pocket. I imagined the knife slicing into Papa John's face and hands. Clement threw my things into my bag and led the way. They put me in the middle, and all the way to the barroom I could hear the heavy tread of the man's feet behind me. The office behind the counter was also a bedroom, Clement's bedroom, and against one wall was a bed with a thin mattress and rumpled sheets that looked as if they hadn't been washed in a long time. There were empty crates of beer in one corner, a desk, a window, and a chair. The man pushed me into the chair, and then he opened the desk drawer and took out a pen. He looked around for a paper in the files and books on the desktop, but there was no paper.

"Get me some paper," he said to Clement.

"Paper don finish," Clement said.

"Go and buy some then, and hurry, we don't have all day," he said angrily. He sat on the bed. It was stormy outside, the wind banging the window loudly against the wall. He stared intently at me; I lowered my head, avoiding his merciless eyes. *He is going to kill me,* I kept telling myself, *I am going to die.* He wanted me to write a statement before killing me, but why? Why not kill me straightaway and dump the body in some dry well and nobody would know. I should scream, make a break for the door, but I knew that I couldn't make it; the bed was nearer the door than my chair, and even if I made it through the door, I wouldn't make it past the counter before he got me.

"You saw the old man, didn't you?" he asked. The pretense was over. He bent over and dragged out the red bag from under the bed. He waved it up and down.

"You did know we have the money, didn't you?"

I said nothing.

"Diaz. What a stupid name."

All I could think of was the old man's mutilated body upstairs, and the contorted agony on his face. We sat in silence broken only by the violence of the wind on the window. Just then a loud knock sounded on the outside door. He ignored it, but it came again, louder, and after a while we heard the door creaking open. Clement was back. "Don't move," the man growled before going out. I heard voices. It was not Clement. It was an early customer garrulously asking for a beer.

"Go away," the man said. He was at the counter, and from where I sat his back looked as insurmountable as a city wall. I opened my mouth to scream for help, but just then the wind blew harder against the window, and when I stood up I could see the road. There were the endless danfo buses, and across the road were the dark, cavelike doorways and alleyways. With my heart racing I realized that the window was big enough for me to pass through. I could stand on the bed and make it through and across the road and into one of the alleyways before the hefty man left the counter. And if I put all my trust in my legs, I could snatch the red bag from the bed as I went. This time my legs obeyed. I started running as soon as I landed in the grass outside; the wind was two giant hands under my arms, lifting me up and hurling me forward.

PAUL HORNSCHEMEIER

■

The Three Paradoxes

an excerpt from the graphic novel The Three Paradoxes

■

Neptune's Navy

FROM *The New Yorker*

ONE AFTERNOON LAST WINTER, two ships lined up side by side in a field of pack ice at the mouth of the Ross Sea, off the coast of Antarctica. They belonged to the Sea Shepherd Conservation Society, a vigilante organization founded by Paul Watson, thirty years ago, to protect the world's marine life from the destructive habits and the voracious appetites of humankind. Watson and a crew of fifty-two volunteers had sailed the ships — the *Farley Mowat*, from Australia, and the *Robert Hunter*, from Scotland — to the Ross Sea with the intention of saving whales in one of their principal habitats. A century ago, when Ernest Shackleton and his crew sailed into the Ross Sea, they discovered so many whales "spouting all around" that they named part of it the Bay of Whales. ("A veritable playground for these monsters," Shackleton wrote.) During much of the twentieth century, though, whales were intensively hunted in the area, and a Japanese fleet still sails into Antarctic waters every winter to catch minke whales and endangered fin whales. Watson believes in coercive conservation, and for several decades he has been using his private navy to ram whaling and fishing vessels on the high seas. Ramming is his signature tactic, and it is what he and his crew intended to do to the Japanese fleet, if they could find it.

Watson is fifty-six years old, pudgy and muscular. His hair, which is white, often hangs over his eyes in unkempt bangs. During trips to Antarctica, he usually grows a beard or a goatee. On January 19, the day he moored his ships together in the Ross Sea, he wore a black, military-style sweater adorned with Sea Shepherd patches, and a rainbow-colored belt that held a sheathed knife. Watson was captaining the *Farley,* a rusty North Sea trawler built in Norway in 1958. The ship, black with yellow trim, featured a skull and crossbones painted across its superstructure and, on the forward deck, a customized device called "the can opener": a sharpened steel I-beam that is propelled outward from the ship's starboard side and is used to scrape the hulls of adversaries. Watson's plan was to transfer as much furniture, equipment, and crew as he could from the *Farley* to the *Hunter,* in part because the *Farley* was old and barely seaworthy, in part because it was operating illegally and could be confiscated upon entry into port, and in part to ready it for a procedure that he called Operation Asshole — so named because it involved ramming one vessel into another's stern.

When Watson is separated from land, he tends to behave like Captain Nemo, which is to say that he does what he thinks is right, even if it involves a violation of custom or the destruction of property. There are a number of rules belonging to civilization that outrage his sense of morality, among them the 1982 United Nations Convention on the Law of the Sea, which asserts that sovereign states alone are the ocean's enforcers. If such rules interfere with his agenda, then, as far as he is concerned, rules be damned. This is particularly true when whales are at issue. Watson believes that whales are more intelligent than people and that their slaughter is tantamount to murder. (He once compared their extermination to the Holocaust.) The Japanese take a different view. They have been hunting whales with a modern industrial fleet since the 1930s, and the more resolutely the rest of the world condemns their hunt the more adamantly their government seems to support it. Watson maintains that if his opponents are forced to defend their actions in public they will demonstrate the untenable nature of their position. A key part of his strategy is to force the issue.

Whaling is not banned, but it is not exactly permitted, either — an ambiguity resulting from political compromise and shortsightedness. In 1946, the world's major whaling nations formed the International Whaling Commission to manage the world's whale fisheries. It did a terrible job. By the 1970s, several species were nearing extinction, and by the early eighties the IWC decided that commercial hunts should be halted. This is often referred to as the "ban" on commercial whaling, but it is more accurate to call it a moratorium. Even so, several leading whaling countries declined to abide by it. Whaling for the sake of science has always been permitted anywhere and without restrictions. The Japanese say that they are hunting whales off Antarctica in order to ascertain when there will be enough to harvest for profit. In the winter of 2005, they killed more than a thousand, nearly double the commercial catch of Norway, which rejected the moratorium. The Japanese fleet is run by the government-subsidized Institute for Cetacean Research, in Tokyo, but the institute has produced virtually no research of any regard, and all the whales that are purported to be under study are also butchered for the purpose of selling whale meat to the Japanese public.

Watson has a tendency to see things in their essence rather than in their particulars. A diplomat might say that the Japanese whaling fleet is technically complying with the rules of the IWC and that to stop it one must first upset the status quo that permits the fleet to hunt whales. Watson, who cannot be bothered with the legal nuances of international regulations, insists that the Japanese fleet is breaking the law, and that, because the IWC refuses to act, he and his crew must. He calls his fleet Neptune's Navy, and he regards it as a law-enforcement agency. Moments before ramming a vessel, Watson will radio its captain and say something that sounds very official, such as "Please remove yourselves from these waters. You are in violation of international conservation regulations." At times, he loses his cool. "We're no protest ship," he once told an intransigent captain. "Now, get out of here." His sense of urgency, his impressive ego, his argumentativeness, his love of theatrics, his tendency to bend the truth, his willingness to risk lives or injury for his beliefs (or for publicity), and his courage (or recklessness) have earned him both loathing and veneration from those who are familiar with his activism.

Watson's celebrity supporters, some of whom he has come to know personally, include Mick Jagger, Pierce Brosnan, Sean Penn, Aidan Quinn, William Shatner, Edward Norton, Orlando Bloom, and Uma Thurman. In 1995, Martin Sheen traveled with Watson and other activists to the Magdalen Islands, in Quebec, to protest the clubbing of baby seals. The group was threatened by a mob of angry sealers, and Watson was badly beaten. "He's one of the gutsiest guys on the planet," Sheen told me. "I am just so grateful to him for his commitment and his courage and his daring and his humanity." Steve Wynn, the Las Vegas casino magnate, once helped Watson buy a submarine (though it was missing essential parts and so couldn't be used). John Paul DeJoria, the CEO of John Paul Mitchell Systems, the hair-care-products company, has raised tens of thousands of dollars for Watson's campaigns. Sea Shepherd's board of advisers includes Elizabeth May, the leader of Canada's Green Party, and Roger Payne, one of the world's foremost experts on whales. Watson is portrayed as a savior in the fiction of Edward Abbey, the author of *The Monkey Wrench Gang* (1975), a seminal book for eco-saboteurs. The Dalai Lama has given him a written endorsement and a statue of Hayagriva, a wrathful deity who, according to early Buddhist texts, yells with a "dreadful voice" and "subdues all demons and all evils." Within the animal-rights community, Watson is treated like a demigod. "I think he's a hero," Peter Singer, the Princeton ethicist and the author of *Animal Liberation,* told me. "He's been prepared to put himself on the line to stop the abuse of animals in places where no one else was prepared to go."

Watson's detractors are no less adamant. Officials in Iceland, Denmark, Norway, Japan, Canada, and Costa Rica have denounced him; some have even called him a terrorist. In the mid-nineties, Norway convicted him of attempting to scuttle a whaler named Nybræna, and he spent eighty days in prison. "He is persona non grata in Iceland," Kristján Loftsson, the managing director of Hvalur, Iceland's largest whaling company, told me. Watson has made enemies of other conservationists, too. For decades, Greenpeace has wanted nothing to do with him — a rebuke that is particularly stinging because he was a founder of the organization. Last year, Watson resigned from the Sierra Club's national board, after feuding with other members about the group's policies. He has been barred from IWC meetings since 1986, when Sea Shepherd scuttled two of Hvalur's ships in Reykjavik's harbor — an act of sabotage that many conservationists believe helped turn Icelandic public opinion against the cause of saving whales. Sidney Holt, one of the principal architects of the whaling moratorium, told me, "I think his involvement in all this is an absolute disaster. Almost everything he has been doing has had blowback for those who want to see an end to whaling. In too many cases, playing piracy on the ocean, and creating danger for other ships, is simply not liked."

As the ships of Neptune's Navy were tied together in the Ross Sea, Watson stood on the deck of the *Farley* and observed his crew transferring equipment to the *Hunter,* a former Scottish-fisheries patrol vessel that was built in 1975. Watson's default temperament is one of detached amusement, and as he surveyed the work of his volunteers — most less than half his age, idealistic, loyal, zealously vegan — he told them, "You guys are like locusts." Sea Shepherd, which has an annual budget of about two million dollars, has a paid staff of fourteen people. Watson is committed to keeping his organization small, and does not believe in spending money on fundraising or recruitment; he raises money by giving lectures and advertising Sea Shepherd's work on the Internet, and by appealing to donors, often celebrities, directly. He has no trouble staffing his ships with volunteers. The *Farley*'s bridge was being stripped bare by a senior officer, a forty-one-year-old electrical engineer from Florida named Pedro Monteiro, who was dismantling redundant navigational equipment: an extra radar console, a global-positioning system. On the main deck, crew members using a crane transferred several tons of steel beams and plating to the other ship. The steel was to be used to construct a platform deck on the *Hunter,* and volunteers wearing welders' masks and gloves began building it almost immediately. On a similar deck at the *Farley*'s stern, under a gray tarp, a Hughes 300c helicopter sat ready to conduct reconnaissance.

Watson had hunted for the Japanese whaling fleet here before: in 2002, he searched for weeks but didn't find it; in 2005, he sideswiped two Japanese vessels. This time, he faced a new predicament: hours after leaving Australia, the *Farley*, which had been registered in Belize, was stripped of its flag by the authorities there. (The Japanese government had been educating other countries about Sea Shepherd's activities.) Without a flag, a ship is considered stateless, which means that if it is attacked on the high seas no government is likely to defend it. The *Farley*, in effect, had become an outlaw ship —

a cause for celebration by its crew. Sea Shepherd volunteers tend to share Watson's frustration with civilization, not only for its relentless expansion into nature but also for the many compromises that come with life on land. As Watson once wrote, "No words can describe the personal liberation that heading seaward bestows upon me. In this aquatic realm no man or woman is subject to the petty decrees of social bureaucracy." From the bow, the ship flew a Sea Shepherd flag, a version of the Jolly Roger featuring a trident crossed with a shepherd's crook. Watson told his crew, "Now you're on a pirate ship."

On the high seas, the greatest danger that the *Farley* posed was to itself. Since 2002, it had nearly sunk three times. On two occasions, divers had had to repair breaches to the hull with wooden stakes to keep the ship afloat. ("Luckily, we weren't in a storm," a crew member recalled. "You can't send divers down when there are five-meter swells.") Watson reasoned that the best way for the *Farley* to end its days at sea was as a battering ram in the service of marine life. To succeed in this, though, the ship would have to overcome a crucial obstacle: speed. Its top speed was ten knots, nowhere near that of any of the Japanese vessels. The *Hunter,* a much faster ship, would have to delay the whalers until the *Farley* could catch up — assuming that the fleet could be found. The Institute for Cetacean Research harvests whales within the Southern Ocean Sanctuary, fifty million square kilometers designated a protected area by the IWC. With two ships and a helicopter, Neptune's Navy hardly had the advantage.

Weeks of searching followed the high-seas rendezvous. By early February, Watson told me, he was preparing to order his navy back to port. His ships were running low on fuel, and the mood among his volunteers was grim. ("Every day that passed, it got a little more dismal," a crew member recalled.) Then, on February 9, a little before 4 A.M., the *Hunter* located a cluster of ships on its radar: an unusual pattern of blips moving across the console at 14.7 knots, faster than drifting icebergs. The sky was black. The air was cold. The *Hunter*'s captain, Alex Cornelissen, could not see more than a few feet off the bow. He decided that before notifying Watson in the *Farley,* twenty-five miles away, he needed more information. He steered toward the closest blip and ordered the helicopter to investigate the largest. At dawn, the sky turned a dark shade of blue, and the helicopter's pilot

saw a lighted ship moving slowly across the water. He radioed Cornelissen to say that he had located a whaler, and a crew member on the
Hunter's bridge announced, "We have found the fleet."

The ship was the *Nisshin Maru*. A colossus at sea, more than four
hundred feet long, it is what whalers call a "factory ship" — the only
one still in operation. Other vessels deliver their catch to the *Nisshin
Maru* for butchering, packaging, refrigeration, and study. For conservationists, it has come to represent everything that is wrong with the
modern whale hunt: mechanized slaughter on a vast scale. Greenpeace crews have frequently sailed to the Southern Ocean to protest
and document the fleet's work. The Institute for Cetacean Research
has painted the word *research* in block letters across the ship's hull;
the word is clearly propaganda, but for Neptune's Navy it serves as a
taunt.

Around 6 A.M., the *Hunter* pulled alongside the *Nisshin Maru*.
The whaling ship blasted its horns and turned on its water cannons,
which sent powerful jets overboard. The two ships were close enough
to collide, but Watson had instructed Cornelissen to delay the ship,
not to ram it. On the *Hunter*'s deck, crew members dressed in black
uniforms, their faces covered by masks, began throwing cannisters
of butyric acid — a relatively harmless substance that smells like
rancid butter — and smoke bombs onto the *Nisshin Maru*'s deck. At
the waterline, motorized dinghies called Zodiacs arced around the
whaler. Most of the Zodiacs had come from the *Farley*, which was not
yet in visible range. Their crews carried cameras and prop-foulers —
long knotted coils of polypropylene — which they hoped would get
entangled in the *Nisshin Maru*'s propellers. Other Zodiac crews were
equipped with nail guns. They drew the dinghies beside the *Nisshin
Maru* and nailed shut scuppers through which whale blood was re-
leased into the ocean. As the confrontation went on, the temperature
dropped. Waves surged, and snow, driven by shifting winds, hit the
ships at wild angles.

One of the *Farley*'s Zodiacs disappeared in the storm. Its crew,
Karl Neilsen and John Gravois, did not respond to radio calls. Watson stood against the back wall of the bridge, near an old brass pilot
wheel, and bit his upper lip. "What?" he said in disbelief to Monteiro.
Referring to Neilsen, the Zodiac's pilot, he asked, "He doesn't have

flares? I don't know why he doesn't have flares." As the *Farley* began to search for the missing boat, Watson grabbed several flares, went to a bridge wing, and fired them into the air. Their light barely penetrated the fog and snow. He faced a difficult decision. Several miles away, the *Hunter* was harassing the *Nisshin Maru*, and if he ordered it to join the search for the Zodiac it would not reach the whaler again. He decided that the *Hunter* should stay on course. "A lot of people were freaking out," he recalled. "But the problem was that I didn't want the Japanese fleet to get away." Cornelissen was having trouble keeping up with the *Nisshin Maru*, which could move faster than the *Hunter* in rough seas, and after several hours he decided to disobey Watson's order and join the search. Watson issued a distress call on the radio, and, moments later, the captain of the *Nisshin Maru* responded, asking how he could help.

What Watson did not know was that the missing Zodiac was badly damaged. It was old and had not been well maintained, and it had slammed into a wave and cracked its hull. As water poured in, it shorted out the radio and the GPS Neilsen and Gravois fell behind the other ships and eventually found themselves alone in the storm. They were wearing wetsuits and, over their wetsuits, foul-weather gear, but, even so, they were cold, and in the event that they became fully submerged they would not have survived for very long. They steered the Zodiac toward an iceberg and took shelter beside it. The men could not climb out, because the ice surface was nearly vertical, and they huddled together for warmth. After four or five hours, the Zodiac began to drift away from the iceberg. Gravois wrestled with the possibility that he might freeze or drown at the bottom of the world. He saw and heard mirages: phantom ships, a nonexistent helicopter. Neilsen did what he could to keep the Zodiac from moving too far from its last known position. Finally, eight or nine hours after the men had fallen behind the fleet, the *Farley* appeared through a wall of fog and rescued them. The *Nisshin Maru*, which had joined in the search, escaped into the Antarctic storm.

Watson had no choice but to order Neptune's Navy to return to Australia. Fuel and supplies were nearly depleted. Some crew members were horrified that he had taken so long to issue a distress call. Others were thrilled by the encounter with the factory ship, convinced that taking life-threatening risks to save animals was central to Sea Shepherd's mission. On February 12, as Neptune's Navy was preparing to leave the Antarctic Circle, the *Hunter* located another Japanese whaling vessel, northeast of the Balleny Islands. The ship, the *Kaiko Maru,* was what whalers call a spotter; it was looking for pods of whales near a field of pack ice. The *Hunter* rapidly closed in on it, and Cornelissen's first mate radioed the Japanese captain to say, "You have been identified as an illegal whaling vessel. We advise that you leave the Southern Ocean Whale Sanctuary immediately."

As the *Hunter* and the *Kaiko Maru* negotiated the floes, they smashed into each other. The *Hunter* tilted port, at an angle close to thirty degrees, and veered into a block of pack ice; the impact caused some structural damage to the hull. The *Kaiko Maru* blasted a looped recording, in English, through loudspeakers on its bridge: "Warning! Warning! This is the *Kaiko Maru*'s captain. Stop your obstructive actions immediately. If you dare to board this vessel, you will be taken into custody and restrained as illegal intruders under Japanese law." The Sea Shepherd crew hurled smoke bombs onto the *Kaiko Maru*'s deck, which soon was covered by an orange cloud. Prop-foulers were again deployed, and one became tangled in the *Kaiko Maru*'s propeller. Sea Shepherd's helicopter, equipped with a film crew, made low-flying passes. When the *Farley* arrived, Watson radioed the *Hunter* and said, "Let's see if we can keep them bottled up." He maneuvered the *Farley* to the other side of the whaler. The *Kaiko Maru*'s captain, in an attempt to free his ship, scraped the *Hunter,* issued a distress call, and complained that his propeller was vibrating in an unusual way. Then, having exhausted all other options, he began to take orders from Watson's crew, which had confined his ship to a tight circle. Watson offered to send a diver into the water to examine the damaged propeller. "Don't need your diver," an officer on the *Kaiko Maru* insisted. "O.K.? Understand?"

For a few hours, the ships remained where they were. Watson had arrested a whaling vessel on the high seas, but he was constrained by the fact that he had no real authority to do so. Using a satellite phone, he called officials in New Zealand and Australia — both countries claim sovereignty over parts of the Southern Ocean and are staunchly against whaling — and requested that a naval vessel take the Japanese ship into custody. Both countries refused. Australia's environment minister, Malcolm Turnbull, publicly denounced the tactics that the Sea Shepherd crew had used. "Threatening to put lives at risk, or vessels at risk, is completely unacceptable," he said. "They must act safely and peacefully. They are not advancing the anti-whaling cause they espouse by threatening lives in this way." Officials from New Zealand's maritime search-and-rescue agency responded to the *Kaiko Maru*'s distress call and spoke to Watson. "These guys are involved in illegal operations down here," Watson told the officials. They ordered him to give the *Kaiko Maru* free passage, and he reluctantly complied.

Since Watson did not have authority, he made use of what he did have: publicity. Earlier in the day, as the *Farley* chased the *Kaiko Maru*, he had conducted interviews with reporters in Australia and New Zealand by satellite phone, in an attempt to get them to write about Japanese whaling. (Complaining about the press to crew members on the bridge, Watson said, "It's all human drama. That's all anybody's interested in, human drama. Nobody is questioning the whales that are dying out here." Then he muttered, "Hominids, man, goddamn hominids.") Watson told the reporters that if Australia and New Zealand didn't take action against the Japanese whaling program he would hunt down the *Nisshin Maru* and give it a "steel enema" by jamming his ship into its slipway. This was unlikely — the *Nisshin Maru* was hundreds of miles away — but the threat had an effect. For several days, members of the political opposition in Australia made use of the incident to criticize the government. A Labor Party minister implied that his party, if elected, would order the Australian Navy into the Southern Ocean to monitor "illegal" whaling. From New Zealand, Chris Carter, the conservation minister, phoned Watson to dissuade him from carrying out Operation Asshole and, shortly afterward, announced, "I have made it clear to Mr. Watson that New Zealand is vigorously opposed to whaling and will continue its efforts on the international stage." Watson responded by telling the *New Zealand Herald* that he was standing down. "We're not going to ram the *Nisshin Maru*, but we will obstruct any whaling activities that we come across," he said. "I will not watch a whale die. I've not seen a whale die since I left Greenpeace, in 1977. When we show up, whales don't die."

The day Watson returned his ships to Australia, on February 19, the *Hunter*, like the *Farley*, lost its flag. It had been registered in the United Kingdom until, presumably, the Japanese saw fit to educate the British, too. In any case, the authorities in Melbourne chose to overlook Sea Shepherd's lack of valid paperwork. (Both ships were soon registered in Holland.) Watson left the *Hunter* in Australia, where it was to undergo preparations for his next Antarctic campaign, in December. The *Farley*, he decided, would cross the Pacific. It would stop in the Galápagos, where Sea Shepherd has an office that helps Ecuador's police fight marine poaching, and then continue to the Grand Banks, off the coast of Newfoundland, where the crew would dump into the ocean twenty tons of steel I-beams welded together to form large spikes. Watson called the spikes "net rippers," because they would be designed to destroy bottom-trawling nets. He planned to scatter them across the Grand Banks seabed and announce that they were there but not say where. The tactic — much like tree spiking, a nineteenth-century method of sabotaging logging equipment, which Watson helped revive in the eighties — would mix propaganda with action, so that fishermen would have to assume the worst. Watson has a habit of blending fact with rhetoric in this way. "You will not ever perceive the truth that is reality," he once wrote. "There are many realities."

Watson spends nearly as much time writing as he does planning for campaigns at sea. He has written several books and, on a Panasonic Toughbook computer that rarely leaves his side, produces a constant stream of poems, essays, and blog postings. Much of his writing is autobiographical, and he seems unable to discuss his personal history without giving it mythic contours. In the opening pages of *Earthforce!*, a strategy manual for radical environmentalists that he self-published in 1993, he wrote, "I was born on December 2, 1950, in the hereditary lands of the Huron on the north shore of Lake Ontario," which was his way of saying that he was born in Toronto. He went on, "I was raised in the east, in the lands of the Alquonquin Micmac on the shores of the Passamaquoddy Bay" — in other words, in the Canadian province of New Brunswick. Watson's descriptions of himself at the age of nine mirror his presentation of himself today: as a fearless and uncompromising defender of animals. In *Seal Wars,* a memoir that he published in 2002, he writes that when he was a young boy his best friend was a wild beaver (which he named Bucky); that he spent much of his time alone in the woods or near a wharf destroying animal traps (after Bucky was killed by one); that he was horrified by a seal hunt, which an uncle took him to see; that he once used his BB gun to shoot a boy who was about to kill a bird; and that he was bullied by other children ("Lost some battles, won most"). By his account, he was an eco-warrior before puberty.

Watson has six younger brothers and sisters. His parents, Anthony Watson (known as Tony), a French-Canadian who grew up in New Brunswick, and Anamarie Larsen, who was from Toronto, endured a difficult marriage. As a child, Watson looked up to his maternal grandfather, Otto Larsen, a painter and bare-knuckled boxer who was a veteran of the Spanish-American War and the Boer War and later became a war resister. (Larsen, a native of Copenhagen, was expelled from Denmark as a teenager after refusing to kneel before the Queen.) Watson lived with Larsen while his father fought in Korea, and when he returned, in the mid-fifties, the family moved to a fishing town on the Atlantic called St. Andrews by-the-Sea. "It is the Atlantic Ocean I remember most vividly from those years, more than I remember my own parents," Watson later wrote. "Looking across the water, I was always curious about what lay beyond." In 1959, the family moved to a village twenty miles inland called Milltown, on the Maine border. Fights between Watson's parents grew intense. In moments of rage, Watson told me, his father was abusive toward him. "When your method of parenting is to beat the hell out of you — I just don't get that," he said. He developed a habit of running away, though never very far, or for very long. In 1962, Tony Watson left for Toronto. "My father just disappeared," Watson told me. "I didn't see him for two years. He was gone."

During his absence, Watson's mother quietly began to see another man, and in 1963 she became pregnant. In January 1964, she was hospitalized as a result of medical complications, and relatives watched over the family. Then Tony Watson suddenly returned. He gathered his children in the living room and told them that their mother had died. (The baby was stillborn.) Watson, who was thirteen years old, jumped up, looked at his father, and yelled, "No, you're lying. It's all your fault." After the funeral, Watson's father moved the family to Toronto. Watson tried several times to run away and lived briefly in a Catholic boarding home for wayward children. His arguments with his father became explosive. "I was sixteen, and my father hit me," Watson told me. "Suddenly, I said to myself, 'I'm bigger than this guy.' I just turned around and slugged him, and actually that was a very therapeutic moment for me, because I took all the animosity I had out on him." He fled to Montreal and found work at Expo 67, as a tour guide. Afterward, he hopped a freight train to Vancouver. "I wanted to get as far away as possible," he told me.

Vancouver in the sixties was a haven for political radicals, draft dodgers, artists, and drifters. "I landed there and I didn't really know where to go," Watson said. He made his way to the University of British Columbia, which was built on a large promontory ringed with wilderness and beaches. Watson climbed down to Wreck Beach, where there were two abandoned gun towers, built during the Second World War to protect Canada from a Pacific invasion. He had brought a sleeping bag with him, and he made his home in one of the towers. In the evenings, to keep warm, he built a fire with driftwood. Sometimes he looked for shelter in town. "At the time, you could go to any police station and say, 'Can I spend the night in the jail?'" he said. "The police would usually throw in a breakfast." He found odd jobs, worked on getting his high-school diploma, and, when he had enough money for rent, stayed in boarding houses. "He was in Vancouver penniless," a friend remembered. "Once, he sat on the steps of the Vancouver General Hospital and swallowed a bottle of aspirin, thinking they must take him in. It looked lovely and warm inside. So he went into the hospital, and they sent him out to the Health Sciences Centre on the UBC campus. He stayed there for a while. They had to get the police to kick him out."

Watson took courses in archaeology, linguistics, and communications at Simon Fraser University, known among students at the time as Berkeley North. (He never finished a degree.) In 1968, in need of work, he skipped a semester to join the Coast Guard, and for several weeks he served aboard a weather ship. He enjoyed the experience enough to enlist, in 1969, on a Norwegian cargo vessel for eight or nine months. Periodically, during the next five years, he left Vancouver for stints in the merchant marine. While at sea, Watson traveled to Southeast Asia, where he watched, from a distance, the bombing of Vietnam; to the South China Sea, where he suffered horrendous weather ("I read Conrad's *Typhoon* during a typhoon"); to Iran, where he says he was detained and interrogated by the Shah's security agents after photographing a military installation ("I was tortured some, nothing too heavy, simply bamboo slivers under the fingernails and a few strokes with a lash"); and to Mozambique ("When I was finally able to see my surroundings, I panicked. I was on a bed in a hut"). Watson possessed what George Orwell once called a "lonely child's habit of making up stories"; through embellishment, he used his adventures to construct an indomitable persona. He loved to impersonate John Wayne. At protests, he was among the angriest radicals. In 1971, several hundred activists built a tent camp in Vancouver's Stanley Park, taking over a portion of it to protest the building of a hotel. The land was already fenced off for construction, and Rod Marining, one of the organizers of the demonstration, recalled, "Paul showed up and he took a crowbar and he began ripping the fence down, and as soon as he did this — the police were right behind him — they arrested him."

At the time, the nexus of countercultural life in Vancouver was a weekly called the *Georgia Straight,* and Watson soon began writing for it. "He virtually lived in the office for a while," Dan McLeod, the paper's longtime editor and publisher, told me. Watson's earliest articles were brief, irate, and punctuation-deprived. In a piece about a rowing club, he wrote with disgust about "the industrious upper class boys straining at their oars as if Caesar himself was watching." About the protest in Stanley Park, Watson wrote, "The cops present were full of contradictions as usual, and couldn't get it through their thick stubborn skulls that the land that they were on was not under their jurisdiction, that it was free land, Indian land, and only subject to natural and tribal law. The pigs expect us to obey their strange laws without question."

In the early seventies, Watson, along with some two dozen other environmental activists, created Greenpeace. In 1975, alarmed by the declining number of whales, the group decided to confront a Soviet whaling fleet off the coast of California. Their plan was to use Zodiacs to put themselves between the harpooners and the whales. When Greenpeace caught up with the fleet, Watson jumped into a Zodiac with Fred Easton, a cameraman. The two men witnessed a Soviet harpooner firing into a pod of whales. At one point, an injured sperm whale charged toward them. "It scared the hell out of us in the beginning," Easton said. "I just remember Paul saying, 'Here he comes!' and we sat there. I couldn't get my camera going, and we both sat at the edge of the Zodiac, on the other side of which the whale was approaching. He swam right past us, and I swear to God he couldn't have been any more than ten feet away, and he was a huge male sperm whale, and he had an eye about the size of a dinner plate, and he did look at us with some sort of compassion, in the sense that he was certainly capable of doing harm to us in the circumstances, and had he been human we might have expected him to." The two men, watching the whale swim away, were overcome with emotion. "In an instant, my life was transformed and a purpose for my life was reverently established," Watson later wrote. He has retold the story countless times. During his recent trip to Antarctica, he composed a sixteen-hundred-line poem titled *Planet of Whales*, which he later read to me in one sitting. It took fifty minutes. The poem's opening segment includes the following lines: "Leviathan's solitary eye haunts me still. / I am obsessed and driven mad with anger."

Fred Easton's footage generated considerable publicity and prompted an outpouring of donations to Greenpeace. Watson desperately wanted to undertake a campaign to save seals, thousands of which are slaughtered as pups every year in northeastern Canada. Some members objected, arguing that the group should focus on whales. Nevertheless, in 1976 and 1977, Watson brought teams of Greenpeace protesters to the ice fields of Newfoundland, where the seals were hunted. During the second trip, Watson spotted a sealer working near a pile of pelts and became furious. He threw the pelts in the water and then tossed the sealer's club in, too. A Greenpeace volunteer had never before acted so aggressively. When the campaign was over, the foundation's twelve-member board met to discuss Watson's behavior.

"It was a crisis point for the organization," Paul Spong, a whale researcher who was on the board, told me. "It was a point at which Greenpeace was trying to clarify itself and its objectives." Many board members believed that Watson's actions violated the group's pacifist ethos. Robert Hunter, a journalist and the group's most influential member (as well as the namesake of Sea Shepherd's ship), argued that Watson should be expelled. Hunter, who nevertheless remained a supporter of Watson's work until his death, two years ago, explained his decision in a history he wrote of Greenpeace, *Warriors of the Rainbow*. Referring to Watson, he wrote, "No one doubted his courage for a moment. He was a great warrior-brother. Yet in terms of the Greenpeace gestalt, he seemed possessed by *too* powerful a drive, too unrelenting a desire to push himself front and center, shouldering everyone else aside." Watson had broken the law and jeopardized Greenpeace's ability to raise money. "People had their different relationships with Watson," Rex Weyler, a board member at the time, told me. "He could be inspiring, but he was not an easy person to get along with. If it wasn't the club, it would be the next thing, and the next thing, and the next thing." The vote to remove Watson was eleven to one. (Watson dissented.) "No one felt good about it," Hunter wrote. "We all felt we'd gotten trapped in a web no one wanted to see develop, yet now that it had, there was nothing to do but bring down the ax, even if it meant bringing it down on the neck of our brother."

Soon after he was expelled from the board, Watson, with a few friends, founded his own group, Earthforce. It had little focus or momentum until, in 1978, he wrote to Cleveland Amory, the writer and animal-welfare advocate, to ask for help. Amory's organization, the Fund for Animals, paid for Watson's first ship, *Sea Shepherd*, which he used to ram and incapacitate a notorious pirate whaling vessel called the *Sierra*, off the coast of Portugal. Watson nearly lost his life in the process, and, after the campaign, he was forced to scuttle *Sea Shepherd*. He wrote an account of his adventure that was optioned by the producer Tony Bill and, with the money, he was able to buy another vessel. (Watson says that he has sold the film rights to his story more than twenty times, though a movie has yet to be made.) After the *Sierra* campaign, Watson told the *Washington Post*, "People sometimes say I have a suicide complex. Well, in fact I enjoy being alive, more than most people. But people can't believe a man will risk death to save whales. That's what they can't understand. So they think I'm crazy or that I attach no value to my life." He added, "I guess I plead guilty to being a vigilante, but I can tell you something, if there are no police then vigilantes will appear because crime will never be given a free rein." He renamed his organization after his first ship and set out to protect the oceans as he saw fit.

A list of Watson's campaigns in the eighties reads like a catalogue of Tintin adventures. In 1981, he secretly entered Siberia to document a Soviet food-processing facility that was converting illegally har-vested whale meat into feed for animals at a fur farm. He succeeded in avoiding the KGB and in outmaneuvering the Soviet Navy around a pod of gray whales. (Greenpeace, which visited the facility the fol-lowing year, got caught; one of the Greenpeace activists told me, "I was taken into a room with a KGB guy who asked, 'Do you know Paul Watson?'") In 1982, from a chartered airplane, Watson dropped paint-filled light bulbs on a Soviet trawler in the northern Pacific. He has used spoiled pie filling, fired from water cannons, as a weapon at sea. During the Falklands War, he contacted the British Navy and of-fered to assist its fleet by ferrying medical supplies to the front — "so I could head off any Argentine move to kill penguins," he told me. The British declined the offer. In 1983, he brought the Canadian seal hunt to a near-standstill by blockading the port of St. John's, New-foundland, and announcing that he would ram any sealing vessel that left the wharf; when the authorities threatened to board his ship, he replied that he would sink it at the mouth of the harbor, thereby creating an impassable reef. Watson eventually left the harbor, un-der cover of fog, and he was later arrested on an ice field where the hunt was taking place. (Since 1977, it has been a crime in Canada to observe the seal hunt without a permit.) His ship was confiscated, he was charged with conspiring to commit mischief and extortion, among other crimes, and he spent several days in jail. He was re-leased after Mike Farrell, the actor who played Captain B. J. Hunnicut on *M*A*S*H*, posted his bail. Watson was acquitted on appeal, and his ship was returned to him.

Watson is a keen tactician. "He generally baffles the police so badly they walk away at times when I would be in handcuffs," Peter Brown, a filmmaker who has been a Sea Shepherd crew member for more than twenty-five years, told me. Watson conducts most of his campaigns in international waters, where the law is vague and enforcement is weak. He nearly always publicizes Sea Shepherd's activities, which helps convey the impression that what he is attempting to do is perfectly legal. One of his preferred tactics is what he calls the Brer Rabbit Ploy: "If you have a political or moral advantage, then let the authorities know and believe that you want to be put on trial." On several occasions, he has demanded to be charged for sinking or ramming vessels, and he has even flown to a country that is considering his arrest. Watson says the ploy works because his adversaries fear that he will use the courts to publicize their own wrongdoing. But he has also claimed responsibility for damage to ships that in fact was caused by accidents or by other activists. "Let me just give you a warning about Paul," an anti-whaling conservationist told me. "He takes credit for more than he's due." (By Watson's count, Sea Shepherd has sunk ten whaling vessels in port. By my count, he and his crew have attempted to scuttle two vessels and have successfully sunk two others.) Still, he is adept at using the judicial system to his advantage. After the incident involving the paint-filled light bulbs, he was charged with four violations of Canada's Aeronautics Act. But, because the Soviet crew could not be subpoenaed, Watson was the government's only witness. According to the Toronto *Globe and Mail,* at a pretrial hearing the judge shook his head in disbelief as he asked the prosecutor, "You have no witnesses other than the accused?" The prosecutor conceded: "That is correct, Your Honor. The location of the incident comes from Watson." The case was eventually dismissed.

In the early nineties, instead of simply claiming the side of morality, as he did after ramming the *Sierra,* Watson began to assert legal authority for his actions. For this, he cited primarily the UN World Charter for Nature, a resolution passed by the General Assembly in 1982, which allows for private citizens to help "safeguard and conserve nature in areas beyond national jurisdiction." But it is not a license for vigilantism. The charter is nonbinding and does not have enforcement provisions. It indicates that individuals should act only "to the extent they are able," a clause that Watson interprets to mean physical capability but which is obviously meant to encompass legal authority as well. No country regards ramming, disabling, or scuttling ships to be legal activities, and, except on rare occasions, even naval ships cannot lawfully interfere with foreign vessels on the high seas. When I described Watson's use of the charter to David Caron, the co-director of the Law of the Sea Institute, at the University of California at Berkeley, he said, "Clearly wrong. There is no ambiguity."

In June, Watson was interviewed on a CBC radio talk show. The host, Susan Bell, asked him about his aggressive tactics, and he explained, "We intervene against illegal activities, and we are simply upholding international conservation law, and the United Nations World Charter for Nature allows for us to do that. It says that any nongovernmental organization, or individual, is empowered to uphold international conservation law. That's why I've sunk ten whaling ships and destroyed tens of millions of dollars' worth of illegal fishing gear, and I'm not in jail." Watson spoke in a calm, authoritative voice, and Bell changed the subject. It was a brilliant evasion. But, the more I heard him invoke the charter, the more I began to suspect that he actually believed that it authorized him to police the sea; some of the people who know him best admitted that they, too, could never be certain when he was tactically stretching the truth and when he was deceiving himself. In *Earthforce!*, Watson advises readers to make up facts and figures when they need to, and to deliver them to reporters confidently, "as Ronald Reagan did." Watson possesses Reagan's intuitive grasp of the media, and, like Reagan, at times he seems astray in the labyrinth of his own illusions.

Several years after ramming the *Sierra*, Watson gave himself the title of captain, though he does not have a captain's license. "He loves to dress up in uniform, as 'Captain Paul Watson,' and suddenly there's enough gold braid on his shoulders to skipper the *Queen Mary*," David Sellers, an old friend and former Sea Shepherd crew member, told me. In the eighties, Sellers and Watson fought so bitterly over the seaworthiness of Watson's ship that they did not speak for fifteen years. (Sellers, a licensed captain, had insisted that it was not safe for ocean travel.) Many of Watson's colleagues from the seventies and eighties no longer work with him; they have grown tired either of the campaigns or of Watson's style of leadership — "anarchy run by God," a longtime volunteer called it. "He doesn't like people who disagree with him."

Watson has been married three times and is currently divorcing his third wife, Allison Lance, whom he met at an animal-rights conference in 1997. His second wife, Lisa DiStefano, was a *Playboy* model. (DiStefano was a Sea Shepherd volunteer, and Lance still is.) His first wife, Starlet Lum, was a Greenpeace bookkeeper. With Lum, Watson had a daughter, Lani. Now twenty-seven, she is a video-game producer living in Seattle. When Watson is not traveling or at sea, he lives in Friday Harbor, Washington, on the grounds of a former Buddhist retreat, which also serves as Sea Shepherd's headquarters. He is close to his daughter now, but for several years he was not. He wrote in one of his memoirs, "I had never felt that a person's vision should be forsaken because of parenthood. In fact, to follow one's bliss is in my opinion the single most important example a father or a mother can set for their child. I would never abandon my dreams for domestic enslavement."

Watson believes that humanity's impulse to organize its surroundings, no matter how benign-seeming or elevating, is inherently destructive. This impulse — dating as far back as the first hoe — has been considered beneficial, Watson argues, because people have assumed that altering the shape of nature does not have real consequences, or because they have measured those consequences only in relation to how they affect humanity, or because they believe that they have a God-given right to do what they wish with plants and animals. Watson considers religion to be the invention of an arrogant species that has spent too much of its existence attempting to remove itself from the animal kingdom. This is why he prefers to call people hominids. "The Hebrew word for man was *adamah* — so there's where you get your Adam — and *adamah* means 'soil,'" he told me. "Cain was a farmer, and farmers began to kill off hunter-gatherers. Our ancestors fed from the table of life; in other words, they fed from nature, but we alienated ourselves from nature by depending upon agriculture, which is what I consider to be the forbidden fruit."

In the seventies, Watson became interested in the writings of

Henry Beston, an early-twentieth-century naturalist, who wrote, "The animal shall not be measured by man. In a world older and more complete than ours they move finished and complete, gifted with extensions of the senses we have lost or never attained." Watson found similar ideas in the work of Henry Fairfield Osborn and William T. Hornaday, and in the Deep Ecology movement, associated with Arne Naess, a Norwegian philosopher and mountaineer, who, in the early seventies, noticed that some environmentalists had begun arguing that no species was of greater worth than another, and that ecosystems should be protected for their own sake, not simply to benefit mankind. A "deep" ecologist would clean up a pond because plants and animals deserve to be free of pollution; a "shallow" ecologist would preserve the pond so that his grandchildren could have a nice place to swim.

Naess believed that the two outlooks could coexist, but Watson argues that they are in profound conflict. He contends that there are only two social currents that really matter, anthropocentrism and biocentrism, and they function in his thinking much like a Marxist dialectic: the former being a dominant and amoral world view that, fixated on the interests of one species, is inherently unstable, violent, and destined to collapse; the latter being a view that is held by a vanguard, egalitarian and just, and that, representing every species' interests, is destined to triumph. There is a strain of misanthropy in this way of thinking, and Watson attracted the attention of the Drudge Report and a number of right-leaning websites recently, after he called for drastic but unspecified measures to reduce the world's human population to under a billion. "He likes people to be shook up," Starlet Lum, his first wife, told me. "Maybe it's a bit of the unrest that's in him." Watson has said that "cancer is a cure to nature's problems," that earthworms are more ecologically important than people, and that humanity resembles a virus on the verge of killing its host, the planet.

"People say, 'You're incredibly arrogant,'" Watson told me. "I say, when you're dealing with a species that's as arrogant as the human race you've got to be arrogant to believe that you can actually change it." He regards civilization's greatest artistic and cultural achievements — from architecture to music and film — as expressions of human vanity, "worthless to the earth." He sometimes asks people to imagine the outrage that would occur if someone were to destroy, say, the Vatican or the *Mona Lisa,* and he compares that with the indifference that people exhibit toward the mass extinction of plants and animals. "In anthropocentric society, a harsh judgment is given to those that destroy or seek to destroy the creations of humanity," he has written. "Monkey-wrench a bulldozer and they will call you a vandal. Spike a tree and they will call you a terrorist. Liberate a coyote from a trap and they will call you a thief. Yet if a human destroys the wonders of creation, the beauty of the natural world, then anthropocentric society calls such people loggers, miners, developers, engineers, and businessmen."

In lectures, Watson often avoids this dialectic and talks mainly about the dying oceans. For many conservationists, the near-extinction of numerous whale populations in the seventies, and their continued threatened status today, is emblematic of a much more severe problem: the wholesale harvesting, whether for human consumption or for industry, of too many living things from the sea. Life in the oceans is being eliminated so rapidly that science can barely measure how much of it is gone. Sea Shepherd exists because Watson is arrogant enough to make sure that it is there, but also, perhaps, because our collective faith in the sea's resiliency runs so deep and has become so dangerously comforting that a certain amount of rage and fantasy is demanded to shake it.

Changes to the ocean have never been easy to document. In the seventies, Jacques Cousteau speculated — without much hard evidence — that roughly a third of all life in the oceans had vanished. In 1984, Farley Mowat, the Canadian naturalist and writer, for whom Watson named his flagship, published *Sea of Slaughter,* a thoroughly researched but primarily anecdotal book that gave substance to Cousteau's claim. "We are now facing the possibility that the seas may become virtual life-deserts in the not-far-distant future," Mowat wrote. Sifting through ship records, some dating as far back as the sixteenth century, he found evidence of startling abundance among whales, seabirds, and fish. ("Cods are so thick by the shore that we hardly have been able to row a boat through them," a skipper observed in the early 1600s.) The records presented a sharp contrast with what Mowat saw in the North Atlantic: the collapse of the cod, haddock, and halibut fisheries, and the virtual extirpation of the right whale — all driven by what he called a "spiral of exploitation." ("As the fish became scarcer, so their value rose," he explained. "They were hunted harder, and became scarcer, and their value rose.") It took Mowat five years to complete the book, and by the end he was despondent. He told me, "I was so depressed that I contemplated blowing myself up. Well, not exactly, but that gives you the idea."

It was not until the mid-nineties that fisheries scientists turned their attention to the spiral of exploitation and attempted to gauge its consequences. They discovered that their discipline had been measuring biodiversity with a very narrow lens: looking, for instance, at habitats only in a particular region of the ocean, or at the rise or decline of a particular species, and usually with respect to benchmarks that had been set just decades earlier. No one had tried to determine what the full spectrum of life in the ocean looked like a hundred years or five hundred years in the past. "We forgot the wonder and splendor of a virgin nature," Watson wrote recently. "We revise history and make it fit into our present perceptions." In 1995, the process of forgetting was given a name — "shifting baseline syndrome" — by Daniel Pauly, a scientist at the University of British Columbia. "Essentially, this syndrome has arisen because each generation of fisheries scientists accepts as a baseline the stock size and species composition that occurred at the beginning of their careers, and uses this to evaluate changes," Pauly argued in the journal *Trends in Ecology and Evolution*. He concluded, "The result obviously is a gradual shift of the baseline, a gradual accommodation of the creeping disappearance of resource species." When Pauly and others took a longer view, they noticed another worrying trend. Humanity had been eating its way down the ocean's food web; as large marine predators became scarce, people developed a taste for smaller and smaller fish. Animals that were once used for bait or that were considered worthless (hagfish, sea cucumber) were later taken in large quantities for human consumption. "Bait thirty years ago was calamari," Pauly told me. "Now it is served in a restaurant. It is very nice. But it was bait before." Future generations, Pauly predicts, only half in jest, will grow up on jellyfish sandwiches.

Technology both furthers the depletion and helps mask it. The tools of industrial fishing (drift nets, bottom trawls, and longlines) compensate for the diminishment of marine life that they cause by taking what little is left all the more intensively. Drift nets — free-floating veils of monofilament webbing that can be as long as twenty-five miles — were essentially banned on the high seas by the United Nations in 1992; at the peak of their use, in the eighties, there was enough drift netting in the ocean on any given day to encircle the planet, if measured end to end. Bottom trawling, which involves raking the ocean floor for food on a huge scale, leaves behind wastelands where there had been complex ecosystems. Like the other forms of industrial fishing, longlines, some of which submerge thousands of hooks in the water, yield immense quantities of bycatch, or unwanted fish, most of which is severely injured or dead. Every year in the United States alone, more than a million tons of bycatch is discarded; in relative terms, this amounts to more than 20 percent of all the fish hauled out of American waters. Some fisheries are more wasteful than others. Among the most notorious is the shrimp harvest in the Gulf of Mexico. Conducted by bottom trawling, it results in more than 80 percent bycatch, and countless plants and corals have been uprooted and dumped overboard. There is no terrestrial equivalent of this type of harvest. Pauly says that it would be like bulldozing whole forests to hunt deer.

Watson refers to our collective misuse of the sea as a tragedy of the commons. The United Nations Food and Agriculture Organization has declared that 69 percent of the world's major fisheries are either "fully exploited" or "overexploited." Among the most pessimistic studies, one published in *Nature* in 2003 estimated that the combined population of large predatory fish — including tuna, marlin, and swordfish — has dropped to a tenth of what it was before the advent of industrial fishing. A more revealing statistic, perhaps, is the number of scientists who have spoken out about the problem. Earlier this year, more than a hundred signed a letter to the World Trade Organization, urging it to scale back subsidies to the fishing sector. "There are only decades left before the damage we have inflicted on the oceans becomes permanent," the scientists wrote. Watson began ramming drift netters in 1987, before the UN ban. In 1993, he pulled his ship alongside a Cuban bottom trawler on the Grand Banks and attacked it with butyric acid. For the past seven years, he has combatted illegal fishing in the Galápagos Islands, one of the ocean's richest and most unspoiled marine habitats. Watson often says, "If we can't save Galápagos, we won't be able to save anything."

In June, after crossing the Pacific from Australia, the *Farley* arrived in Puerto Ayora, on Santa Cruz, the most populous island in the Galápagos. In a harbor filled with small pleasure boats, it seemed out of place. According to Watson, although the *Farley* was designed as a North Sea trawler, it was never used for fishing and during the Cold War it was a NATO spy vessel. Some furniture and equipment had been returned to the ship since the Antarctic expedition, but not much. Among the few remaining decorations were paintings of sea animals, including one of Mocha Dick, the whale that apparently inspired Melville's novel.

Unlike campaigns at sea, Watson's work in the Galápagos requires him to negotiate a complicated government bureaucracy. The Galápagos National Park manages the protection of wildlife in the third-largest marine protected area in the world. The Ecuadoran Navy, which monitors and controls the movement of all ships in the area, is reluctant to fight environmental crimes and, at times, has blocked other agencies from combatting them. Ecuador's Environmental Police has the authority to make arrests in the Galápagos but has no real presence on the islands. And the Galápagos National Park, which patrols the waters, is eager to end illegal fishing there and is not permitted to use force to prevent criminal activity. In April, Ecuador's president, Rafael Correa, declared that the Galápagos was in a state of environmental crisis, and in June UNESCO announced that the islands were on the World Heritage in Danger List. As many as three hundred thousand sharks are killed annually in the reserve, where shark hunts and industrial fishing are banned.

Conservationists often complain that it is difficult to gain popular support for saving sharks — animals that tend to evoke fear rather than sympathy. In 1975, in the *Georgia Straight*, Watson wrote an angry critique of *Jaws*. ("The movie has proven itself more dangerous to marine life than sharks are or ever have been to human life.") Since then, numerous species, including oceanic whitetip sharks, scalloped hammerheads, and daggernose sharks, have experienced catastrophic declines in population. Many sharks perish as bycatch, but increasingly they are being hunted for their fins, a delicacy in China and a lucrative commodity. (The annual export of fins is thought to be worth about a billion dollars.) One study, published in *Ecology Letters* last year, estimates that between twenty-six million and seventy-three million sharks are killed for their fins every year. Not long ago, Watson was nearly imprisoned in Costa Rica after confronting shark hunters in Cocos Island National Park, another UNESCO Heritage site, and seizing some of their equipment. He fled the country as the authorities were trying to apprehend him. (The events are documented in a new film, *Sharkwater*.)

In 2000, Watson sailed a Sea Shepherd ship to the Galápagos for the first time and lent (and eventually donated) a ninety-five-foot former Coast Guard vessel to the park, to help the rangers patrol. Several years later, when a ranger needed to learn how to fly light aircraft to expand the park's reach, Watson provided money for lessons. Sea Shepherd volunteers joined park rangers on their missions, to document their effectiveness. If they believed that the rangers were not aggressive enough, they protested, sometimes publicly. "It's been a rocky road," Watson told me. "Over the last seven years, we've been chased out of here three times by the Navy. Fishermen once seized the park and tried to kick us out." Still, Watson persisted. Last year, he decided to open an office in Puerto Ayora and hired Sean O'Hearn-Gimenez, a thirty-three-year-old computer specialist, to run it.

O'Hearn-Gimenez, who was born in Puerto Rico, first went to the Galápagos in 2000 as a Sea Shepherd observer. One afternoon while we were on the *Farley*, he told me about a day that changed his life. He was at sea with the rangers, who had found shark poachers in the reserve; the men argued over what to do with a shark that had become tangled in a line off the poaching vessel's transom. "One of the fishermen got angry and just hooked the shark, gaffed it, and slammed it against the deck. And he goes, 'There you go, there's your shark.' And there is this live shark flapping on deck, bleeding, and they're discussing exactly what to do, and finally one of the fishermen cut the line and threw him overboard. But before he cut the line you could see that the shark was flapping around, injuring himself, because he was desperate to survive. And it was horrible. It was probably the moment where I said —" O'Hearn-Gimenez's eyes began to fill with tears. After a moment, he said, "Sorry. I didn't care. I was willing to die. I didn't give a shit, because the shark almost broke his own tail, trying." He paused again. "And then the shark stood still, gasping, and that's when they just cut the line and threw him back into the water, like he was a piece of nothing."

By May of this year, O'Hearn-Gimenez had turned the Puerto Ayora office into a private intelligence service designed to fight environmental crimes. He identified poachers who were trying to move contraband out of the country and provided the authorities with the resources — fuel, food, lodging — that they needed to apprehend the criminals. Sea Shepherd began making the Ecuadoran papers. When O'Hearn-Gimenez learned that the mayor of the Galápagos' Isabela Island had cut down a ninety-year-old mangrove forest, he publicized the incident, and the mayor was prosecuted. (The case is pending.) In late June, O'Hearn-Gimenez provided the Environmental Police with information that led to the seizure of nearly nineteen thousand shark fins that were being smuggled to Peru, presumably for shipment to Asia. It was one of the largest shark-fin busts in Ecuador's history.

Watson was due in the Galápagos in early July, after a short trip to Quito, Ecuador's capital, to accept an award from the government for Sea Shepherd's work. In the meantime, Alex Cornelissen was captaining the *Farley*, and he decided to take the ship out to sea for a couple of days to patrol for illegal long-lining within the reserve. He did this without notifying the park, much to the annoyance of some senior rangers. During the ship's first evening out of port, Cornelissen gathered the crew and announced, "I just want you to know that Sean was supposed to come with us, but the reason why he is in Quito is because there was another bust. With our help, the police confiscated twenty thousand sea cucumbers." The crew cheered.

The next morning during breakfast, three high-pitched alarms rang in the galley. Everyone ran to the deck or to the bridge. A deck-

hand in the crow's nest had spotted a fishing vessel that was dropping miles of line into the marine reserve. Behind the vessel, a speedboat, a series of empty plastic oil jugs — blue, green, yellow, black
— bobbed in the water. The containers were being used as buoys
for the longline, braided polypropylene cording. Cornelissen, looking through his binoculars, announced, "Speedboat five miles away."
The first mate, Peter Hammarstedt, yelled from the bridge to the
deckhands, "Get some grappling hooks. Get a ladder in case someone is going in the water." The plan was to pull up the line. Hammarstedt hung his head out the window to try to gauge the ship's distance from the line.

"It's just off the starboard bow," he said.

"Get it away from the propeller," Cornelissen said.

The line became taut. The crew tried to pull it in, hand over hand,
but each pull seemed to edge the line closer to the propeller. Cornelissen turned to Hammarstedt and said, "Get that line out of the water, dude, now!" Hammarstedt ordered the line to be cut. The crew
lifted another portion of the line on deck and, this time, brought it to
an eyelet at the bow, through which it could be threaded and brought
on board with minimum danger to the propellers. Miles of line were
pulled through the eyelet. Because the line had not been in the water
for very long, most of the hooks were either baited or empty; only a
few had snared fish, nearly all of them yellowfin tuna.

As the crew hauled in the line, someone on the bridge noticed that
the poachers had fled, and a plan quickly developed to pursue them in
a Zodiac. Cornelissen wanted video footage of the speedboat's name
and registration number. As a crane hoisted the Zodiac overboard,
three crew members leaped in. One was carrying a video camera and
a handheld GPS, which he had been instructed to frame at the bottom of his shot, to prove that the poachers were in the reserve.

The speedboat was not visible from the Zodiac, which sits very
close to the water, but it could be seen from the *Farley*'s bridge. By radio, Cornelissen provided the Zodiac with directions, and for the first
mile or so the dinghy, driven by a volunteer named Adam Conniss,
raced across the empty water. Conniss's face was sunburned, and his
dreadlocks were blowing behind his ears. "Ahaaa, you motherfuck-

ers!" he screamed. After a few minutes, the *Farley* radioed to tell him that he was going the wrong way. He adjusted the Zodiac's course, and the poachers came into view.

The Zodiac was moving faster than the speedboat, and when the poachers noticed this they began to jettison evidence of long-lining. They threw bait into the water — the trail of fish oil in their wake was visible more than a mile away — and dumped spools of polypropylene cording, which floated near the surface. The first spool became tangled in the Zodiac's propeller. Conniss stopped to cut it away, and after that he steered more carefully. Minutes later, the Zodiac pulled alongside the poachers. The speedboat contained three men, and its name, *Siempre Maximo,* was painted on the bow. As the two vessels raced side by side, the fishermen looked at the Zodiac with befuddlement. Clearly, the *Farley* did not belong to the Navy or to the park, and yet its crew was acting as if it had authority to police the area. Stranger still, perhaps, was the end to the pursuit. Once the video footage was shot, the Zodiac veered away from the *Siempre Maximo* and headed back toward the *Farley.*

The rest of the afternoon was spent pulling in lines, an arduous task. When a longline is taut, it is likely to cause blisters in the hands of the person pulling it aboard; when the line is slack, there is a danger that some part of it will drift into a propeller. Longlines are slippery in the water and, in this case, the line was coated with broken jellyfish tentacles that stung. By evening, the crew had pulled in roughly ten miles of line and about two hundred and fifty hooks. It had untangled fifteen tunas, most of them carcasses, and two rays. All the animals, alive or dead, were returned to the sea.

That night, I climbed into my bunk thinking about the fishermen we had pursued. The *Siempre Maximo* did not belong to a commercial fleet; its lines were handmade. And yet, even if one could confirm that the men's financial predicament was dire, it would not make the ocean seem less vulnerable. In a day's catch, assuming for the sake of argument that the *Farley* had interrupted the fishermen while they were in the middle of their work, and that only 10 percent of their hooks caught anything, the lines could have snared about fifty animals; in a week of solid fishing, about three hundred and fifty; in a year, nearly twenty thousand — all this, potentially, from just three poachers in a tiny boat off the coast of South America.

Watson and O'Hearn-Gimenez arrived in Puerto Ayora on July 5. "We met with the Vice President and the Minister of Foreign Affairs," Watson told me. The ceremony had been followed by talks with the general commander of the National Police, who wanted to discuss how Sea Shepherd could assist the police in fighting poachers. The talks concluded with a signed pledge formalizing the relationship. One clause stated that Ecuador might grant Watson's crew the authority to conduct joint patrols with the police in the reserve. "This was a surprise," O'Hearn-Gimenez said. "I'm sure this was the result of the successful operations we had. I didn't think that we were going to have meetings, and then last night the general —"

"Get this," Watson interrupted. "The general wants to go on the Antarctica campaign —"

"He came to the ceremony, and in the end he mentioned this joint cooperation," O'Hearn-Gimenez continued. The two men spoke excitedly about the meetings. "The problem is the goddam Navy," Watson said. "Everybody in Quito knows the Navy is on the take." Earlier in the year, rangers had attempted to prevent the Navy from giving illegal tours in the Galápagos; in return, members of the Navy and the Air Force had assaulted the director of the park, Raquel Molina, and several rangers. (The Ministry of Defense is investigating the incident.) When Watson met with Molina to find out how he could further help the park, she spoke about the assault and seemed shaken. It was obvious that the more involved with the government Sea Shepherd became, the more it would have to compromise.

Watson's initial plan had been to take the *Farley* through the Panama Canal to the Grand Banks, to dump the net rippers, and then, possibly, to Iceland, to combat whaling there. Most of the crew had joined with the hope of going to Iceland, which now appeared to be suspending its planned whale hunt. In any case, Watson, excited about the agreement he had signed in Quito, decided to linger in Ecuador. He had also learned that an American company called Planktos was planning to send a ship into international waters about three hundred miles from the marine reserve; Planktos had announced that it would dump tons of iron dust in the ocean to spark the growth of phytoplankton, and then sell credits based on how much carbon the phytoplankton consumed. Activists and government officials in Ecuador and in the United States had expressed concern about the project's environmental impact; Watson thought that he might intervene. He spent hours at his computer, researching the project, and continued to meet with officials. The head of the Environmental Police, Colonel Teresa Carranza, came to Puerto Ayora for a tour of the *Farley*. At a dinner that Watson held for her, she raised her glass and announced, "Paul Watson and all of you here, what you've been doing is very contagious. I have been influenced by what you do." Then she turned to Watson and handed him a gold pin. She continued, "Now, with everything that has happened, Sea Shepherd is part of the Environmental Police, an extension of the Environmental Police, and this shield is a great honor. It is only worn by police officers." Watson smiled. The pin was a symbolic gesture, another step toward being given real authority to protect the sea, but the praise seemed to make him uncomfortable. He glanced down, pointed to O'Hearn-Gimenez, and said, "I haven't done anything. He's done it all."

In the morning, droplets of seawater and precipitation pricked faces, arms, and legs. From the *Farley*'s deck, the panorama was one of humanity pushing into nature: ships, noise, people, and the mundane detritus of civilization — water bottles and diesel exhaust — spreading out from the shoreline. Since 1990, the population of the Galápagos has grown from under ten thousand to thirty thousand. On board the *Farley*, the crew was restless. Watson's volunteers had spent more than a month crossing the Pacific, determined to save whales in Iceland. For many crew members, the campaign against Planktos presented a confusing moral calculus, and it wasn't even certain that Watson would pursue the company's ship. Without a clear objective, the cycle of chores that kept the *Farley* running — the continuous battle against rust and decrepitude — became tedious, eroding morale each day. At least ten people planned to leave the ship. One volunteer said, "It's getting a little silly, just feeling useless." Watson told me that there were worse places to sit idle than the Galápagos. "They can all jump ship," he said.

*

"I have received death threats, and I'm pretty much in a safe house right now," O'Hearn-Gimenez told me from his cell phone on August 3. I was back in New York, and he was on the Ecuadoran mainland. He had orchestrated another huge shark-fin bust — as much as three tons, he speculated, in three hiding places. But during the seizures mobs of fishermen had gathered at two of the hideouts, and a high-ranking officer had called off the bust. O'Hearn-Gimenez told me that the contraband belonged to "one of the biggest Mafia leaders in Ecuador," whom he suspected of interfering. Whether or not corrupt officials were involved, the government's position on the shark-fin trade was changing. In late July, the President decreed that sharks accidentally caught could legally be sold — a significant loosening of the ban. On August 4, he announced, "We are not going to allow Americans from Sea Shepherd or wherever else to come here to tell us what to do." He ordered that O'Hearn-Gimenez be deported. As O'Hearn-Gimenez was packing his bags, however, the order was rescinded.

Still, it seemed that Sea Shepherd's position in the country had grown much more tenuous. The *Farley*'s port clearance had expired, and the Ecuadoran Navy was anxious to see the ship leave the Galápagos. As the *Farley* sailed from Puerto Ayora, Watson wrote me a long e-mail from the radio room, in which he declared his intention to stay and look for poachers in Ecuadoran waters. His defiance reminded me of something he had once said about Conan the Barbarian, the comic-book hero. "It's a wonderful ethic that this guy has," Watson said. "You know, he wouldn't hesitate to take your head off. But there is a code: always doing the honorable thing, even when it put him in life-threatening situations. He always honored everything that was weaker than he was. He had that mercy quality. But, at the same time, strength. And he never hesitated. He would never stop to think, Am I doing the right thing? He knew he was doing the right thing."

Watson was also doing, not thinking. He wrote, "We are making our way in the darkness between the islands and we should be in the area where we suspect illegal long-lining is taking place by early morning. The Navy has been hailing us on the radio but we have been ignoring them. I don't think they have any idea where we are or where we are heading. We were ordered to go due east and out of the Galápagos marine reserve. Instead we are going southwest and deep into the marine reserve." Humpback and sperm whales had surfaced near the ship; a red-throated frigate bird had perched on the foremast for most of the day. "The seas are calm," Watson wrote. "The night sky is inky black, without a star in sight and no moon. It is like cruising through deep space. In the far distance we can see the dull glow of Puerto Ayora to our stern. It's amazing cruising through these waters flying our black-and-white Jolly Roger, in defiance of the Ecuadoran Navy. Not much different than the pirates of the seventeenth century, really, challenging authority in defense of the living treasures of the Enchanted Islands."

STEPHEN KING

■

Ayana

FROM *The Paris Review*

I DIDN'T THINK I would ever tell this story. My wife told me not to; she said no one would believe it and I'd only embarrass myself. What she meant, of course, was that it would embarrass her. "What about Ralph and Trudy?" I asked her. "They were there. They saw it too."

"Trudy will tell him to keep his mouth shut," Ruth said, "and your brother won't need much persuading."

This was probably true. Ralph was at that time superintendent of New Hampshire School Administrative Unit 43, and the last thing a Department of Education bureaucrat from a small state wants is to wind up on one of the cable news outlets, in the end-of-the-hour slot reserved for UFOs over Phoenix and coyotes that can count to ten. Besides, a miracle story isn't much good without a miracle worker, and Ayana was gone.

But now my wife is dead — she had a heart attack while flying to Colorado to help out with our first grandchild and died almost instantly. (Or so the airline people said, but you can't even trust them with your luggage these days.) My brother Ralph is also dead — a stroke while playing in a golden-ager golf tournament — and Trudy is gaga. My father is long gone; if he were still alive, he'd be a centenarian. I'm the last one standing, so I'll tell the story. It *is* unbelievable, Ruth was right about that, and it means nothing in any case — miracles never do, except to those lucky lunatics who see them everywhere. But it's interesting. And it *is* true. We all saw it.

*

My father was dying of pancreatic cancer. I think you can tell a lot about people by listening to how they speak about that sort of situation (and the fact that I describe cancer as "that sort of situation" probably tells you something about your narrator, who spent his life teaching English to boys and girls whose most serious health problems were acne and sports injuries).

Ralph said, "He's nearly finished his journey."

My sister-in-law Trudy said, "He's rife with it." At first I thought she said "He's ripe with it," which struck me as jarringly poetic. I knew it couldn't be right, not from her, but I wanted it to be right.

Ruth said, "He's down for the count."

I didn't say, "And may he stay down," but I thought it. Because he suffered. This was twenty-five years ago — 1982 — and suffering was still an accepted part of end-stage cancer. I remember reading ten or twelve years later that most cancer patients go out silently only because they're too weak to scream. That brought back memories of my father's sickroom so strong that I went into the bathroom and knelt in front of the toilet bowl, sure I was going to vomit.

But my father actually died four years later, in 1986. He was in assisted living then, and it wasn't pancreatic cancer that got him, after all. He choked to death on a piece of steak.

Don "Doc" Gentry and his wife, Bernadette — my mother and father — retired to a suburban home in Ford City, not too far from Pittsburgh. After his wife died, Doc considered moving to Florida, decided he couldn't afford it, and stayed in Pennsylvania. When his cancer was diagnosed, he spent a brief time in the hospital, where he explained again and again that his nickname came from his years as a veterinarian. After he'd explained this to anyone who cared, they sent him home to die, and such family as he had left — Ralph, Trudy, Ruth, and me — came to Ford City to see him out.

I remember his back bedroom very well. On the wall was a picture of Christ suffering the little children to come unto him. On the floor was a rag rug my mother had made: shades of nauseous green, not one of her better ones. Beside the bed was an IV pole with a Pittsburgh Pirates decal on it. Each day I approached that room with increasing dread, and each day the hours I spent there stretched longer. I remembered Doc sitting on the porch glider when we were growing up in Derby, Connecticut — a can of beer in one hand, a cig in the other, the sleeves of a blinding white T-shirt always turned up twice to reveal the smooth curve of his biceps and the rose tattoo just above his left elbow. He was of a generation that did not feel strange going about in dark blue unfaded jeans — and who called jeans "dungarees." He combed his hair like Elvis and had a slightly dangerous look, like a sailor two drinks into a shore leave that will end badly. He was a tall man who walked like a cat. And I remember a summer street dance in Derby where he and my mother stopped the show, jitterbugging to "Rocket 88" by Ike Turner and the Kings of Rhythm. Ralph was sixteen then, I think, and I was eleven. We watched our parents with our mouths open, and for the first time I understood that they did it at night, did it with all their clothes off and never thought of us.

At eighty, turned loose from the hospital, my somehow dangerously graceful father had become just another skeleton in pajamas (his had the Pirates logo on them). His eyes lurked beneath wild and bushy brows. He sweated steadily in spite of two fans, and the smell that rose from his damp skin reminded me of old wallpaper in a deserted house. His breath was black with the perfume of decomposition.

Ralph and I were a long way from rich, but when we put a little of our money together with the remains of Doc's own savings, we had enough to hire a part-time private nurse and a housekeeper who came in five days a week. They did well at keeping the old man clean and changed, but by the day my sister-in-law said that Doc was ripe with it (I still prefer to think that was what she said), the Battle of the Smells was almost over. That scarred old pro shit was rounds ahead of the newcomer Johnson's baby powder; soon, I thought, the ref would stop the fight. Doc was no longer able to get to the toilet (which he invariably called "the can"), so he wore diapers and continence pants. He was still aware enough to know, and to be ashamed. Sometimes tears rolled from the corners of his eyes, and half-formed cries of desperate, disgusted amusement came from the throat that had once sent "Hey, Good Lookin'" out into the world.

The pain settled in, first in the midsection and then radiating outward until he would complain that even his eyelids and fingertips hurt. The painkillers stopped working. The nurse could have given him more, but that might have killed him and she refused. I wanted to give him more even if it did kill him. And I might have, with support from Ruth, but my wife wasn't the sort to provide that kind of prop.

"She'll know," Ruth said, meaning the nurse, "and then you'll be in trouble."

"He's my dad!"

"That won't stop her." Ruth had always been a glass-half-empty person. It wasn't the way she was raised; it was the way she was born. "She'll report it. You might go to jail."

So I didn't kill him. None of us killed him. What we did was mark time. We read to him, not knowing how much he understood. We changed him and kept the medication chart on the wall updated. The days were viciously hot and we periodically changed the location of the two fans, hoping to create a cross draft. We watched the Pirates games on a little color TV that made the grass look purple, and we told him that the Pirates looked great this year. We talked to each other above his ever-sharpening profile. We watched him suffer and waited for him to die. And one day while he was sleeping and rattling snores, I looked up from *Best American Poets of the Twentieth Century* and saw a tall, heavyset black woman and a black girl in dark glasses standing at the bedroom door.

That girl — I remember her as if it were this morning. I think she might have been seven, although extremely small for her age. Tiny, really. She was wearing a pink dress that stopped above her knobby knees. There was a Band-Aid printed with Warner Bros. cartoon characters on one equally knobby shin; I remember Yosemite Sam, with his long red mustache and a pistol in each hand. The dark glasses looked like a yard-sale consolation prize. They were far too big and had slid down to the end of the kid's snub nose, revealing eyes that were fixed, heavy-lidded, sheathed in blue-white film. Her hair was in cornrows. Over one arm was a pink plastic child's purse split down the side. On her feet were dirty sneakers. Her skin wasn't really black at all but a soapy gray. She was on her feet, but otherwise looked almost as sick as my father.

The woman I remember less clearly, because the child so drew my attention. The woman could have been forty or sixty. She had a close-cropped afro and a serene aspect. Beyond that, I recall nothing — not even the color of her dress, if she was wearing a dress. I think she was, but it might have been slacks.

"Who are you?" I asked. I sounded stupid, as if awakened from a doze rather than reading — although there is a similarity.

Trudy appeared from behind them and said the same thing. She sounded wide awake. And from behind her, Ruth said in an oh-for-Pete's-sake voice: "The door must have come open, it won't ever stay on the latch. They must have walked right in."

Ralph, standing beside Trudy, looked back over his shoulder. "It's shut now. They must have closed it behind them." As if that were a mark in their favor.

"You can't come in here," Trudy told the woman. "We're busy. There's sickness here. I don't know what you want, but you have to go."

"You can't just walk into a place, you know," Ralph added. The three of them were crowded together in the sickroom doorway.

Ruth tapped the woman on the shoulder, and not gently. "Unless you want us to call the police, you have to go. Do you want us to do that?"

The woman took no notice. She pushed the little girl forward and said, "Straight on. Four steps. There's a poley thing, mind you don't trip. Let me hear you count."

The little girl counted like this: "One . . . two . . . free . . . four." She stepped over the metal feet of the IV pole on *free* without ever looking down — surely not looking at anything through the smeary lenses of her too-big yard-sale glasses. Not with those milky eyes. She passed close enough to me for the skirt of her dress to draw across my forearm like a thought. She smelled dirty and sweaty and — like Doc — sick. There were dark marks on both of her arms, not scabs but sores.

"Stop her!" my brother said to me, but I didn't. All this happened very quickly. The little girl bent over the stubbly hollow of my father's cheek and kissed it. A big kiss, not a little one. A smacky kiss.

Her little plastic purse swung lightly against the side of his head as she did it and my father opened his eyes. Later, both Trudy and Ruth said it was getting whacked with the purse that woke him. Ralph was less sure, and I didn't believe it at all. It didn't make a sound when it struck, not even a little one. There was nothing in that purse except maybe a Kleenex.

"Who are you, kiddo?" my father asked in his raspy fixing-to-die voice.

"Ayana," the child said.

"I'm Doc." He looked up at her from those dark caves where he now lived, but with more comprehension than I'd seen in the two weeks we'd been in Ford City. He'd reached a point where not even a ninth-inning walk-off home run could do much to crack his deepening glaze.

Trudy pushed past the woman and started to push past me, meaning to grab the child who had suddenly thrust herself into Doc's dying regard. I grabbed her wrist and stopped her. "Wait."

"What do you mean, wait? They're trespassers!"

"I'm sick, I have to go," the little girl said. Then she kissed him again and stepped back. This time she tripped over the feet of the IV pole, almost upending it and herself. Trudy grabbed the pole and I grabbed the child. There was nothing to her, only skin wrapped on a complex armature of bone. Her glasses fell off into my lap, and for a moment those milky eyes looked into mine.

"You be all right," Ayana said, and touched my mouth with her tiny palm. It burned me like an ember, but I didn't pull away. "You be all right."

"Ayana, come," the woman said. "We ought to leave these folks. Two steps. Let me hear you count."

"One . . . two," Ayana said, putting her glasses on and then poking them up her nose, where they would not stay for long. The woman took her hand.

"You folks have a blessed day, now," she said, and looked at me. "I'm sorry for you," she said, "but this child's dreams are over."

They walked back across the living room, the woman holding the girl's hand. Ralph trailed after them like a sheepdog, I think to make sure neither of them stole anything. Ruth and Trudy were bent over Doc, whose eyes were still open.

"Who was that child?" he asked.

"I don't know, Dad," Trudy said. "Don't let it concern you."

"I want her to come back," he said. "I want another kiss."

Ruth turned to me, her lips sucked into her mouth. This was an unlovely expression she had perfected over the years. "She pulled his IV line halfway out . . . he's bleeding . . . and you just sat there."

"I'll put it back," I said, and someone else seemed to be speaking. Inside myself was a man standing off to one side, silent and stunned. I could still feel the warm pressure of her palm on my mouth.

"Oh, don't bother! I already did."

Ralph came back. "They're gone," he said. "Walking down the street toward the bus stop." He turned to my wife. "Do you really want me to call the police, Ruth?"

"No. We'd just be all day filling out forms and answering questions." She paused. "We might even have to testify in court."

"Testify to what?" Ralph asked.

"I don't know what, how should I know what? Will one of you get the adhesive tape so we can keep this christing needle still? It's on the kitchen counter, I think."

"I want another kiss," my father said.

"I'll go," I said, but first I went to the front door — which Ralph had locked as well as closed — and looked out. The little green plastic bus shelter was only a block down, but no one was standing by the pole or under the shelter's plastic roof. And the sidewalk was empty. Ayana and the woman — whether mother or minder — were gone. All I had was the kid's touch on my mouth, still warm but starting to fade.

Now comes the miracle part. I'm not going to skimp it — if I'm going to tell this story, I'll try to tell it right — but I'm not going to dwell on it either. Miracle stories are always satisfying but rarely interesting, because they're all the same.

We were staying at one of the motels on Ford City's main road, a Ramada Inn with thin walls. Ralph annoyed my wife by calling it the Rammit Inn. "If you keep doing that, you'll eventually forget and say it in front of a stranger," my wife said. "Then you'll have a red face."

The walls were so thin that it was possible for us to hear Ralph and Trudy arguing next door about how long they could afford to stay. "He's my father," Ralph said, to which Trudy replied: "Try telling that to Connecticut Light and Power when the bill comes due. Or the state commissioner when your sick days run out."

It was a little past seven on a hot August evening. Soon Ralph would be leaving for my father's, where the part-time nurse was on duty until 8 P.M. I found the Pirates on TV and jacked the volume to drown out the depressing and predictable argument going on next door. Ruth was folding clothes and telling me the next time I bought cheap discount-store underwear, she was going to divorce me. Or shoot me for a stranger. The phone rang. It was Nurse Chloe. (This was what she called herself, as in "Drink a little more of this soup for Nurse Chloe.")

She wasted no time on pleasantries. "I think you should come right away," she said. "Not just Ralph for the night shift. All of you."

"Is he going?" I asked. Ruth stopped folding things and came over. She put a hand on my shoulder. We had been expecting this — hoping for it, really — but now that it was here, it was too absurd to hurt. Doc had taught me how to use a Bolo-Bouncer when I was a kid no older than that day's little blind intruder. He had caught me smoking under the grape arbor and had told me — not angrily but kindly — that it was a stupid habit, and I'd do well not to let it get a hold on me. The idea that he might not be alive when tomorrow's paper came? Absurd.

"I don't think so," Nurse Chloe said. "He seems better." She paused. "I've never seen anything like it in my life."

He was better. When we got there fifteen minutes later, he was sitting on the living room sofa and watching the Pirates on the house's larger TV — no technological marvel, but at least colorfast. He was sipping a protein shake through a straw. He had some color. His cheeks seemed plumper, perhaps because he was freshly shaved. He had regained himself. That was what I thought then; the impression has only grown stronger with the passage of time. And one other thing, which we all agreed on — even the doubting Thomasina to whom I was married: the yellow smell that had hung around him like ether ever since the doctors sent him home to die was gone.

He greeted us all by name, and told us that Willie Stargell had just hit a home run for the Buckos. Ralph and I looked at each other, as if to confirm we were actually there. Trudy sat on the couch beside Doc, only it was more of a whoomping down. Ruth went into the kitchen and got herself a beer. A miracle in itself.

"I wouldn't mind one of those, Ruthie-doo," my father said, and then — probably misinterpreting my slack and flabbergasted face for an expression of disapproval: "I feel better. Gut hardly hurts at all."

"No beer for you, I think," Nurse Chloe said. She was sitting in an easy chair across the room and showed no sign of gathering her things, a ritual that usually began twenty minutes before the end of her shift. Her annoying do-it-for-mommy authority seemed to have grown thin.

"When did this start?" I asked, not even sure what I meant by *this*, because the changes for the better seemed so general. But if I had any specific thing in mind, I suppose it was the departure of the smell.

"He was getting better when we left this afternoon," Trudy said. "I just didn't believe it."

"Bolsheveky," Ruth said. It was as close as she allowed herself to cursing.

Trudy paid no attention. "It was that little girl," she said.

"Bolsheveky!" Ruth cried.

"What little girl?" my father asked. It was between innings. On the television, a fellow with no hair, big teeth, and mad eyes was telling us the carpets at Juker's were so cheap they were almost free. And, dear God, no finance charges on layaway. Before any of us could reply to Ruth, Doc asked Nurse Chloe if he could have *half* a beer. She refused him. But Nurse Chloe's days of authority in that little house were almost over, and during the next four years — before a chunk of half-chewed meat stopped his throat forever — my father drank a great many beers. And enjoyed every one, I hope. Beer is a miracle in itself.

It was that night, while lying sleepless in our hard Rammit Inn bed and listening to the air conditioner rattle, that Ruth told me to keep my mouth shut about the blind girl, whom she called not Ayana but "the magic negro child," speaking in a tone of ugly sarcasm that was very unlike her.

"Besides," she said, "it won't last. Sometimes a light bulb will brighten up just before it burns out for good. I'm sure that happens to people too."

Maybe, but Doc Gentry's miracle took. By the end of the week he was walking in his backyard with me or Ralph supporting him. After that, we all went home. I got a call from Nurse Chloe on our first night back.

"We're not going, no matter how sick he is," Ruth said half-hysterically. "Tell her that."

But Nurse Chloe only wanted to say that she'd happened to see Doc coming out of the Ford City Veterinary Clinic, where he had gone to consult with the young head of practice about a horse with the staggers. He had his cane, she said, but wasn't using it. Nurse Chloe said she'd never seen a man "of his years" who looked any better. "Bright-eyed and ring-tailed," she said. "I still don't believe it." A month later he was walking (caneless) around the block, and that winter he was swimming every day at the local Y. He looked like a man of sixty-five. Everyone said so.

I talked to my father's entire medical team in the wake of his recovery. I did it because what had happened to him reminded me of the so-called miracle plays that were big in the sticksville burgs of Europe in medieval times. I told myself if I changed Dad's name (or perhaps just called him Mr. G.) it could make an interesting article for some journal or other. It might have even been true — sort of — but I never did write the article.

It was Stan Sloan, Doc's family practice guy, who first raised the red flag. He had sent Doc to the University of Pittsburgh Cancer Institute and so was able to blame the consequent misdiagnosis on Drs. Retif and Zamachowski, who were my dad's oncologists there. They in turn blamed the radiologists for sloppy imaging. Retif said the chief of radiology was an incompetent who didn't know a pancreas from a liver. He asked not to be quoted, but after twenty-five years, I am assuming the statute of limitations on that one has run out.

Dr. Zamachowski said it was a simple case of organ malformation. "I was never comfortable with the original diagnosis," he confided. I talked to Retif on the phone, Zamachowski in person. He was wearing a white lab coat with a red T-shirt beneath that appeared to read I'D RATHER BE GOLFING. "I always thought it was Von Hippel–Lindau."

"Wouldn't that also have killed him?" I asked.

Zamachowski gave me the mysterious smile doctors reserve for clueless plumbers, housewives, and English teachers. Then he said he was late for an appointment.

When I talked to the chief of radiology, he spread his hands. "Here we are responsible for photography, not interpretation," he said. "In another ten years, we will be using equipment that will make such misinterpretations as this one all but impossible. In the meantime, why not just be glad your pop is alive? Enjoy him."

I did my best on that score. And during my brief investigation, which I of course called research, I learned an interesting thing: the medical definition of *miracle* is misdiagnosis.

Nineteen eighty-three was my sabbatical year. I had a contract with a scholarly press for a book called *Teaching the Unteachable: Strategies for Creative Writing*, but like my miracle-play article it never got written. In July, while Ruth and I were making plans for a camping trip, my urine abruptly turned pink. The pain came after that, first deep in my left buttock, then growing stronger as it migrated to my groin. By the time I started to piss actual blood — this was I think four days after the first twinges, and while I was still playing that famous game known the world over as Maybe It Will Go Away on Its Own — the pain had passed from serious into the realm of excruciating.

"I'm sure it's not cancer," Ruth said, which coming from her meant she was sure it was. The look in her eyes was even more alarming. She would deny this on her deathbed — her practicality was her pride — but I'm sure it occurred to her just then that the cancer that had left my father had battened on me.

It wasn't cancer. It was kidney stones. My miracle was called extracorporeal shock wave lithotripsy, which — in tandem with diuretic pills — dissolved them. I told my doctor I had never felt such pain in my life.

"I should think you never will again, even if you suffer a coronary," he said. "Women who've had stones compare the pain to that of childbirth. Difficult childbirth."

I was still in considerable pain but able to read a magazine while waiting for my follow-up doctor's appointment, and I considered this a great improvement. Someone sat down beside me and said, "Come on now, it's time."

I looked up. It wasn't the woman who had come into my father's sickroom; it was a man in a perfectly ordinary brown business suit. Nevertheless, I knew why he was there. It was never even a question. I also felt sure that if I didn't go with him, all the lithotripsy in the world would not help me.

We went out. The receptionist was away from her desk, so I didn't have to explain my sudden decampment. I'm not sure what I would have said, anyway. That my groin had suddenly stopped smoldering? That was absurd as well as untrue.

The man in the business suit looked a fit thirty-five: an ex-marine, maybe, who hadn't been able to part with the bristly gung-ho haircut. He didn't talk. We cut around the medical center where my doctor keeps his practice, then made our way down the block to Groves of Healing Hospital, me walking slightly bent over because of the pain, which no longer snarled but still glowered.

We went up to pedes and made our way down a corridor with Disney murals on the walls and "It's a Small World" drifting down from the overhead speakers. The ex-marine walked briskly, with his head up, as if he belonged there. I didn't, and I knew it. I had never felt so far from my home and the life I understood. If I had floated up to the ceiling like a child's Mylar GET WELL SOON balloon, I wouldn't have been surprised.

At the central nurses' station, the ex-marine squeezed my arm to make me stop until the two nurses there — one male, one female — were occupied. Then we crossed into another hall where a bald girl sitting in a wheelchair looked at us with starving eyes. She held out one hand.

"No," the ex-marine said, and simply led me on. But not before I got another look into those bright, dying eyes.

He took us into a room where a boy of about three was playing with blocks in a clear plastic tent that belled down over his bed. The boy stared at us with lively interest. He looked much healthier than the girl in the wheelchair — he had a full shock of red curls — but his skin was the color of lead, and when the ex-marine pushed me forward and then fell back into a position like parade rest, I sensed the kid was very ill indeed. When I unzipped the tent, taking no notice of the sign on the wall reading THIS IS A STERILE ENVIRONMENT, I thought his remaining time could have been measured in days rather than weeks.

I reached for him, registering my father's sick smell. The odor was a little lighter, but essentially the same. The kid lifted his own arms without reservation. When I kissed him on the corner of the mouth, he kissed back with a longing eagerness that suggested he hadn't been touched in a long time. At least not by something that didn't hurt.

No one came in to ask us what we were doing, or to threaten the police, as Ruth had that day in my father's sickroom. I zipped up the tent again. In the doorway I looked back and saw him sitting in his clear plastic tent with a block in his hands. He dropped it and waved to me — a child's wigwag, fingers opening and closing twice. I waved back the same way. He looked better already.

Once more the ex-marine squeezed my arm at the nurses' station, but this time we were spotted by the male nurse, a man with the kind of disapproving smile the head of my English department had raised to the level of art. He asked what we were doing there.

"Sorry, mate, wrong floor," the ex-marine said.

On the hospital steps a few minutes later, he said, "You can find your own way back, can't you?"

"Sure," I said, "but I'll have to make another appointment with my doctor."

"Yes, I suppose you will."

"Will I see you again?"

"Yes," he said, and walked off toward the hospital parking lot. He didn't look back.

He came again in 1987, while Ruth was at the market and I was cutting the grass and hoping the sick thud in the back of my head wasn't the beginning of a migraine but knowing it was. Since the little boy in Groves of Healing, I had been subject to them. But it was hardly ever him I thought of when I lay in the dark with a damp rag over my eyes. I thought of the little girl.

That time we went to see a woman at St. Jude's. When I kissed her, she put my hand on her left breast. It was the only one she had; the doctors had already taken the other.

"I love you, mister," she said, crying. I didn't know what to say. The ex-marine stood in the doorway, legs apart, hands behind his back. Parade rest.

Years passed before he came again: mid-December of 1997. That was the last time. By then my problem was arthritis, and it still is. The bristles standing up from the ex-marine's block of a head had gone mostly gray, and lines so deep they made him look a little like a ventriloquist's dummy had carved down from the corners of his lips. He took me out to an I-95 exit ramp north of town, where there had been a wreck. A panel truck had collided with a Ford Escort. The Escort was pretty well trashed. The paramedics had strapped the driver, a middle-aged man, to a stretcher. The cops were talking to the uniformed panel truck driver, who appeared shaken but unhurt.

The paramedics slammed the doors of the ambulance, and the ex-marine said, "Now. Shag your ass."

I shagged my elderly ass to the rear of the ambulance. The ex-marine hustled forward, pointing. "Yo! Yo! Is that one of those medical bracelets?"

The paramedics turned to look; one of them, and one of the cops who had been talking to the panel truck driver, went to where the ex-marine was pointing. I opened the rear door of the ambulance and crawled up to the Escort driver's head. At the same time I clutched my father's pocket watch, which I had carried since he gave it to me as a wedding present. Its delicate gold chain was attached to one of my belt loops. There was no time to be gentle; I tore it free.

The man on the stretcher stared up at me from the gloom, his broken neck bulging in a shiny skin-covered doorknob at the nape. "I can't move my fucking toes," he said.

I kissed him on the corner of the mouth (it was my special place, I guess) and was backing out when one of the paramedics grabbed me. "What in the hell do you think you're doing?" he asked.

I pointed to the watch, which now lay beside the stretcher. "That was in the grass. I thought he'd want it." By the time the Escort driver was able to tell someone that it wasn't his watch and the initials engraved on the inside of the lid meant nothing to him, we would be gone. "Did you get his medical bracelet?"

The paramedic looked disgusted. "It was just a piece of chrome," he said. "Get out of here." Then, not quite grudgingly: "Thanks. You could have kept that."

It was true. I loved that watch. But . . . spur of the moment. It was all I had.

"You've got blood on the back of your hand," the ex-marine said as we drove back to my house. We were in his car, a nondescript Chevrolet sedan. There was a dog leash lying on the backseat and a St. Christopher medal hanging from the rearview mirror on a silver chain. "You ought to wash it off when you get home."

I said I would.

"You won't be seeing me again," he said.

I thought of what the black woman had said about Ayana then. I hadn't thought of it in years. "Are my dreams over?" I asked.

He looked puzzled, then shrugged. "Your work is," he said. "I sure don't know anything about your dreams."

I asked him three more questions before he dropped me off for the last time and disappeared from my life. I didn't expect him to answer them, but he did.

"Those people I kiss — do they go on to other people? Kiss their boo-boos and make them all gone?"

"Some do," he said. "That's how it works. Others can't." He shrugged. "Or won't." He shrugged again. "It comes to the same."

"Do you know a little girl named Ayana? Although I suppose she'd be a big girl now."

"She's dead."

My heart dropped, but not too far. I suppose I had known. I thought again of the little girl in the wheelchair.

"She kissed my father," I said. "She only touched me. So why was I the one?"

"Because you were," he said, and pulled into my driveway. "Here we are."

An idea occurred to me. It seemed like a good one, God knows why. "Come for Christmas," I said. "Come for Christmas dinner. We have plenty. I'll tell Ruth you're my cousin from New Mexico." Because I had never told her about the ex-marine. Knowing about my father was enough for her. Too much, really.

The ex-marine smiled. That might not have been the only time I saw it, but it's the only time I remember. "Think I'll give it a miss, mate. Although I thank you. I don't celebrate Christmas. I'm an atheist."

That's really it, I guess — except for kissing Trudy. I told you she went gaga, remember? Alzheimer's. Ralph made good investments that left her well-off, and the kids saw that she went to a nice place when she was no longer OK to live at home. Ruth and I went to see her together until Ruth had her heart attack on the approach into Denver International. I went to see Trudy on my own not long after that, because I was lonely and sad and wanted some connection with the old days. But seeing Trudy as she had become, looking out the window instead of at me, munching at her lower lip while clear spit grizzled from the corners of her mouth, only made me feel worse. Like going back to your hometown to look at the house you grew up in and discovering a vacant lot.

I kissed the corner of her mouth before I left, but of course nothing happened. A miracle is no good without a miracle worker, and my miracle days are behind me now. Except late at night when I can't sleep. Then I can come downstairs and watch almost any movie I want. Even skin flicks. I have a satellite dish, you see, and something called Global Movies. I could even get the Pirates, if I wanted to order the MLB package. But I live on a fixed income these days, and while I'm comfortable, I also have to keep an eye on my discretionary spending. I can read about the Pirates on the Internet. All those movies are miracle enough for me.

RUTU MODAN

Queen of the Scottish Fairies

FROM *www.nytimes.com*

During the next few weeks, the toddler and his pink tutu were inseparable. The more content he was with it, the more gloomy his father grew. "The classification of gender along color lines, namely pink and blue, is an invention of the mid-19th century," I lectured him. "And up until the 1920s, boys wore dresses and skirts to the age of 3."

Ofer was unimpressed with my historical overview. "Nowadays it's not accepted," he mumbled.

"What about Mel Gibson? He wore a skirt and he didn't look half bad in it."

Albert Einstein in childhood

"But why can't he be... be more..." He was fishing.

"What? More like everybody else?"

"No...That's not what I meant...I just want him to be..."

"What? Come out with it already..." I said, preparing my feminist arguments.

"More like ...more like a guy." he finally admitted. "He looks guy enough to me."

His gaze shifted doubtfully toward our son, who was sitting on the floor in his glamorous attire and playing with a Barbie doll.

"So he likes blondes," I said. "Surely you can identify with that?"

A week later, while I was sorting a package of old clothes we'd been sent by a friend, Max showed up and retrieved from it a pair of lavender floral Mary-Janes.

Ofer practically fainted when he met us later at the playground.

"You're doing that to me in purpose," he whispered.

"He doesn't have any sandals," I shrugged. "And besides, it's too hot for shoes."

"You're only encouraging him so that everyone can see how progressive you are," my husband said angrily.

"I'm letting him be who he chooses to be," I countered.

"Stop being so self-righteous!"

"And you stop being such a homophobe!"

"Don't patronize me!"

"You're the only one who even cares," I added.

"If you have issues with your masculinity, that's your problem—don't project that on the kid."

"You want a cookie, princess?" a nice lady asked Max.

"He's a boy!" Ofer exclaimed.

"Really?" She gaped and called her husband over: "David, come here! You've got to see this!"

"That's it!" Ofer concluded. "We're going to get him some normal sandals RIGHT NOW!" Max, for his part, was actually happy about the new purchase. And when we got to the store he knew exactly what he wanted: Crocs, just like everyone else in his school.

"Crocs?" I snapped. "No way!"

"Aha!" Ofer called out triumphantly. "Now what happened to letting him 'express himself'? Pick a color, sport."

"Pink Crocs! Pink Crocs!" Max shouted and we left the store, without buying a thing.

The pink tutu continued to attract a lot of attention.

The Cousin

When my Ronny asked me to buy him a tutu, **I** agreed immediately.

Then, at the store, he chose a Batman outfit, didn't you Ronny?

The Gay Friend

I don't think he'll turn out Gee-Ay-Why. See how he loves his computer?

The Psychologist Friend

He simply identifies with his big sister.

Pink? Peeew!

The Grandmother

Look what I got you. Blue suits you so well!

Meanwhile, unaware of the political maelstrom around him, Goldilocks scanned himself in the mirror, frowning. "I wish I were blond," he muttered mournfully.

Being mature adults, however, Ofer and I arrived at a compromise. I explained to Max that dresses are like costumes and that for kindergarten we wear regular clothes. And then Ofer bought him a pair of wings and a tiara when Max announced that he wanted to dress up as a fairy.

Last March there was a costume ball at our daughter's school. Max was overjoyed at the opportunity to show off his get-up, but an unexpected snag arrived when we were about to leave the house.

I'm not going with him dressed like that! My friends will laugh at me!

What do you care? It's him, not you!

If he's going like that, I'm not going, and that's that!

It seemed there was no way out of this impasse. The two kids were bawling, and their father was standing between them, looking at me, his expression very clearly reading "THIS IS YOUR FAULT—NOW FIX IT." With a sudden inspiration known only to mothers and commanders of large armies, I retrieved a plaid skirt from the dresser.

"Everybody knows Scottish men wear kilts," I explained to my daughter.

After she gave her permission for him to wear it, Max quickly donned the improvised costume.

You should have seen him at that party.
He was so happy! And he proudly told
anyone who asked that he was
the Queen of the Scottish Fairies.

Story Editor: Dana Modan

EMILY RABOTEAU

■

Searching for Zion

FROM *Transition*

THE SECURITY PERSONNEL OF El Al Airlines descended upon me at Newark International Airport like a flock of vultures. There were five of them, in uniform, blockading the check-in counter. They looked old enough to have finished their obligatory service in the Israeli Defense Forces but not old enough to have finished college, which put them beneath me in age. I was prepared for their initial question, "What are you?" which I've been asked my entire life, and, though it chafed me, I knew the canned answer that would satisfy: "I look the way I do because my mother is white and my father is black." This time the usual reply wasn't good enough. This time the interrogation was tribal.

"What do you mean black? Where are you from?"

"New Jersey."

"Why are you going to Israel?"

"To visit a friend."

"What is your friend?"

"She's a Cancer."

"She has cancer?"

"No, no. I'm kidding. She's healthy."

"She's Jewish?"

"Yes."

"How do you know her?"

"We grew up together."

"Do you speak Hebrew?"

"*Shalom,*" I began. "*Barukh atah Adonai . . .*" I couldn't remember the rest, so I finished with a word I remembered for its perfect ono-matopoetic rendering of the sound of liquid being poured from the narrow neck of a vessel: *"Bakbuk."*

It means bottle. I must have sounded to them like a babbling idiot.

"That's all I know," I said. I felt ashamed somehow, but also pissed off at them for making me feel that way.

"Where is your father from?"

"Mississippi."

"No." By now they were exasperated. "Where are your *people* from?"

"The United States."

"Before that. Your ancestors. Where did they come from?"

"Ireland."

They looked doubtful. "What kind of name is this?" They pointed at my opened passport.

"A surname," I joked.

"How do you say it?"

"Don't ask me. It's French."

"You're French?"

"No, I *told* you. I'm American."

"This!" They stabbed at my middle name, which is *Ishem.* "What is the meaning of this name?"

"I don't know," I answered, honestly. I was named after my father's great-aunt, Emily Ishem, who died of cancer long before I was born. I have no idea where the name came from. Possibly it's a slave name.

"It sounds Arabic."

"Thank you."

"Do you speak Arabic?"

"I know better than to try."

"What do you mean?"

"No, I don't speak Arabic."

"What are your origins?"

I felt caught in a loop of that Abbott and Costello routine, "Who's on first?" There was no place for me inside their rhetoric. I didn't have the right vocabulary. I didn't have the right pedigree. This is what my mixed race has made me: a perpetual unanswered question. This is what the Atlantic slave trade has made me: a mongrel and a threat.

"Ms. Raboteau. Do you want to get on that plane?"

I was beginning to wonder.

"Do you?"

"Yes."

"Answer the question then! What are your origins?"

What else was I supposed to say?

"A sperm and an egg," I snapped.

That's when they grabbed my luggage, whisked me to the basement, stripped off my clothes, and probed every orifice of my body for explosives. When they didn't find any, they focused on my tattoo, a Japanese character that means *different, precious, unique*. I was completely naked, and the room was cold. My nipples were hard. I tried to cover myself with my hands. I remember feeling incredibly thirsty. One of them flicked my left shoulder with a latex glove. "What does it mean?" he asked. This was the first time I'd ever been racially profiled, not that the experience would have been any less humiliating had it been my five hundredth. "It means *Fuck you*," I wanted to say, not because they'd stripped me of my dignity but because they'd shoved my face into my own rootlessness. I have never felt more black in my life than I did when I was mistaken for an Arab.

I was going to visit Tamar Cohen, my best friend from childhood. We loved each other with the fierce infatuation particular to friendships between preadolescent girls — a love that found its form in bike rides along the towpath, notes written in lemon juice, and pantomimed tea parties at the bottom of swimming pools. Looking back on the years we spent growing up in the privileged, picturesque, and predominantly white town of Princeton, New Jersey, where both of our fathers were history professors, I can see that what grounded our friendship was a shared sense of being different. She was Jewish. I was black. Well, I was half black, but in a land where one must be one thing or the other, that was enough to set me apart.

Being different was, for both of us, a source of pride and, I'm ashamed to say, enabled us to hold everyone else in slight disdain (especially if they happened to play field hockey or football). Tamar and I were a unified front against conformity. We stood next to each other in navy blue robes in the first row of the soprano section of the high school choir like two petite soldiers, sharing a folder of sheet music between us with a synchronicity of spirit that could trick a listener into believing that we possessed a single voice. When I received my confirmation in Christ, I wore Tamar's bat mitzvah dress.

We were bookish girls, intense and watchful. Our afternoons were spent sprawled out on my living room rug doing algebra homework while listening to my dad's old Aretha Franklin records. Our Friday nights were spent eating *Shabbat* dinner at her house around the corner on Murray Place. I felt proud being able to recite the Hebrew blessing with her family after the sun went down and the candles were lit: *"Barukh atah Adonai, Eloheinu melech ha'olam . . ."* The solemn ritual made me feel as though I belonged to something larger than myself.

Perhaps stemming from that warm feeling, much to my father's chagrin, I started to keep kosher, daintily picking the shrimp and crab legs out of his Mississippi jambalaya until all that remained on my plate was a muck of soupy rice. It was her father's turn to be chagrined when we turned eighteen and got matching tattoos on our left shoulder blades. The Torah forbids tattooing (Leviticus 19:28). Tamar's might someday disqualify her from burial in a Jewish cemetery, but we relished the idea that, no matter where in the world we might end up, no matter how much time might pass, even when we were old and ugly and gray, we would always be able to recognize each other.

Tamar's father was an expert in medieval Jewish history, while mine specialized in antebellum African American Christianity. Both men made careers of retrieving and reconstructing the rich histories of ingloriously interrupted peoples. Both were quietly angry men, and Tamar and I were sensitive to their anger, which was at once historical and personal. I was acutely aware of the grandfather I had lost to a racially motivated hate crime under Jim Crow, though my father didn't discuss the murder with me. He didn't need to give words to my grandfather's absence anymore than Tamar's father had to give words to the Holocaust. There were ghosts in our houses.

Both of us knew at a relatively young age what the word *diaspora* meant — though to this day that word makes me visualize the white Afro-puff of a dandelion spore being blown by my lips into a series of wishes across our old backyard: to be known, to be loved, to belong. I didn't fit in. I looked different from the white kids, though I didn't exactly look black. Tamar didn't fit in either. In her case, the "otherness" was cultural: her summers were spent in Israel; her Saturdays at synagogue; and, up until the seventh grade, she attended a yeshiva. I didn't see Tamar as white any more than I did my own mother. Consequently, it didn't confuse or surprise me when Tamar suddenly turned to me in choir practice one snowy morning and proclaimed, *"I'm not white."*

We had been rehearsing the French composer Jean L'Héritier's sonorous, sacred motet, *"Nigra sum sed formosa,"* whose Latin text is taken from the Song of Songs, and reads:

> *Nigra sum sed formosa filiae Jherusalem*
> I am black but comely, daughters of Jerusalem

> *Ideo dilexit me rex*
> Therefore have I pleased the Lord

> *Et introduxit me in cubiculum suum.*
> And he hath brought me into his chamber.

I thought I understood why she made her proclamation at that particular moment in choir practice. *"Nigra sum sed formosa"* is a heartbreakingly succulent song, one that brought tears to my father's eyes when we sang it a few weeks later at the winter concert. It was a song you wanted to be about yourself.

Tamar felt the same way about the freedom songs being broadcast at an exhibit held by the Jewish Museum in New York in collaboration with the NAACP, an exhibit linking Jewish and African American experience. My father brought the two of us there a few years after the Crown Heights Riot during what must have been Passover, because I can remember nibbling on matzoh bread and leaving a trail of unleavened crumbs. Klezmer music played in a room showcasing a sil-

ver candlestick bent by a bullet in a Russian pogrom. The adjacent
room displayed photographs of lynched black men. In each of those
men's tortured faces I saw my grandfather, and I found myself on the
verge of tears, more from anger than from sadness. "Go Down Moses (Let My People Go!)" issued from the speakers:

> *When Israel was in Egypt's land,*
> *Let My people go!*
> *Oppressed so hard they could not stand,*
> *Let My people go!*
> *Go down, Moses,*
> *Way down in Egypt's land;*
> *Tell old Pharaoh*
> *To let My people go!*

"I like this music better than klezmer," Tamar admitted. I trained
my ears on the lyrics I knew so well, and they soothed me in my anger, just as they are meant to do.

"This is a liberation song," my father explained. "Do you girls
know where Canaan is?"

"Israel," Tamar answered.

"In a sense. But that's not the place this song is about. Look." He
pointed to a picture of Frederick Douglass with an attending quota-
tion that read: "We meant to reach the North, and the North was our
Canaan." My father continued talking to us that afternoon about how
pivotal the Old Testament story of Exodus and the Promised Land
was for African slaves in America, whose early involvement with
Christian tradition was born out of a feeling of kinship with the Hebrew slaves. They found redemptive hope in the scripture about Moses, the trials and tribulations of the Israelites, and their journey
from bondage into Canaan. "I'll meet you in de mornin', when you
reach de promised land: On de oder side of Jordan, For I'm boun' for
de promised land . . ."

"Maybe that's why you like this music, Tamar," my father finished.
"When we sang freedom songs about the ancient Israelites, we linked
ourselves to you. Our people have a lot in common."

*

Tamar and I had promised to stay in touch when we parted ways for college. But while I was busy reading Hurston, Ellison, Wright, and Fanon, she was busy attending Hillel Society. We called each other less and less. Shortly after we graduated, she moved to Israel and became a citizen under the Law of Return. I hadn't heard from her in months when she phoned at the start of the Second Intifada to ask me to visit. The desperation in her voice surprised me — it nearly had the quality of begging. I decided to go.

I fell in love with Jerusalem. How could I not? I was expecting to land in a desert place, hostile and khaki and hard as a tank, because that's what I'd seen on TV, and that's how El Al's security had behaved at Newark International Airport — hostile and hard. But when Tamar led me through that ancient city of soft hills and olive trees, its white stone going rosy in the sunset, when we entered the mouth of Lion's Gate and walked along the Via Dolorosa, when I smelled the peach tobacco smoke from a narghile pipe, when I saw the red wool of the Bedouin rugs on display in the Old City, when I heard the calls to prayer from a hundred mosques at dusk, my heart swelled round as the Dome of the Rock with a sense of holy longing, and I halfway understood why men would fight rock over stick, hand over fist, bomb over gun, in order to call this place their home. There is no real word in the Hebrew language for *home*. Yet Tamar had chosen to expatriate and make this place hers. As problematic as that choice was, no matter at whose expense, I felt enormously jealous of her ability to make it, and not a little rejected that she had.

As a consequence of growing up half black in a nation divided along unhealthy racial lines, I had never felt at home in the United States. I identified with the line James Baldwin wrote in *The Fire Next Time* about the experience of black GIs returning from war only to discover the democracy they'd risked their lives to defend abroad continued to elude them at home: "*Home!* The very word begins to have a despairing and diabolical ring."

Tamar, on the other hand, now had a divine Promised Land, a place to belong, and a people who embraced her. Here she was in Zion. It was a real place: a providential, politically sanctioned place, with roots and dirt she could hold in her hand. This wasn't the imagined heaven that black slaves (and their descendants) had to look forward to in the afterlife once they had reached the North, realized its spiritual bankruptcy, rubbed their eyes, and asked each other, "Where's de milk an' honey at? An' de streets all paved wit gold?" No, this was the real deal. Jerusalem seemed to me a place where the very *air* was gold — I swear the light had that imperial quality against my skin. It was a place I could lust after and visit, where my price of admission was a slight degradation, and where Tamar could have a physical address. Her beautiful old Arab house had tile floors, arched doorways, and room enough for a piano. It was situated in a dusty alley in the German Colony off Emek Refaim, a street name meaning "valley of the ghosts."

One of the ghosts was a woman named Hala Sakakini. She once lived a few doors down at no. 10 Emek Refaim but left her home along with her family to escape mortar attacks during the Arab-Israeli War. That was in 1948, the year the State of Israel was proclaimed. Over 700,000 Palestinian refugees fled at that time. Their houses were quickly expropriated by Holocaust survivors and Jewish immigrants from Arab lands. Many Palestinians, including Hala Sakakini, expected to return. They refer to their exodus as the *Nakba*, or "cataclysm." In her memoir, *Jerusalem and I*, there is a photo of Hala Sakakini in her living room, shortly before *Nakba*. She sits in an armchair before a large ornate radio, in the light of a gooseneck floor lamp, usmiling, with a hard set to her jaw. She describes the painful experience of revisiting her occupied home years later:

We knocked on the door. Two ladies appeared . . . We tried to explain: "this is our house. We used to live here before 1948 . . ." The elderly lady was apparently moved but she immediately began telling us that she too had lost a house in Poland, as though we personally or the Arabs in general were to blame for that. We saw it was no use arguing with her. We went through all the house room by room — our parents bedroom, our bedroom, Aunt Melia's bedroom, the sitting room and the library . . . the dining room, the kitchen . . . everything was so different. It was no more home . . . we stood there as in a daze looking across the street and the square at our neighbour's houses . . . It is people that make up a neighbourhood and when they are gone it will never be the same again. We left . . . with a sense of emptiness, with a feeling of deep disappointment and frustration.

Reconciliation over property ownership remains a controversy between Israel and Palestine.

Who used to own the house Tamar had usurped? Where was that displaced person now? What kind of Zion was this, superimposed on top of another nation? What kind of screwed-up Canaan has an *intifada*? I was pondering these kinds of questions when Tamar's boyfriend, Yonatan, laid *Lady Sings the Blues* on the turntable, told me he loved Billie Holiday with all his might, and asked me in earnest if I thought he understood her as well as I did. "Of course you don't," I scoffed, because my broken, darling Billie was singing "God Bless the Child" in her ripped-satin voice, and what could he possibly be thinking? He could have his Canaan land, but Lady Day belonged to me.

Once upon a time, Tamar had been a part of my tribe, but a shadow wall had crept up between us. I couldn't shake the uneasy feeling that, in spite of her leftist stance, which was about as far left as she could stand without falling off the edge into the unknown, she was complicit in an unjust occupation. It didn't matter that the State of Israel was declared, in large part, in reparation for the Holocaust. Palestine was under its colonial thumb. It didn't matter that Tamar didn't live in a settlement, or that she participated in peace protests and rallies, or that she rolled her eyes at the slogans in her neighbors' windows (*"Golan Heights Is Ours!"*). They were still her neighbors, and she'd chosen to leave me in order to live among them. It didn't matter that she wasn't the one who shined a flashlight between my legs to look for a bomb. I couldn't shake the feeling that her choice to be Israeli had turned my best friend white.

We were floating. Our twin tattoos were on display, but there were no living fish in the Dead Sea to look up at our naked backs and notice. It was nighttime at the nadir, literally the lowest point on the planet. Home was halfway around the world, and we were floating in the still, still water, whose salt lifted us up like hands. The lights of Jordan twinkled on the distant shore, and above us wheeled a soup of stars thick enough to stir with a spoon.

"It's so good to see you again," she whispered.

"You too. I'm glad I came here," I answered, "but I miss black people."

I was surprised to hear myself say it, but I realized it was true. With the exception of Maine, I'd never traveled to a place without black people.

"There are black people here, silly," Tamar said. "You're not the only one."

"Where are they?"

"All over."

"Really?" Where were they hiding? I hadn't seen them.

"Sure. The Falashas."

"Who?"

"Beta Israel. The Ethiopian Jews. And there's a bunch of black Americans squatting in the desert — the Black Hebrews. I think they're from Chicago."

"What are they doing here?"

"Why don't you ask them? They're not far away. Israel's only the size of New Jersey, remember?" She splashed me. "If you really want to see 'your people' that badly, we can find them."

"I'd like to, but I'm leaving in two days."

Tamar sighed. "I wish you didn't have to go."

There is such a thing as a black Jew. I rotated the thought in my mind. I'd always considered the two groups to be mutually exclusive. A light wind rippled the water. I shivered. I closed my eyes and perceived the imperceptible tilt of the earth on its axis. The pigeonholes I knew were collapsing. It was a delightful feeling.

Six months later, from my rooftop in Brooklyn, I witnessed the Twin Towers collapse. Two weeks after that, Tamar was in the States for Rosh Hashanah. We walked across the Brooklyn Bridge and found ourselves in the quiet ash at the foot of a twisted twenty-foot waffle of metal at Ground Zero. I gagged on the smell of burnt wire and flesh. Sickened and stunned, I said what we all said then: "It feels like a movie." Tamar looked at me sideways. "You know," she said, "in most of the world, this kind of thing goes on all the time."

She was right, of course. How could I have been so quick to judge her status as an Israeli without judging my own status as an American? She, at least, lived with the daily consequences of her nation's bullying, lived with the ruptures, the bombs, the protests. She had to confront this strife and examine her place within it.

I had to do the same. I began to see how globally hated my government was and, by extension, the citizens of my country. It didn't matter that my black friends and I hated our government too, or that we didn't support it. In my travels, I began to feel ashamed. If someone asked me where I was from, I said "New York," rather than "the United States."

When Hurricane Katrina set her wrath upon the Gulf of Mexico, I sat glued to the TV screen in a state of near paralysis, scanning the black bodies abandoned in the Superdome and marooned on the rooftops of those spoiled houses for the faces of my relatives, who lived in Bay Saint Louis, Mississippi, a beach town sixty miles from New Orleans now under fifteen feet of water. My grief didn't protect my cousins from the deluge, nor did it bring them to dry land. My outrage at the infrastructure that had failed my family didn't serve them either. Even in this age of information, it took months for us to locate them in their great disbursal. This was another diaspora. But what did my sense of loss matter to my homeless Mississippi aunties as I sat in a yoga class and walked my dog?

I published a book and was made a professor, like my father. I moved to Harlem to be closer to the university that employed me. Harlem was shifting. It didn't matter that I belonged halfway to the race being slowly squeezed out of Manhattan's final frontier of affordable real estate. As much as I hated to watch the sad, slow effects of gentrification spill over the stately brownstones of Sugar Hill and Strivers' Row, home of Madam C. J. Walker and Langston Hughes and all those wild jazzmen I loved so much, I couldn't pretend, with my Ivy League degree, that I wasn't a member of the gentry. I myself was not disinherited. Recognizing this, I began to feel my terrible whiteness, and I was ashamed.

Avoiding my reflection in storefront windows, I meandered

through Harlem and beyond: northward to the Cloisters of Fort Tryon Park, eastward to the movable Macombs Dam Bridge and into the Bronx, westward over the Washington Bridge across the dirty Hudson, southward down the long finger of Manhattan. On one of these rambles, in the shadow of the elevated subway tracks off 125th Street, I stumbled upon a short stretch of alleyway called *Old Broadway*. And there, in the middle of the alley, stood a small, sweet shul with a dirty façade and bricked-up windows. Here was Harlem's last remaining synagogue, a remnant from the neighborhood's former days of Yiddish theaters and crowded Jewish tenements. I stopped in front of it and cocked my head. Why did I feel I'd been there before? It was Friday night, and the sun was setting. Slowly I pushed open the heavy wooden door.

"Welcome!" cried an old black man in a *kippah*. "Good Shabbos." He adjusted the tallit on his shoulders and took my hands in his. "This is wonderful," he smiled. He had the whitest teeth. "Another wandering Jew has found their way home." Home! Either as a result of his kindness or as a result of his mistake, I was afraid I might begin to weep.

Meanwhile, Tamar had settled down with an Argentine Jew who shared her last name, and together they bore a daughter. Somehow six years had gone by. I returned to Israel in order to visit them and also to find those black folks. Did they think they were home? Did Tamar?

On the flight, I worked on the patchwork quilt I was nearly done sewing for Tamar's baby, Nina, who had just celebrated her first birthday, and whose first steps I was hoping to witness. I labored over this quilt. It was hand stitched in strips, chromatically schemed like a rainbow. The last step was to finish the border, now fastened by forty little pins, ten on each side. I was worried that security would mistake the pins for tiny explosive devices. I was worried that they wouldn't let me bring my gift into their country. They didn't take the baby's quilt. They didn't strip-search me in the basement. Instead, they brought me behind a heavy black curtain, rifled through my luggage, and confiscated my iPod.

Without my music to comfort me, I grew restless on the long flight to Tel Aviv. The plane was almost empty. Israel was in its sixth day of war with Lebanon, exchanging escalating fire with the Hezbollah militia. It was a grossly lopsided exchange — Beirut was being steadily, smolderingly, mercilessly destroyed — but northern Israel was not a safe place either. My mother had begged me to postpone my trip. I was flying headlong into a war zone.

The first place I went looking for black folks was a reggae club on Tel Aviv's Harakevet Street. THE RASTA was painted in block letters on a pan-African green, gold, and red sign hanging above a chain-locked doorway being guarded by a stocky Russian Jew in a leather jacket.

"You don't want to go in there," he warned me.

A fighter plane roared above us, and then another, flying north.

"Oh, yes I do."

"No." He crossed his arms.

"Isn't there a show tonight?" I looked at my watch. A band called Tony Ray and the Amjah was supposed to play at ten. It was now rounding midnight.

"It's not for you. Karaoke is next door."

"But I came for this."

"You won't like it. Believe me. They get drunk and fight like animals. It's messy."

"Look," I said. "I came all the way from New York for this."

"It's not safe."

"Are you going to let me in or not?"

The guard sighed with annoyance, got down from his stool, unlocked the door, and called for the club owner, none other than Tony Ray himself, a tall man in his early fifties from Jamaica by way of England. He had a head of graying beaded dreadlocks, a gold tooth, and an easy manner.

"Don't pay that bald-head guard no mind. You're just early, little daughter. We on colored-people time," he said, leading me to the bar and pouring me a liberal shot of cheap rum. Behind the bar hung an embossed picture of Haile Selassie, a small felt banner of the Lion of Judah, and a poster of Bob Marley. On the shelf with all the liquor bottles sat a glow-in-the-dark plastic alien smoking ganja.

As a Rastafarian, Tony Ray believes that he is ancestrally tied to

Ethiopia, that his captive forebears originated from that homeland, that the messiah has come and gone in the form of Ethiopia's last emperor, the Conquering Lion of Judah — formerly known as Ras Tafari/Haile Selassie (who claimed to descend directly from King Solomon and the Queen of Sheba), and that Ethiopia is the Promised Land.

"How'd you wind up here instead of Addis Ababa?" I asked him, thinking of Marcus Garvey's nationalist "Back to Africa" repatriation platform.

He explained that he'd come for a three-month tour with his band as a young man, "And I tell you, I din like it one bit. Israeli folk are rude and out of order. Yuh see me?"

I nodded.

"Then I return to London, where they act so civilized, but underneath their smile they want to kick their boot inside I and I mouth. I start miss Israel. My gut was craving for figs! So I came back, and now it's thirty years gone. I and I is a natty Nazarite now. Is my place this." He spanked the bar with a wet rag for emphasis and began wiping it down.

The door burst open and a young man sauntered in with an electric bass. "Jamaican-boy!" he cried.

"Etiopian-bwoy!" Tony Ray answered, embracing him. "You ready to make music, my brethren?"

By three in the morning, in my beer-soaked haze, I thought I may as well have been in Addis Ababa. The Rasta was packed shoulder to shoulder with Ethiopians, stirring it up to the reggae of Tony Ray, backed by the Amjah on trombone, bass, drums, and krar. Hardly anyone in the crowd spoke English, but they all knew the lyrics of the Bob Marley covers — "Redemption Song," "Buffalo Soldier," and the rest. So we danced and sang "I'm gonna be Iron like a Lion in Zion" until somebody opened the door allowing a shock of July sunlight to land in a trapezoidal wedge on the edge of the dance floor, and I realized it was morning. The guard was snoring on his stool in the entryway, slumped like an overstuffed rag doll. Out on the sidewalk of Harakevet Street, it took me a full minute to remember where I was. I blinked. The fighter jets were still droning overhead.

*

The second place I went looking for black folks was an absorption center in the northern port city of Haifa, roughly thirty miles from the Lebanese border.

"What exactly is an *absorption center*?" I asked Tamar's friend Yitzhak on the taxi drive from Tel Aviv up the coastal highway. I couldn't help noticing that all the cars were traveling in the opposite direction. I would rather have put my question to Yizthak's friend Abate, who actually lived in an absorption center when he made *aliyah* from Ethiopia in 1999, but Abate's English was limited. He sat in the front seat, cradling the beat-up case of his soprano saxophone as if it were a baby. I watched his face in the rearview mirror. He had a pencil-thin mustache, a slightly receding hairline, and preternaturally large eyes — Louis Armstrong eyes — through which he looked out at the passing road signs in studied silence.

Abate's integration into Israel was a painful one. While he'd enjoyed a successful jazz career in Addis Ababa and had toured Europe several times over, he wasn't recognized as a musician in Israel, he didn't speak Hebrew, and he had to work several menial jobs in order to support his family. One was washing dishes in a restaurant; another was at a chemical factory. He worked nights as a security guard. A grant from the Ethiopian Jewry Heritage organization eventually enabled him to quit all but the night job, leaving him enough time to practice his instrument in the day, but not before the chemicals and dishwater had damaged his hands. He had to wait a long, long time for his fingers to heal.

Tamar had introduced me to Yitzhak, a serious, bespectacled composer in his thirties who described his sound as "third-stream jazz." Yitzhak had two things on his lap in the backseat of the taxicab that day: an electric keyboard and a rolled-up marriage license that had just been rejected by the Rabbinate Council on the grounds that it didn't conform to their standards.

"What did you say?" he asked me. He seemed distracted.

"An *absorption center*," I repeated, "what is it?"

Before he could answer, his cell phone rang. It was his fiancée.

"Don't go to Haifa!" she screamed, loud enough for me to hear.

Yitzhak pacified her in Hebrew. I'm guessing he told her the same thing he'd told me in English, which was that, as an army reservist, it was his civic duty to go. It was the will of *ha-Sokhnut*, the Jewish Agency. This bureaucratic arm of Israeli government facilitates immigrant absorption into Israel. Tamar later described it to me as "floundering" and "inept." The Jewish Agency had ordered Yitzhak to play music for the Falashas. A USO sort of thing.

In the ancient ecclesiastical language Ge'ez, the word *falasha* means "landless one" and, by association, "wanderer," "exile," "stranger." It is used to describe the Beta Israel, Ethiopian Jews whose tradition holds that they descend from the line of Moses himself — specifically from the lost tribe of Dan — though the origin of their Judaism remains contested by scholars (unlike the Lemba, a South African tribe of black Jews whose DNA has linked them to ancient Judea). Many scholars theorize that Ethiopian Jews converted from the Christian faith during the thirteenth and fourteenth centuries. Ethiopisant Ephraim Isaac, on the other hand, believes that Jewish presence in Ethiopia dates back to the period of the First Temple. He points out that the Bible mentions Ethiopia more than fifty times, "but Poland, not once." One thing is certain: The Beta Israel have longed for Jerusalem for centuries. Maybe for millennia.

The Israeli Rabbinate recognized the status of Ethiopian Jewry in the mid-seventies and, in so doing, paved the way for a mass exodus under the Law of Return. Coming mostly from the mountainous northern Gondar region, where they made up only a small minority of Ethiopia's population and were denied the right to inherit land unless they converted to Christianity, their number in the State of Israel is now approaching 100,000. This is thanks in large part to two massive, highly publicized "rescue" efforts, Operation Moses (1984) and Operation Solomon (1991), which airlifted the Beta Israel by the planeload from Africa. *Falasha* is decreasingly used in Israel to describe Ethiopian Jews like Abate, because they themselves prefer that the term not be used. It has a pejorative tinge, like the Hebrew word *kushi* (darkie) but is not as strong a word as *nigger* in the United States.

As Yitzhak finished placating his fiancée, Oz, the taxi driver, directed my attention to a sprawl of modest white houses around Hadera. Oz was in his early fifties and looked like he spent the better part of his time lifting barbells in a gym. "Look at their ugly houses!" he spat. "They're not like us. They have ten, twelve children, and they don't take care of them. They're like cockroaches." He was speaking, of course, about a community of Palestinians. I wondered if Abate could understand Oz's speech, and, if so, whether it made him as uncomfortable as it made me. I wondered if his allegiance was torn, if the return to the Promised Land, whose government had "saved" him from the Dark Continent, was worth the harsh decline in his status as a musician. I wanted to ask him if this was home.

"Are you American?" Oz asked me.

"I'm from New York," I said.

"Israel is the America of the Middle East!" He meant modernity.

"I know." I meant the malignancy of Manifest Destiny.

"Do you have children?" Oz asked me.

"No," I replied as coldly as possible, having summarily dismissed him as a racist. I was trying to figure out how to discourage further conversation when he tightened his greasy ponytail and started talking again.

"Me? I have four children. Two of them are mine, and two of them I adopted from my best buddy. He was killed when we were soldiers in Lebanon, so this war is nothing new to me. Maybe you heard about the missile that hit a car in Haifa yesterday? Don't worry, Miss. You can be comfortable in my cab because I know what to do. If we hear a siren, I will park, and we will find a safe place."

Oz offered me a piece of hard candy, which I refused. Then he fisted his right hand to flex a muscle in his forearm, which was marred by an ugly keloid scar. "You see that? I got that in '82 from the bullet that went into my buddy's face."

I was horrified.

"These people are animals," he reasoned. "They want to kill us."

"What a coincidence!" said Yitzhak, who had shut off his phone by this point. "Abate! Show them *your* scar."

Abate rolled up the long sleeve of his button-down shirt.

"He got that in an Ethiopian war."

The scar on Abate's left arm looked just like the one on Oz's right. The two of them clasped hands in the front seat in a gesture of solidarity. I'd seen this symbol before, a white hand holding a black one. In my lexicon, it was supposed to mean *Peace*.

Yitzhak gave me a loaded look over the top of his spectacles. "You see?" he asked. "We have a lot in common."

Abate lowered his sleeve.

"We have a lot to learn from the Ethiopians in this country," Yitzhak continued. Do you know the word *chutzpah*? We have a lot of *chutzpah* in our personality. It makes us prickly. But the Ethiopians are a gentle people."

I'd heard the Beta Israel characterized as gentle before. In my experience, they tend to be talked about in two contradictory, yet equally patronizing ways by the Alphas of the greater society: either in terms of docility — *humble, peaceful, quiet, soft* — or with regard to their inability to hold their liquor — *drunk, messy, sloppy, loud.*

"I wasn't interested in playing music with Abate at first," Yitzhak revealed. "I don't like world music, but I've really learned a lot from him. He's an amazing musician. Do you want to hear a song he wrote for the Ethiopian radio station? Put on that CD, Abate. . . . That's Abate singing. You'll hear him sing later today, too. It's in Amharic. I don't know what he's saying. Hey, Abate, what do the words mean?"

Abate carefully translated the lyrics into Hebrew. Oz laughed and slapped his thigh. Then he corrected Abate's pronunciation.

Yitzhak translated into English for my benefit: "Abate is singing, 'The fool who tries to crush the State of Israel will himself be crushed.'"

Haifa was a ghost town. The beach was empty. The streets were empty. The stores were closed. The absorption center was an ugly four-story building complex with a Star of David and the Lion of Judah painted on the wall next to the front door. Almost all immigrants from Ethiopia move through way stations like this on their path to Israeli citizenship.

This particular center housed three hundred Beta Israelites, some of whom had immigrated as recently as two weeks before — others who had already lived there for as long as eight months — in overcrowded rooms crammed with bunk beds and fold-up cots. In the kitchen, foil-wrapped trays of unappetizing food were rationed out to the head of each household, anemic-looking vegetables and congealing globs of macaroni and cheese. There was no *berbere* spice in the kitchen. There were not enough bathrooms in the building. In a classroom furnished with child-size desks, both adults and children were given lessons in dietary laws, Hebrew, and hygiene. A picture of Theodor Herzl, the founding father of Zionism, hung on the wall.

In such rooms, the Beta Israel are halfheartedly assimilated before being shunted to the ghettos of Netanya, Rehovot, and Ashdod. They are not given proper job-skills training nor oriented to the shock of Western society. Instead, they are given Orthodox lessons in how to pray and eat. While some of the Beta Israel express gratitude for these lessons, others find them humiliating. They can't be granted full Jewish status or marry religiously unless they undergo formal conversion by immersion in a *mikveh*. People like the *Kessim* (Jewish priests) who led the spiritual community back in Ethiopia don't want their brand of Judaism converted to mainline Israeli Rabbinate standards. The Kessim's status in the community has dropped precipitously as a consequence of the conversion efforts made in classrooms like these. This is where they begin to lose institutional power.

In a concrete lot behind the absorption center, two uniformed female Israeli soldiers corralled dozens of Ethiopian kids into a moon-bounce, one of those air-inflated nylon pleasure-houses you might find at a carnival. A third soldier, with a rifle strapped to his chest, was busily spinning cotton candy onto cardboard wands and distributing them to the kids, who stuffed the sugar into their mouths with sticky fingers. These kids looked dirty, like they hadn't had a bath in a good long while.

I wondered if they would grow up and join "the lost generation." Israeli schools make few allowances for cultural difference. As a result, twenty thousand Ethiopian teenagers have fallen behind, grown disaffected and dropped out, with no plans to join the army or go to college. This generation identifies less with Ethiopian or Israeli culture than with the black pride, oppositional politics, and the message of self-reliance found in the music of rap artists like Tupac Shakur and in reggae clubs like The Rasta. This is a weird circularity. The Jamaican searches for Ethiopia. The Ethiopian searches for Israel, arrives, then searches for Jamaica. And me, the African American searching for what, exactly? The Promised Land seems always out of reach, somewhere on the other side of the planet. Maybe Jamaica will turn into the Promised Land for those bouncing doe-eyed children someday. Maybe America will.

In the meantime, the children were walking on the moon. Their parents looked afraid. A rocket had ripped into the building across the street the day before. This was the landscape of their new home. I suspected that today's concert and candy were meant to keep the Ethiopians quiet.

"You don't see this on the news," said Oz, "but you should. You see what we do for these people, because we are Jews? *This*," he indicated the bright moonbounce, "is Israel."

Assuming he was right, I wondered what the hell those children were doing there. Everyone else in the city with the means to leave had left. Why *wasn't* this in the news? Tamar had shown me an article in the *Haaretz Daily* newspaper about the pets that got left behind by evacuees:

> More than 8,000 dogs and cats have been abandoned in the north by owners who have fled south. These include street cats who lost their food supply. . . . "Numerous abandoned dogs are roaming the streets in the Galilee," says veterinarian Gil Shavit of Yesod Hama'ala. . . . "There is no excuse to abandon a dog. This is a very sensitive creature that is adversely affected by being deserted."

Where was the article about the Ethiopians? Where does one even find a cotton candy machine in the middle of a war? I thought of Katrina — the dispossessed being left behind in the face of disaster. Then I tried to put things in perspective. It seemed an Ethiopian Jew in Israel had less value than a dog — but not too much less, since the Ethiopian was being taught Hebrew and fed candy. Still, an Ethiopian was worth far more than an Arab, whose value was only that of a cockroach.

Of course, it was ridiculous for me to identify Ethiopian Jews as my kinsmen just because their skin appeared to be black, and for me to think they were black just because they appeared to be second-class citizens. Actually, several groups in Israel can lay claim to "blackness" as far as marginalization, disenfranchisement, and second-class citizenship are concerned.

When Sephardic Jews began immigrating to Israel in the 1950s from the Arab nations of North Africa and the Middle East, they met with poverty, low-paying jobs, life in the slums, and widespread discrimination by the European Ashkenazi Jews who preceded them. In 1970, an antiestablishment group of Sephardic youth organized to struggle for their civil rights. What did they call themselves? The Black Panthers. Later waves of *aliyot* brought Mizrahi and Russian Jews who met with a similar fate.

One of the overtaxed workers at the absorption center in Haifa told me, "We have never dealt well with immigrants. Maybe it's worse for the Falashas because they're black, but it's always been hard for immigrants here. We haven't learned from our mistakes." She shut her eyes and pinched the bridge of her nose between her forefingers, as if trying to relieve herself of a migraine headache. Then she said, "You have to realize how hard this is. Imagine if the United States had to absorb all of Mexico. Can you imagine? Where would you put all those people?"

I'm not sure that she intended this as a rhetorical question, but I'm afraid I treated it as one. "These people don't like to be called *Falashas*," I said, somewhat possessively, still clinging to my association as if it mattered at all.

The Beta Israel don't even think of themselves as black — at least they didn't while they were in Africa. They thought of themselves as *queyy* — red or brown, a harmonious shade that God finally got right after botching his palette on white and black people. Furthermore, they distinguished themselves racially from their black African slaves. Like non-Jewish Ethiopians, Beta Israel is separated into a master caste, the *chewa*, and a slave caste, the *barya*. This hierarchical relationship has not been dismantled through the process of immigration because the *chewa* have had the good sense to keep quiet about their slaves in Israel. The *chewa* justify their slave ownership by maintaining that the *barya* have different bones and descend from the cursed line of Ham. It was a slap in the face for the *chewa* to arrive in Israel along with their chattel and be referred to as *kushis*, or blacks.

As for their participation in the Israeli Defense Forces, the Beta Israel soldiers are known for being fearless, for fighting as though they have something to prove — which they probably do. They often volunteer for the most dangerous posts, like border patrol, where their duty is to frisk and humiliate Arabs, while letting Israelis pass. They might be "black" to white Israelis, and the object of some race prejudice, but the most consistently profiled racial group in Israel is the Arabs — the truest niggers of the Holy Land.

Before I could peel my notion of blackness off of Beta Israel and paste it onto Palestine, Yitzhak yanked me away from the moon-bounce by the elbow and told me a story.

"I don't agree with everything Oz said in the cab. I don't think all Arabs are inhuman. I even went to protest the building of the separation wall. It's true. I marched on their side because it was too much like apartheid for my taste. The Israeli soldiers came to stop us. One of them pointed a M16 at my chest. He was Ethiopian. I thought, 'He could kill me. I might die today. What am I dying for? Which side am I on?' Do you know what the Palestinian standing next to me said? 'Look at that filthy *kushi* who wants to shoot us. I can't believe it's come to this. My homeland is being run by monkeys.' I was scared the Arab would yell 'Go back to Africa!' and the soldier would open fire. It gets so confusing here sometimes."

"I see what you mean," I said.

Then a siren wailed and the whole lot of us — children, soldiers, masters, slaves, black, white, and *queyy* — flew down into the basement. The basement was set up for the concert with folding chairs. The soldiers walked around the dank periphery, spraying bottles of perfume, presumably to mask the fetid odor of sweat. Something cracked outside. It sounded like the scratch of a needle on a record followed by a low boom. "Was that a *katuba* rocket?" I asked.

"No," said Yitzhak, laughing at my poor Hebrew. He held up his marriage license like a baton. *This* is a *katuba*. *That* was a *katyusha*." I didn't think it was a funny joke, but right on cue to spike the punch line, a second explosion sounded. I had to pee suddenly, but there was nowhere to go. Instead, I helped Yitzhak set up his keyboard while Abate warmed up the crowd. I wondered what he was telling them. I wondered what I was doing there. And then they began to play the blues.

Let me be precise. It was unbearably hot. The women sat on the left. They wore colorful head wraps and Jewish-star necklaces, seemingly at odds with the Coptic crosses tattooed on their foreheads, though these are less a symbol of Christianity than a phylactery protective charm against evil. The men sat on the right. They wore *kippahs*. The children sat on the floor, holding hands. The room reeked of perfume. Everyone was very still. Everyone was watching Abate. Abate had his saxophone strapped around his neck. When he closed his eyes and opened his mouth, the basement widened into a vast space. He sang in Amharic, backed by Yitzhak on stride piano, and when his voice grew jagged, he wet the reed of his horn and transformed the line of the Ethiopian song into indefinable flights of improvised jazz. Then Abate circled back to the plaintive root of his own voice.

The two-man band played in a minor pentatonic scale, one mode of which is called *tezeta*. The word means nostalgia. I looked at the delicate faces of the women, some of whom were nursing babies. Some of the women were beginning to smile. I could sense that they recognized Abate's song. *Tezeta* is the mode in which the Jews in Ethiopia express their longing for Jerusalem, but that's not what Abate was singing about. This song expressed his longing for *Ethiopia*. I recognized it as the mode of the blues — a sound that goes straight to the heart, the sound of the Negro spirituals, the sound of "Amazing Grace." It didn't matter that I didn't understand the words. Everyone in that basement understood the song, including me. It was a sorrow song about homesickness, and it soothed us in our fear, just as it was meant to do. While it was being sung, the war outside went away. I realized then that I had done Billie Holiday a great disservice when I told Yonatan that he couldn't comprehend her depth.

Tezeta was also the name of the woman I talked to at the Israeli Association for Ethiopian Jews. The IAEJ office was inside a Jerusalem shopping mall and decorated with children's artwork that portrayed the dramatic exodus of the Beta Israel from Africa in sequential order, like the Stations of the Cross. I was particularly taken by a tempera painting of a fat blue propeller plane with white stars on its wings. It flew above several brown-faced figures in a yellow desert landscape.

All but one of these figures held the Torah in their upraised hands. The one who didn't belong stood in the lower right-hand corner holding a red umbrella, as if she knew it was going to rain.

"Why are you interested in us?" Tezeta asked with suspicion. She was a fiercely determined and articulate woman in her late twenties with a wild, natural hairdo, kohl-rimmed eyes, and a direct stare. She had recently quit her job as anchorwoman on the Ethiopian cable access channel in favor of championing basic civil rights for Beta Israel. Her organization is primarily sponsored by American Jews, as are the majority of Ethiopian causes in Israel. In fact, Jews in America financially support Ethiopians above all other Israeli immigrant groups. What is behind this charitable giving? I don't mean to undermine their acts of much-needed generosity, but I do believe that guilt is a factor — guilt over race relations in America and fear that such relations might take hold in Zion. Tezeta herself had an American sponsor for a while. This benefactor sent her five hundred shekels a month but abruptly withdrew funding when Tezeta went backpacking through Europe and forgot to send him the personal letters he'd come to expect about how grateful she was for his money. Understandably, she was suspicious of me.

A postcard of Martin Luther King Jr. was tacked to the wall by Tezeta's desk. I pointed at his picture. "I'm interested in you because his dream is important to me," I said.

And then, because I was still thinking about the meaning of her name and the transformative power of Abate's music, I asked Tezeta what she thought of Idan Raichel. Raichel is a white Israeli musician whose eponymous debut album, *Idan Raichel Project*, went triple platinum when it was released in 2002 and won him such national accolades as "artist of the year," "album of the year," and "song of the year." His success was due in large part to the Ethiopian folk music sampled in his songs. Idan Raichel has toured the United States during Black History Month and has been described as the "Israeli Bob Marley." Since he doesn't play reggae, I can only assume he's called this on account of his waist-length dreadlocks. He is widely lauded for exposing Israel both to Amharic music and to the gift of diversity that Beta Israel has delivered.

"I know Idan Raichel," said Tezeta. "You want to talk to him?"

"I'm more interested in talking to one of the Ethiopians he exploited by neglecting to pay them for his success," I said.

Tezeta laughed and leaned toward me conspiratorially. "My best friend sings in one of the hit songs — 'Bo'i.' She's really mad. He doesn't give her any money, and do you know how much money he has from her voice? His pockets are fat from our music. Ever since Idan Raichel made it big, I want to run and see what kind of car he drives because I can remember when he drove a jalopy."

"Maybe he's a necessary evil," I suggested. I told her about how much Abate's music moved me. Then I told her about the Rasta, how its door had been guarded, effectively segregating the club. "Maybe it takes someone like Idan Raichel to get Israel to open its ears to what you have to offer. Maybe he's a cultural bridge."

"I don't think so," she said. "Ethiopian music can only make it in Israel if it has white in the middle. If you take away the white, they don't want it. I know Abate. He is saying something deep. For Israeli listeners, they will be amazed to hear him play the sax. He will give them something rich they don't know. But they are deaf and blind to him. We all hear Idan Raichel on the radio. He sounds like cheap popcorn. He doesn't have anything new to give to an Ethiopian."

I tried to extend the implied metaphor about unfair trade to her own experience by asking Tezeta what she'd given Israel and what Israel had given her in return, but she was reluctant to talk about her service in the army and dismissive about her journey from Ethiopia during Operation Solomon fifteen years before. Maybe these personal topics were too painful to discuss.

"I'm supposed to be grateful to Israel for saving me" was all she would say.

This is the image the world has, that a fleet of planes swooped down like a flock of angels, scooped up the endangered black Jews in the knick of time, and delivered them from starvation into Israel's bosom. It's true that Operation Solomon rescued the Beta Israel from violence in Addis Ababa during a civil war, but their journey to Jerusalem began long before that. At the start of their journey, they weren't at risk, they weren't starving, and they weren't particularly impoverished. Jerusalem was a magnet, and the force of its pull was stronger than the force of Ethiopia's push. What prompted tens of thousands of the Beta Israel to abandon their relatively safe and comfortable lives to risk everything by migrating to the point where those planes would pick them up? Perhaps opportunism was a factor, but more than that, the pull was their longing for Zion.

I pointed again at Dr. King's picture. "He said he went to the mountaintop and saw the Promised Land. I'm guessing this isn't it?"

Tezeta snorted. "I'm not a Zionist. Zionism was a bad idea. Israel wants to be a melting pot for all the world's Jews to make them one thing. She is very sexy. She has what every strong nation wants — a stable economy and an atom bomb. But we don't have any tolerance."

"Are you saying multiculturalism can't exist here?"

"I am saying this does not exist in Israel."

"And absorption is the price of Zionism? Everybody must conform?"

"Yes. You are right. Maybe we embrace Ethiopian music when a white man brings it on a plate, but they cannot see them as a full human. They want them to be white."

I pointed out Tezeta's pronoun confusion. She alternated between *we, they, us, them, ours,* and *theirs* to talk about both Israelis and Ethiopians, and I didn't think it was because English was her third language. Which did she feel she was — Israeli or Ethiopian?

"I don't know. I have my feet in two lands. I don't know what I am."

"I understand what that's like," I said. "Tezeta, are you black?"

"There are a lot of blacks here. The Mizrahi is black, the Bedouin is black, the Yemenite is black, the Moroccan is black, and the Ethiopian is the most black, because we came to Israel last. The next to come will be more black than us. It doesn't matter the color of their skin."

"Are the Palestinians black?"

"No. They are not playing in the game. We don't absorb them."

The next day, Tezeta and her boyfriend, Tsuri, brought me and Tamar to Mt. Herzl National Memorial Park. Tamar described the park as "the heart of the Zionist commemoration machine." The Holocaust memorial complex, Yad Vashem, is there, as are the military cemetery, the burial sites of Golda Meir and Yitzhak Rabin, and the construction site of a brand-new memorial whose design Tsuri consulted on. It is being erected to commemorate the thousands of Beta Israel who died trying to reach Israel. Tsuri showed me the architectural design for the memorial, which included four round thatch-roofed huts. Tamar served as translator: "He says those are what their houses looked like in Gondar."

Tsuri pointed to a part of the construction site where a backhoe was lazily kicking up yellow dust. Tamar tried to keep up with his torrent of words. "He says the huts will go there in a diamond. One, two, three, four. . . . The idea was for each house to have text on the walls, a monologue about the exodus by four different Ethiopian characters . . . a mother, a child, a father who leads the family, and a holy man. He wanted visitors to be able to go inside their houses and read their stories."

Tsuri seemed angry.

"What's he saying?" I asked. Tamar struggled to keep up with his tirade. "He's saying that the Jewish Agency didn't approve the design."

"Why not?"

"He says they were afraid the Falashas would go in there to drink and do drugs. . . . Sorry, he's talking really fast. They're allowed to have the structures, but they have to be closed."

"So nobody can go inside," I clarified.

"That's right," Tamar translated. "No doors. You can only see the huts from the outside."

"But that's ridiculous," I said. "If the story remains hidden, then this is a memorial with no memory."

"I *told* you," Tezeta interrupted, gesticulating wildly. "They do not want what is in our heart. They only want what is in *her* heart." She meant Tamar. "For us they only want to pat themselves on their backs. Do you think they asked Tsuri to work for this memorial?"

She turned to her boyfriend and spoke animatedly at him. It took me a moment to realize her torrent of words were Amharic. Amharic is a softer-sounding language than Hebrew, but she was speaking it hard.

Tsuri sighed and tucked the blueprints into his bag. Then he said something brief and looked with resignation at the backhoe. "He says they didn't ask him," Tamar translated. "He heard they were building the memorial, and he fought to be included on the steering committee."

"He is the only Ethiopian making this. They think they know better than us how to make it," Tezeta hissed.

On our way through the cypress trees down the mountain, Tamar admitted that when she'd come to Israel for summer camp in her youth, she'd felt the land belonged to her, and she to it. "The counselors instilled a sense of ownership in us," she said. "I thought the Falashas were foreigners, but I didn't think of myself as a foreigner. It's ironic, isn't it? They were living here. I was only visiting."

"It is not ironic," said Tezeta. *Chutzpah*. That is the word for how she said this: "Israel does belong to you. Not to us."

"Do you guys think of this place as your homeland?" I asked the young couple.

Tsuri was tight-lipped. Tezeta was fed up. "I have told you! I'm not a Zionist! The Ethiopians dream of Zion as a place that our grandfathers dreamed. But they need to wake up from that dream and see how this Zion treats us. That dream is not real. The day we say our dream is just a dream is the day we will stand up for our rights. But the Ethiopians want to stay asleep. They say, 'I dreamed to be here. I am a Zionist and I belong to Zion.' Israel doesn't want them. She only wants them if they play the game by her rules, pray the way she tells us, think the way she tells us, be the Jew she wants. It was not my dream to be a citizen of Israel. If you want to listen to that kind of talk, you should go and see my boss."

Dany Admasu was a chain-smoking, poetic man in his early thirties who looked like he hadn't slept in months. He had been airlifted in from Sudan during Operation Moses in 1984, an era I remember for Live Aid, Hands Across America, the hit song "We Are the World," and starving Ethiopians on the cover of *Time* magazine. Having been in Israel longer than Tezeta, Dany's English was more assured.

"I wrote this," he said, pulling a yellowed clipping of an article from the *Jerusalem Post* off the bulletin board in his office. "It gives you an idea of my politics." The headline read: "Which Way for Ethiopian Israelis?" The article focused on discrimination against the Beta Israel in the school system, the civil service, the private sector, and the housing market, as well as their lack of representation in government and all other centers of power.

"What about the Ethiopian on *The Ambassador*?" I teased, referring to the reality show that pitted fourteen young Israelis against each other in tasks designed to boost Israel's disintegrating world image. "And wasn't there an Ethiopian singer represented on *Israeli Idol*?"

"They didn't win," he said. "They were just window dressing to complete Israel's cultural menagerie."

"What about Addisu Messele?" I asked about the former lone Ethiopian-born member of the one-hundred-and-twenty-person Knesset. "Window dressing?"

"More or less."

"I bet your article got you in trouble," I guessed. "You called the Ministry of Absorption a *disgrace*. That's pretty bold."

"I am bold — I'm an Israeli. We know how to shout to get our point across. But you're right. The government doesn't like me because I'm speaking the truth. My goal is to change their idea that we're not worthy. They don't understand. They think Jewish means white."

He offered me a cigarette, which I declined.

"They want you to think they love us because we're all Jews, but they don't think we have the same bones and blood."

"I heard about how they dumped all the Beta Israel blood out of the blood bank because they thought it was infected with AIDS."

"How did you hear about that?"

"I read about it."

"Are you American?"

"I'm from New York."

"Americans have a tendency to talk about the ethos of the community, and not of the individual. You think this war is between Israel and Lebanon, for example. You think about who is right and wrong, but you don't think about the experience of the soldier."

I thought about what he said and how quickly I'd written Oz off.

He was a man who had seen his best friend's face blown away. Who would I have turned against, if I had witnessed the same thing done to Tamar?

"I will tell you my individual story," Dany offered. "Imagine you are me. You are a little Jewish boy in Gondar, where you shepherd goats. Every morning you drink fresh milk from the goats you tend. But the real food in your life as you grow up is the dream of Jerusalem. This dream is in everything you do — the way you pray, the blessing, all the Jewish ceremonies. In every sentence the word *Jerusalem* comes up."

He stopped to ash his cigarette.

"One day, your father says to you, 'We're going to Jerusalem.' Imagine your surprise. You didn't know it was a real place. You thought it was a dream as far away as the moon. Your father has sold your goats and everything else but the donkey to carry the food. You begin walking with everyone else from your village. You're doing what Moses did to get to Israel. Every father in the village is a Moses.

"They knew there would be sacrifice. Somebody was going to die along the way. They were willing to pay whatever it cost to get to Jerusalem. Looking back, it was crazy. The government regime did not allow emigration. They arrested us along the way and sent us back to the village. So we began again. We walked at night and hid in the day. My sister was arrested three times, and she bore a kid in jail.

"Imagine you are walking. You walk from Ethiopia to Sudan. It takes two months. The weak ones didn't make it this far. You made it, but you have to stop walking because you ran out of food and water. You are so thirsty you would gladly drink your own urine, only you are too dehydrated to urinate. You live in a refugee camp, and it is hell. Sometimes the Red Cross brings medicine, but forty to sixty people die there every day from starvation and snakebites. Israel finally hears about you, but they don't think you're a Jew because you're *black*. You yourself didn't know there were white Jews. You have never seen a white person before.

"America is putting pressure on Israel to save you. A big safari truck comes to pick you up and drives you for three hours with your father to a big airplane. You have never seen an airplane, so you don't know it's strange that they ripped out the seats to fit more of you inside. On the airplane they feed you bananas. You eat so many you get sick. When you arrive in Israel your father is crying because he thinks he's in heaven. You made it. You know you are home.

"That is *my* story. The story the world knows is how Israel endangered herself to bring poor people from Africa. That's a big lie. I started my way to this land that I knew from the stomach of my mother without their help. My father put me in danger for this dream. He made it come true. I don't need permission from anyone to prove I'm Jewish. Israel doesn't need to feed me lies to turn me into an Orthodox Jew. I was Jewish before I was born."

Dany lit another cigarette, leaned back, took a long drag, and exhaled a slow rhapsodic haze of smoke. I noticed that he finished the narrative of his amazing journey homeward at the exact spot where spiritual Zion butts heads with political Zion. I am sure the euphoria of his arrival must have worn away painfully fast, perhaps beginning right when he stepped off the plane onto the tarmac and, along with everyone else on board, was bestowed a Hebrew name. Or did he like to be called Daniel? I wondered what his name used to be, the one his father gave him. I wondered when exactly the word *home* began to take on a "diabolical ring" for him and his father, but I didn't ask Dany about the second half of his journey. I understood that, along with his activism, the dream was what kept him alive. It didn't matter if home was a myth he was still walking toward. Maybe it mattered that he was walking on other people's backs to get there, but I don't think Dany thought about that. It only mattered to him that he hadn't stopped walking.

We were quiet for a while. Then I asked, "Do you know who James Baldwin is?"

He didn't.

"You'd like him. He's a black American writer. He said, 'I criticize my home because I love it.' Or something like that. This paragraph in your article made me think of him." I read it aloud:

More than two decades have passed since the first significant wave of Jewish immigration from Ethiopia to the promised "Land of Milk and Honey" began. While coming on aliyah and being physically present in Israel fulfilled half of the dream, the intolerance towards their language, culture and color, which they have encountered in every aspect of life since their arrival in Israel, has buried the other half of Ethiopian Jewry's dream. Today we can speak more aptly in terms of the crushed dream.

Dany nodded. "I love Jerusalem. I am speaking the truth."

"I am speaking the truth," said the priest. I was at a Sabbath service in the multipurpose room at the Kingdom of Yah, home of the African Hebrew Israelites of Jerusalem, and I was wearing a white head wrap and a loose black dress that came down to my sandaled feet. The room was lit by a dozen *menorahs*. I sat between my hosts, Crowned Dr. Khazriel, head of the School of the Prophets, and one of his many wives, Sister Aturah. She had lent me the dress because the clothes I showed up in were immodest.

The priest was reading from the book of their prophet, Ben Ammi Ben-Israel, a former foundry worker from Chicago, born Ben Carter, whom the African Hebrew Israelites call "Abba" and believe to be the messiah. In 1966, he claims to have had a forty-five-second vision from an angel who told him it was time for him and the rest of his lost tribe to return to Jerusalem. Their tradition holds that they were exiled from the Holy Land during the Roman Invasion nearly two thousand years ago, migrated southward, down the Nile, through the centuries, and westward to the coast of Africa, where a great number of them were captured and shipped into modern Babylon as a curse for sinning against God's law. They distinguish their progenitor from Judah, the Jewish father. Their father is Adam, the original man. They distinguish their curse (referred to in Leviticus and Deuteronomy as a great disbursal and a voyage into captivity by boat) from the eternal curse of Ham, which was used by white slave owners to justify slavery. While Ham's curse cannot be redressed, the African Hebrew Israelites believe their curse *can* be, by living according to certain principles, including a vegan diet.

This is a seductive idea for people who have grown up in inner-city slums, who can only reach four hundred years into their history and then bump against a wall. Being a charismatic leader, Ben Ammi convinced thirty black folks of his angelic vision. First, they traveled to Liberia to cleanse themselves of their slave mentality. In 1969, they showed up in Israel and were told by the Rabbinate that they were not Jews. But the African Hebrew Israelites saw themselves as the original Jews. They refused to convert, calling the Israelis "heathens" and publicly threatening to run them into the sea.

The priest read some more scripture from Ben Ammi's holy book — *God, The Black Man and Truth* — and then launched into a sermon, much of which I agreed with. Up to a point.

"You can't get to freedom on an airplane."

"Tell it!"

"An airplane won't take you there. Brothers and sisters, I'm here to tell you, freedom is a place in your *mind*."

"That's right!"

"Back there we were sick."

"I was dying!"

"Sickness, perversion, and death abound in the land of Great Captivity, but our greatest sickness there was of our *spirit*. We didn't choose to live there."

"No!"

"They took us in chains! That place of wickedness was not our home. Theirs was not our way. Why would you want a house for your car when your brother was homeless? Because you were sick. You were thinking like them. Why would you poison your body with cigarettes, knowing they would kill you?"

"Because I was sick!"

"You were thinking like them. Why would you believe the earth moves around the sun? Does that make sense?"

"No!"

"No. The earth is the center of the universe. Jerusalem is the center of the earth. If the earth moved around the sun, how could the sun rise and set every day? You didn't use your *mind*. You listened to their lies. You let them tell you Jesus was white, Adam was white. Jesus wasn't white. Neither was Adam. They were black men with wooly hair."

"That's right!"

"Why would you let your child play with a toy gun? If you let your child shoot water, he will grow up and think it's a game to shoot a bullet! Why would you allow him to shoot a brother over a pair of hundred-dollar sneakers or a vial of crack? Because you were sick. Our bodies weren't in shackles, but our minds were. They told us we were nothing, and we believed them, but we're not at the bottom of their boat no more. They told us we couldn't do it, but we did. We built the boat. We drive the boat."

"Amen!"

"They want you to believe we're a cult. Say the whole word!"

"Culture!"

I started to feel a little uneasy. I wasn't sure if it was the sermon or the head scarf — Sister Aturah had wrapped mine too tight, and I was afraid I might pass out.

"You don't go to Japan and say, 'That's a cult.' That's a *culture*. We're a *culture*. They say we're a weird sect. Say the whole word. We're a *section* of the Hebrew Israelite nation living in Dimona, Israel, Northeast Africa. If you conform to our vision, you will not be sick. You will not need a medicine chest. Diabetes — what's that? Cancer — what's that? Depression — what's that? Can I get a witness?"

"I haven't been sick since I came to the Kingdom nineteen years ago — not once!"

"The Torah speaks of people who lived nine hundred years, so why can't we? This is possible, people. Nine hundred years is a blink of Yah's eye and we are his *chosen* people. We don't have to die. Heaven is possible in the mind and body, and we are living proof. We don't use the word *death* around our children. Our children don't know the meaning of that word. We are making new people, with new minds, befitting of this new world."

"Hallelujah!"

After the service was over, Dr. Khazriel and Sister Aturah walked me through the Village of Peace to the guesthouse where I was staying in a room decorated with generic Afrocentric prints, a tall wooden giraffe, and a two-by-three-foot poster of Ben Ammi's benevolent face. Aturah was quiet in her husband's presence. I learned that they'd been married only a few weeks before, and that none of his fourteen children was hers. I imagine that being middle-aged and childless was hard for her in a community that forbids birth control and puts a high premium on a woman's ability to bear children.

All of the women I met in the Village of Peace introduced themselves to me in terms of their motherhood, as in, "I'm Sister Ze-horah, mother of eight." They told me that a man's wife is a piece of him just as Adam's rib is a piece of him, and that while Man keeps his hands in the hands of Yah, Woman keeps her hands in the hands of Man.

Aturah walked a few steps behind her new husband and me, her head bowed. I turned to ask her if the priest was using a metaphor when he spoke about immortality.

"Oh, no," she said.

"You don't believe in death?"

"We call it *transitioning*," she said softly.

I thought it would be gauche to ask where they put their dead peo-ple. "Do you celebrate funerals?" I asked.

Dr. Khazriel gave her a look.

"Everything we do promotes life and healing," she said. "What we put in our bodies, what we put into the earth, how we sing. We don't sing the blues anymore."

Dr. Khazriel had a slight lisp. He waved at the crooked little tar-pa-pered shacks that make up the Kingdom of Yah with his cane. "None of this was here when I came," he said, fingering his gray beard. Al-though he is not one of the founders of the kingdom, Dr. Khazriel arrived a few short years after its inception. He was seventeen years old when he came to join his aunt and the swelling number of other African Americans who'd settled in the Negev Desert near a nuclear reactor, where the State of Israel had allowed them to squat. Now there are an estimated 2,500 members of their community living in Israel, where they have recently gained permanent residency status. Their population has grown thanks to the practice of polygamy and to widespread proselytizing efforts in "the provinces," which include Baltimore, Houston, Detroit, Atlanta, and New York. In fact, the Af-rican Hebrew Israelites make up the largest community of African Americans living outside the United States and, Dr. Khazriel told me, "the only progressive one — a historic fact in itself. We built this na-tion with our own hands."

At first, the sprawling shantytown didn't look like much to me, but then I considered the amazing accomplishment. My hosts pointed out their school, their sewing center, their bakery, their gym, their library, their "House of Life" (there is no need for a hospital in a land without sickness) — all of this was built from scratch in thirty-some-odd years. These people make their own clothes, grow most of their own food, and, most importantly, govern themselves.

Where the Beta Israel represent the bitterness, disorientation, and disillusionment of Zionism's dream deferred, members of the African Hebrew Israelite community believe, or are indoctrinated to believe, that they have fully arrived in Canaan. Because the Israeli Rabbinate has never acknowledged them as Jews, they've never enjoyed any of the rights of citizenship that Israel has to offer. This rejection has forced them to fashion their own Zion. Because they've never been forced to assimilate to dominant Orthodox Judaism, they've managed to maintain and forge their own unique Judaic identity. Theirs is truly a fully operable, self-sustained nation-inside-a-nation with one interesting concession — about seventy African Hebrew Israelite youth are enlisted in the Israeli Defense Forces.

I asked Dr. Khazriel if their participation in the IDF conflicted with the African Hebrew Israelite's governing practice of promoting life. "The priest said it was sick for a child to play with a toy gun, but some of your young people are handling real guns right now in Lebanon. What are they fighting for?"

"That's a good question, Sister Emily. I see you have a sharp mind. What you see surrounding you is our spiritual home but it's also a physical realm. We have to protect our village. We're a spiritual entity in a secular world with social realities. Those scuds and rockets are real. Outside of a war atmosphere, killing is not acceptable, but we live in a punishing atmosphere of war. We're not disconnected from greater Israel," Dr. Khazriel reasoned. "We live here, and so we have to show solidarity. But our involvement in the army is only transitional."

I told him I'd been witness to the hard transition Beta Israel was making into Zion. "It's truly a shame what's happening to them," he said, shaking his head. "They're African Hebrew Israelites too. We all descend from Judea, but when they returned home, they began to lose their original form."

We arrived at the guesthouse. "There used to be a baseball diamond scratched in the sand right here," Dr. Khazriel said. "The day I arrived, there was a pickup game going on. My aunt said, 'Boy, this is the kingdom of heaven, and these are the saints.' I said, 'If this is heaven, then where's Jesus?' She pointed at the pitcher and said, 'Right there.' Do you know who she was pointing at?"

"Abba?" I guessed.

"See that, Aturah? She's sharp as a sword." He laid his hand on my shoulder. "We could use a mind like yours in the Kingdom."

Abba stood in a resplendent, canary-yellow robe, in the center of a large painting hanging above the table in the conference room of the School of the Prophets where Dr. Khazriel sat me down to instruct me further in his beliefs. Twelve other men figured in the painting, just like the apostles at the Last Supper. The other decorations of note in the classroom were a picture of Martin Luther King Jr. and a world map.

"Do you really believe Ben Ammi is the messiah?" I asked.

Dr. Khazriel gestured at the painting. "Those men represent our governing body," he began. "Our government must remain in a prophetic mode. Many men have had visions — Frederick Douglass, Martin Delaney, Father Divine, Garvey, King, Malcolm — and all of their visions failed. Why? Because all black visionaries in America become martyrs. The man who can electrify and unify a black movement is an automatic target. We had to authenticate Ben Ammi's vision by calling him the *Messiah*. That title gives him absolute authority."

"As the son of God?"

"As the anointed leader of the Kingdom of Yah. He's our ruler. We couldn't be free until we had our own nation. 'He who rules Jerusalem rules the world.'"

"Sounds like a crusade."

"It is. All men have focused on Jerusalem since the dawn of mankind. Do you know why?"

"Your priest said Jerusalem is the center of the universe."

"Good listening. Israel began with correct socialist aims, but you don't see too many *kibbutzim* anymore. Jerusalem has fallen under the control of profane and perverted European empires. Their dominion has brought the world to darkness. Euro-gentiles have corrupted earth-centered concepts more than any other people. They have distorted the institutions of liberalism and democracy. You'd have to be blind not to recognize this as a fallen world." Dr. Khazriel pushed up the loose sleeves of his *dashiki* and counted out a list of recent calamities on his fingers: tsunami, Katrina, global warming . . . The list had more than ten items and it included the present war with Lebanon. He fisted and unfisted his hands.

"We're at a time of transition. Those empowered to administrate the earth are about to have a rude awakening. Their time of rule is up." He pounded the table with his fists. "Our purpose is to restore Jerusalem, Africa, and the earth. The diaspora cannot save Africa, but Africa can save the diaspora."

"Can you repeat that?"

"There's no spiritual impetus for the black diaspora to save Africa. With all its resources, scholars, and religious leaders, the black diaspora is out of focus. Sister Emily, let me ask you a question. Do you think of Africa as a prophetic or pathetic realm?"

"Um . . ."

"You can admit it."

"Well, I've never been there."

"You're there right now! This is it. You're in Africa." He swiveled his chair and pointed a pen at little Israel on the world map, hanging off Egypt like an earlobe. "All that separates you from the mother continent is the Suez Canal. "The Kingdom of Yah is the New Jerusalem. We're not built out of brick and mortar alone. We're building a new mind beyond the shackles we once knew. We've recovered from chattel slavery. We've saved ourselves from stress and harm, trauma and drama, from the dialysis machine, hypertension and heart attack, from kidney failure, self-hatred, and jail. We've reversed all that impurity by restoring Hebraic concepts of interdependent community, love, and humanity. By doing that, we're restoring Africa, which will in turn restore the earth populace. No brag, just fact."

Dr. Khazriel held out his hand. "This hand is humble. This hand reaching out to save the earth is black. People don't want to hold this hand. They are selective about salvation. Look at this mess." He brought out a copy of the *Economist* and slapped it on the table. Bill Gates was on the cover, holding a black baby. "What does that say?"

"Billanthropy."

"That man has thirty-four *billion* dollars. His impulse is greed, profit, big business, tax-deductible philanthropy. When is it enough? There is no possibility for contentment in the framework of capitalism. Do you know why they crucified *him?*"

Dr. Khazriel signaled the picture of Martin Luther King Jr., which was the same image as the one in Tezeta's office, only much bigger. "Because he was a Hebrew. Their edict was to stop the rise of the black messiah."

"COINTELPRO?"

"Yes, Sister. They got rid of him, of our king, because he spoke the powerful phrase 'Promised Land.' That's a Hebrewism. It comes from Old Testament theology. Hebrewisms are the basis of all black protest social movements. Did you ever read about us in school? Had you ever heard of a Black Jew?"

"No," I admitted.

Dr. Khazriel shook his head, sadly. "We've been omitted from the annals of history. But I want you to see that we're not a fringe. We're not a myth blown out of a vacuum. I want you to read this," he held up the holy book, "as a history text. Begin with Genesis. That's our history."

Sister Aturah, in a purple robe and a matching head wrap, entered the room quietly to serve us watermelon. "This was grown on our farm," she whispered, setting it down. "It's very sweet."

"Thank you, Aturah," said Dr. Khazriel. "Do you have something you want to tell Sister Emily on her search for truth?"

"Yes, I do."

"Tell it."

"This is an island of sanity. This is the place our soul was crying out for."

"Aturah might also have said that we see ourselves as the fulfillment of Dr. King's dream," Dr. Khazriel added. "Isn't that right?"

"Yes," she answered, looking at her feet.

I began picking out the little black seeds from the fruit. Pathetic and prophetic. To me their world was both. "So this is Canaan Land?" I asked Dr. Khazriel. The reason I didn't put my question to his wife was that I didn't think she was at liberty to say "No."

"I was born into a Detroit ghetto," he answered, biting into a slice of watermelon. "If I wasn't here, I would be dead."

On my last day before leaving Israel, Tamar and I walked Nina through a mob of displaced Israeli settlers dressed in orange. It was *Tisha B'Av*, the Fast of the Ninth of Av, a holiday which observes the many tragedies that have stricken Jews throughout history, including the destruction of the First Temple, the Second Temple, and the expulsion of the Jews from Spain. These settlers were using the day to mourn the loss of their homes in Palestinian territory. We hadn't foreseen the march, and soon we were tangled in its masses. There were thousands of settlers, shouting, singing, waving the Israeli flag, flooding us in a rage of orange.

"I can't believe these people," Tamar said, plowing her way through the crowd with the stroller. "Move!"

We escaped behind the walls of the Old City, wended through the maze of its narrow, cobbled streets, bypassed all of its wares — the blue and white Armenian ceramics, the backgammon sets inlaid with mother of pearl, the beads, the baklava, the incense sticks, and *doumbek* drums. We wound up outside the compound of St. Anne's Church. This compound contains the ruins of the curative Bethesda pool where, according to the Gospel of John, Jesus is said to have performed a miracle of faith. "Do you want to be healed?" Jesus asked a lame man with useless legs. The man said yes. "Then get up and walk!" Christ commanded. Which is just what the invalid did.

"I want to show you something special," said Tamar, leading me into the basilica. Except for two middle-aged French women sitting with their hands folded in the back pew, the church was empty. Tamar unstrapped Nina from her stroller. "This church has a fifteen-second echo," she whispered. Nina squealed and her voice ballooned outward to fill the unadorned space, as high as the vaulted ceilings. She widened her eyes in wonder.

"*Excusez-moi. Êtes-vous américaines?*" asked the French woman with the paisley silk scarf at her throat.

"Sort of," said Tamar.

Sort of.

Sort of.

"Ah!" clapped the woman, and her clap became a cannon's boom. "Do you know how to sing?"

"*Dites-leur de chanter* 'Amazing Grace,'" her friend suggested. The last word bloomed from her lipsticked mouth.

Grace.

Grace.

"*J'aime cette chanson.*"

"We know it," Tamar smiled.

We know it.

We know it.

We know it.

We do. We walked up the aisle side by side, sat Nina in the first pew with her quilt, took our places at the altar, looked at each other and began. We sang that mournful hymn composed by a white man who'd sailed the seas on slave ships, witnessed the shackled hold, and attempted to expiate the sin of his complicity through the act of composition.

We sang it in two-part harmony. Our voices cast out like fishing lines into the void where they unraveled. They unraveled into water and swam back to us, doubling and quadrupling in volume, backward and forward, a current running in all directions. This was our sweet sound. Wanting to be cradled in it, the baby scooted backwards off the pew and crawled toward us in her sagging diaper across the marble floor.

We transposed from major to minor key. Nina stopped three feet from us and stood. In the end, this is Zion: the song about our wretchedness lifting up to save us, our voices leashing us together, the child walking toward us on unsteady legs. Two steps. Her first. She will fall down, but right now our song holds her up like hands, and this is Zion, right here, in the moment before she does.

GEORGE SAUNDERS

■

Bill Clinton, Public Citizen

FROM *GQ*

Who Moved That Tiny Crutch in the Corner?

IMAGINE A CLASSROOM IN a hospital in the Dominican Republic filled with little sweethearts in First Communion frocks and white dress shirts, doing what little kids tend to do when grouped, which is roughly the same thing eighty-year-olds tend to do when grouped, i.e., chatter while ignoring the instructions being issued with increasing urgency by those in charge: in this case, a handful of tiny nuns who look as if they've been specially recruited not to tower over the kids. A guest is coming, an important guest, will they please — children, will you please be calm, will you please quiet down?

The guest is in the doorway.

It's Bill Clinton.

The kids continue to be a blur of hair-bow adjustments and dance-like half spins and smirks from ornery boys whose orneriness has been subdued but not vanquished by the occasion, two of whom are at the moment engaged in feeling each other's biceps.

Clinton doesn't say a word as he enters. I'm expecting the affable, gregarious, at ease president of legend to exude a burst of tension-diffusing warmth. But no. He's tall, thin, white-haired, and solemn, like the ghost of Jimmy Stewart, if death had made Jimmy Stewart watchful and biblically dour. Clinton nods gravely to a nun, touches one kid on the head, stares at another a beat longer than you'd expect, as if he's met the kid before and is trying to remember where. The silence goes on an uncomfortably long time. It begins to feel, possibly, like sullenness, or confusion. Is he exhausted? Has he had it with all the traveling, the attention, the continual expectation that he will exude bursts of tension-diffusing warmth?

The silence has the effect of bringing the room to attention. The kids go quiet. Even we Press, behind our green rope, stop jostling and photographing and just *look*. Suddenly, whether it's accidental, intentional, or some sort of visceral Zen body-sense he's acquired over many years of doing this kind of thing, we're all more in the room than we were a few seconds earlier. We're having — he is causing us to have — a moment.

In this little Clinton-caused moment, something occurs to me: if not for —

At this point, a warning about an encroaching moment of possible corniness of a type you'll see again in this story: that which results when a virtuous action, reported objectively, is so virtuous it still sounds corny.

So:

In this little Clinton-caused moment, something occurs to me: If not for the William J. Clinton Foundation, every one of these little kids would be dead or dying soon, since every one of them is HIV positive, and until the foundation intervened, almost no one in the Dominican Republic had access to life-prolonging antiretroviral drugs (ARVs). And for most kids this young, the life expectancy for someone with HIV not on ARVs is five years.

"I see a vacant seat in the poor chimney corner, and a crutch without an owner, carefully preserved," the Ghost of Christmas Present says to Scrooge, re Tiny Tim. "If these shadows remain unaltered by the Future, the child will die."

The kids — these twenty altered shadows — present Clinton with a poster: CHILDREN LIVING WITH AIDS. A BIG CHALLENGE FOR THE DOMINICAN REPUBLIC.

The teachers count off: "*Uno, dos, tres . . .*"

"DENK YOU!" the kids shout.

The Once and Future Murderous Inequity

In 2002, approximately thirty-five million people in the world had HIV. Two million of these lived in the developed nations and had access to ARVs. The remaining thirty-three million people, in the developing nations, had essentially no access to ARVs, i.e., were living under a virtual death sentence.

As Person One will sometimes say to Person Two when Person Two's in a bad situation from which Person One is trying to disassociate himself: *Sucks for you.*

If I were to type one *sucks for you* for each person with AIDS in the developing world in 2002 with no access to ARVs, the page you are reading would be followed by about 54,000 pages filled with the words *sucks for you*, each *sucks for you* representing one man, woman, or child on the way to the grave before his or her time. Wherever you were in 2002 (remember U2 at the Super Bowl, Bush's "axis of evil" speech, the release of *Yankee Hotel Foxtrot*?), they were out there: thirty-three million people waiting to die, though a cure of sorts existed for what was killing them.

If you're like me, you vaguely knew about this and took it as proof of the essential powerlessness of man and the cruelty of a universe in which certain horrible problems were simply too complex to solve.

If you were Bill Clinton, you called Ira Magaziner, senior adviser for policy development in your White House and key architect of your universal health care plan, and together you went off and brokered a deal with some Indian and South African generic-drug companies, a deal now legendary for the judoistic, zero-sum beauty of its logic. Clinton/Magaziner made the case that, given the enormous potential market for ARVs (i.e., those thirty-three million people), the companies could profit even if they drastically reduced their prices, on the principle that, revenue-wise, selling a thousand widgets at $10 apiece is identical to selling ten at $1,000 each (that is, a low-margin, high-volume model).

The price of ARVs dropped from around $600/person/year in 2003 to around $140 today.

The Clinton Foundation estimates that some 750,000 people are now taking reduced-price ARVs purchased under the Clinton HIV-

AIDS Initiative–negotiated agreements. The *New York Times* puts this figure at 400,000.

Either way, it's huge: half a million people, sentenced to die, given a reprieve.

Who We Are/How We Roll

How are we Press (about a dozen of us, representing various magazines, newspapers, wire services, and a major television network) traveling as we go forth from Santo Domingo to four African countries to observe various Clinton Foundation projects related to HIV-AIDS, malaria, and poverty eradication?

On a private plane, jack, thanks for asking.

Is the plane nice?

Holy crap.

Our Plane — within just a few hours we Press go from *Beverly Hillbillies*–style gawking (*"A COUCH! Dang! A COUCH on a PLANE! Yee-haw, let's sit on her!"*), to very naturally calling it "Our Plane," to craving planes of our own — sleeps sixteen via a system of couches/recliners/foldout tables and has three big-screen TVs; wood paneling/leather trim everywhere you look; a live orchid in a perma-mounted end-table vase; an onboard iPod system; original paintings by Frank Johnston and Robert Genn, who, to the extent this phrase is not oxymoronic, are *famous Canadian painters;* three glistening mod bathrooms, each with a basket of Freshening-Up Products and an electric sliding James Bond–ish door; and a king-size bed in the master bedroom, where Clinton sleeps when he flies on this plane but which now belongs to whichever Press dude or chick can, on reboarding, haul ass in there fastest to claim it.

Our Plane has been loaned to the foundation for this trip by a Canadian friend of Clinton's — hence the famous Canadian painters — who recently pledged $100 million for a Clinton Foundation global poverty initiative, as well as half of all the profits from one of the most profitable segments of the donor's business for as long as he lives.

On Our Plane are we Press and our Clinton Foundation press liaisons. Clinton, his staff, the Secret Service, and some Donors, who paid as much as $750,000 to be on this trip, are on another plane, supposedly even nicer than Our Plane.

But Our Plane is good enough for us.

The owner of Our Plane is also donating some insane hospitality: A predinner seafood appetizer tray will miraculously appear; we get omelets in the morning, gourmet Indian food in the evening. The most gracious flight attendants imaginable remember our coffee orders from country to country and generously lead us to a hidden drawer of Tic Tacs when, about to disembark, we find ourselves foul-mouthed from sleep. All they ask, ever, is that, if so inclined, we might kindly sign a guest book previously signed by (for example) Rod Stewart, Dan Rather, Faith Hill/Tim McGraw, and various Central American presidents, all of whom have scrawled some variation of: "Hi, [Plane Owner's First Name]! Great flight!"

As we leave the Dominican Republic, dinner is served. We've already had dinner, back in Santo Domingo, but have it again, because it's free and being served to us on Our Plane. *Caddyshack* is shown on the primary big-screen. Crashing seems passé. One senses it isn't done. As night deepens, our flight attendant reappears, soundlessly unfolding the various couches/chairs/tables into beds into which we, the Press, exhausted from all our redundant eating, collapse.

The plan is: refuel in Brazil, fly across the Atlantic to South Africa.

Okay, excellent, carry on! We will be here in our foldout beds, which are more comfortable than our beds at home, waking now and then to crane up our heads and see if the coast of Africa is nigh.

We have, it seems, ascended into some kind of God Realm, where, because we're special, everything's nice, and whenever we get used to how nice it is, it suddenly gets better.

The War against Trouble Will Be Led by the Young

Word problem: Fifteen young men stand on a corner in South Africa, wearing those familiar dude-in-South-Africa wool hats, waving at your sleek hotel bus. Statistically speaking, how many are unemployed?

Four.

How many have HIV?

Three.

Of those three, how many have access to ARVs?

Just one.

Avert.org reports that 1,000 South Africans die of AIDS-related causes every day; that in South Africa, people attend more funerals than weddings; that half of all deaths in South Africa (and 71 percent for people between the ages of fifteen and forty-nine) are AIDS-related. In Johannesburg, the gap between rich and poor is the largest of any major city in the world, and the crime rate is among the highest in the world, ditto the rape rate.

But this morning, Johannesburg manifests as a town in a kids' book: all bright colors, basic shapes, and Simple Useful Activities. Some men paint a building. Others dig up a vacant lot by hand. Work, men, work! Dig, dig, dig! Build your city, eradicating the socioeconomic effects of the cruel system of apartheid!

We visit an elementary school participating in a program called City Year, in which recent high school grads mentor younger, at-risk kids. City Year is near and dear to Clinton's heart and was the inspiration and early model for his AmeriCorps project.

In a courtyard, some students conduct a lively mock/memorized Q and A to show how much they've learned about AIDS. As a chubby kid steps up, an anticipatory ripple shoots through the crowd, indicating: Possible Class Clown.

"You're right!" he shouts like a carnival busker, and the laughter begins. "Yeah, you're right! When the mother takes ARVs, the mother is also affecting the child's future! When the mother takes ARVs when the baby is still inside, the baby can be blind! Future's just not that bright!"

Their startling absence of cynicism/smart-assism makes these kids appear, relative to American kids, like members of another species. They're bright, exuberant, and supportive of one another. There are no slouchers, nobody mocking-out anybody else, no ironic eye rolling to indicate unwilling participation. This positivity seems to be in response to some very real Trouble. It's like we've walked in on some kind of odd survivors' group or a new religion whose central tenet is: We will bond together and, through positive action, beat back the Trouble and endeavor to be continually expanding our circle of the saved.

The Trouble is real. These kids, you sense, have seen it. Their mentors have seen it and are trying to stay clear of it themselves. The presence of Trouble seems to have had the effect of producing wisdom on a quicker schedule. A seventh grader named Faith describes her pre–City Year self as "a loner who had dreams" but "lacked hope of having some special someone to listen" to her. Her mentor, she says, "brought me out of the dark and into the light portion of my life."

In another part of the courtyard, I approach a reading circle and implement my sophisticated interviewing technique: (1) Thrust tape recorder into group; (2) say: "Anybody want to say anything?"

One little girl does want to say something but loses her nerve, drops chin to chest.

"She's the quiet one," says her City Year mentor. "She doesn't speak much."

I go around to the others but return to the quiet one before I leave.

She pulls the recorder close and whispers into it, as if her words are being beamed directly home.

"I like to say," she says, "to my mom, I'm by school and not worry about me. I'm by you, and same time I'm by City Year: Please don't worry about me. And say that . . . shout out to my mom and dad, and by schooled by City Year, but I want, I was going, I like to say that: Mom, I love you so much. [*pause*] And Father."

That's what she says. What I hear, in her tone and inflection, goes something like this: *Mom, I know you worry. And I know why you worry. But right now I'm in school, getting help, being good. I hope you don't mind that I like it here. I miss you. But this help I'm getting may save me from the Trouble, and in this way, I'm proving my love for you, and for Father.*

Then she's done.

I can tell because her eyes close in a long, amen-like blink.

Does That Guy Look Like Bill Clinton or What?

Every so often, wandering around the school's blacktop playground, I'll look over and there he is: Bill Clinton, the man who was president when my daughters were small; whose inaugural ("force the spring") choked me up in my cubicle; whose State of the Unions my wife and I watched year after year in our little house in Rochester; whom I let slip off my personal radar somewhat during that long second term because, having admired him, I felt let down and sick about the whole mess: his mistakes and the way some people jumped on those mistakes, exulting in what was a complex, personal issue, the infantile streak it revealed in us as a culture.

I don't, you know, *say* any of the above when he looks over — just give what I hope is a professional-looking nod-smile combo.

The reserved, somber quality I saw in the Dominican Republic is gone today. He's animated, looks happy to be here: moving energetically around the schoolyard, reaching down to hold hands with a schoolkid, evincing a comic look of shock — a kind of Arkansas gape — at something somebody's telling him.

His role on this trip seems (to paraphrase Ken Kesey) to be to function as both lightning rod and seismograph, to create excitement while absorbing information. He's asking questions, checking progress, being seen, offering praise. Toward the end of the City Year event, he makes a speech in the gym. He was very impressed by the level of HIV awareness he saw today, he says; there are adults in the United States who couldn't have answered some of those questions. There's only one reason for him ("an old white-haired guy who's got more yesterdays than tomorrows") to be up here and that's to get publicity for this program, so people will give money, so more good things can be accomplished.

A little ripple of delight passes through the crowd of kids at the frankness of this reference to his own mortality.

Set Those Aromatic Atomizers to "Dark Continent"

Over the next six days, we travel from South Africa to Malawi, from Malawi to Zambia, from Zambia to Tanzania.

It's strange travel, somehow reminiscent of the holodeck on *Star Trek:* we emerge from Our Plane into various African vignettes, which vary in hut style and soil color and native costume and extent of urban-ness, but not in any other way discernible to us, because we don't stay long enough to discern it.

There is beauty, of course, my God (in a shantytown of lopsided shipping containers, a roaring garbage-can fire silhouettes two drunks bent at the waist in a scene that might be titled *Two Variations on Full-Body Wincing;* at a stand where floor-polishing powder is sold, bright red, orange, and yellow dust coats the hands of the women selling the dust, who look like rainbow-making fairies in a kids' book, except their hands are banged up, and they look exhausted and cowed; during an event in Johannesburg, as Clinton helps Nelson Mandela — frail, silent, and smiling — to his seat, the way a grateful son might), but the beauty doesn't cohere into anything, or it coheres into a feeble attempt to generalize from too few data points. Zambians, I conclude, are friendlier than Tanzanians, based on a day in each country and my patented How Quick Do They Smile Back test. Malawians, I conclude, tend to live in the country, and are thus more simple and rural, compared with South Africans, all of whom, in my experience, live in cities, namely Johannesburg, the only place in South Africa we go.

When it's time to leave, there's no customs, no security. We just get on Our Plane and go. The world feels different when you leave it so effortlessly: more like a big mysterious borderless ball with forests and rivers on it, and less like a series of discrete checkpoints you have to pass through in order to arrive at other, similar checkpoints. Our Plane, in other words, liberates us. We can talk on our cell phones, even during landing. We may use portable electronic devices whenever we like. We are continually free to move about the cabin. We can even, if we like, ass-surf on a piece of cardboard as Our Plane inclines on takeoff, proceeding joyfully down the carpeted downhill run until we whack, at speed, into the coffee table.

On the ground, we experience the secret joys of the motorcade. All traffic is stopped, and we zip along unopposed, waving to the people we've inconvenienced. We're not Clinton, but we're in his motorcade, which confers on us a kind of mini celebrity, and we try to be generous to the little people.

Wave, wave, check out that dude with the bike basket full of NGO rice.

Look at that yellow-flowering tree, in that yard where a father and his kids are enacting a kind of *African Gothic.*

A regal head-scarved woman, chatting with her shorter but equally regal friend, makes a little hand gesture at us, indicating: *Speed it along, get out of my life.*

Our mode of travel puts me in mind of those nineteenth-century bourgeoisie who'd set up camp on a hill overlooking a battlefield and watch the killing go down while eating well under parasols. We've brought our stuff with us — our BlackBerrys, laptops, boom microphones; we maintain contact with New York (someone reads aloud an e-vite to a Manhattan party; someone synopsizes footage for her distant producer; someone checks the Drudge Report to see how Clinton is perceived to have done on *Good Morning America*); we cellphone home at will (from airport tarmacs; from a high-end "crafts bazaar" filled with $10,000 twenty-foot-tall, all-carved-from-one-piece-of-wood sculptures depicting hundreds of naked primal humans crawling over one another to reach, I guess, God; from our van, when we've lost the motorcade and are stalled in traffic, as women in the roadside ditch arrange their wares in the dusk, getting ready for the night market).

Is Africa really a dark continent on the edge of chaos, full of menacing shadows but also ethereal beauty, where glowering child soldiers roam majestic landscapes filled with grazing gazelles and ghostly starving diseased metaphors lean weakly on walking sticks while pointing bony fingers of accusation at the Indifferent West?

I have no idea.

Because I don't feel I've ever really been to Africa, though I have passed through something *resembling* Africa, ensconced in a mobile nation called Junket.

The irony of this is not lost on us Press: we're traveling like royalty through some of the poorest places on earth, where people are truly suffering, to write about some people nobly working to alleviate that suffering, although we aren't in a position to see much of that suffering ourselves.

And we're traveling with some of the wealthiest people on earth,

these millionaire and even billionaire Donors. At first it's a little off-
putting: all those Gucci shoes; all their tourist joy at being photographed in the belly of the beast; the way they have, at first, of avoiding us Press. They seem like a kind of rare animal species that runs
on very expensive food, and you want — part of you does, the re-
flexively middle-class part — to discount them. But over the week I
change my mind. Because while it's true that the rich are different
from you and me (less shabby and desperate and ad hoc, more at
home in the God Realm), it's also true that the rich are different *from
one another*. And these rich — our rich — are actually doing something with their wealth: underwriting the fight against AIDS while
looking for new ways to benevolently spend more of their money.

In a fight as desperate as this one, against an enemy as voracious
as the AIDS pandemic, we should be glad when the big dogs show
up, no matter how extravagant their collars.

Because even with everything the Clinton Foundation and countless other NGOs are doing, even with President Bush's astonishing
PEPFAR program (a five-year, $15 billion assault on AIDS — the larg-
est commitment by any country, ever), there are still some twenty-
three million people in the developing world with no access to ARVs
(seven million of whom need them urgently): Instead of 54,000
pages of *sucks for yous*, we're down to 38,000.

My Friend in Real Estate

What I see of African suffering might best be called *refracted suffering*, in the person, for example, of an older gentleman I meet outside
the Taj Hotel in Lusaka, Zambia, near a sap-stained, feudal-looking
wall keeping street from hotel.

He's maybe sixty-five, wearing a sport coat over a white polo shirt;
well-spoken, round-bellied, genteel, borderline jolly even, missing a
couple teeth in front. He's on his way into the Taj to meet some potential Brazilian investors. He's a real estate agent, representing certain high-end properties that foreigners may be particularly —

From his back pocket he produces a sad little two-page photo-
copied list. I look it over. Descriptions, bordering on gibberish, of expensive properties: "KABULONGA: 4 BD HSE 2 MSC, 3 BD GUEST

HSE MASTER BD 1.5 MSC. CHALIMBANA: 810 Hᴀ DEV. FARM BOREHOLE FARM HOUSE. MAIN ROAD SHED WITH OFFICE BLOCK."

I tell him I'm not living in Zambia and so, uh, as far as being interested in —

Perhaps, he suggests, once back in America, I will *become* interested, or may know someone who might be interested, in these excellent properties.

He used to work for the Ministry of Health, he says, but not anymore. This is his work now: the selling of the houses on the copy.

Suddenly he looks a little despondent, and the conversation begins to sprout odd corridors. He has nothing at home, he says. No food. No money. That is why, at the present time, he cannot afford — he has just come from the InterContinental, hoping to sell some of his homes over there, from the copy — he has given me the copy? Yes. That is why he is selling in this manner, person-to-person, because he cannot, at this time, afford to advertise on the Internet. A friend is helping him out, by supplying him with this list of houses, on the copy. Also, his situation has made it necessary for him to come on foot from the InterContinental to the Taj — no short distance — because he cannot, at this time, afford the additional expense of a taxi.

Also, he is diabetic. He finds himself needing to do business even now, during the lunch hour, when he should be going for his injection. But he must work during lunch, because they have, sir, at this time, as he may have said, nothing. Nothing in the home.

He, yes, has children. Eight. Then he corrects himself: five. He has five. Three have died.

He dabs at his forehead with a handkerchief.

I'm sorry, I say. Were they . . . did they die of . . . ?

Various diseases, he says.

Not AIDS, I say.

Not AIDS, he says. Various diseases.

(A foundation staffer later tells me that denial is rampant in Zambia. People will say a relative or friend or child died of TB or pneumonia — but not of AIDS. Never of AIDS. Yet people are dying of AIDS in droves. You see no old people here, she says.)

He looks dolefully over the wall at the Taj. This, he says, is a challenging way of doing business. Now he must go inside and try to locate the Brazilian investors he read about in the newspaper.

He doesn't have an appointment?

No. He is hoping to "meet with them," i.e., meet with them by chance, i.e., basically collar them in the lobby.

Oh, poor man, I think. You'll never get in there with the increased Clinton-related security, and second of all, Jesus, imagine the long-shot quality of (1) locating the Brazilians and (2) not scaring them off, while (3) avoiding being ejected by hotel security so you can (4) close the deal, selling a half-million-dollar house, sans even photo of the house, to some total strangers who aren't even looking for a house, or if they were, would know a reputable way to find one.

The impossibility of his situation makes me a little giddy. Christ, I'm glad I'm not him.

Well, he says, I am in trouble.

He says it the way I would say it, or you would, if after working all our lives, we suddenly found ourselves destitute and nearly seventy: one man to another, awed by the sudden crushing weight of the bare cupboard. He says it as if he's never said it aloud before and is only saying it now because I'm a foreigner who will soon be gone forever.

Goodbye, he says, goodbye, sir. And please try to help me on this copy.

Based on the Results You Obtain, I Was Rather Expecting You to Be Yoda

Here's a sentence I never thought I'd type:

I was scheduled to head for Neno, Malawi, on a helicopter belonging to the Malawi Army, but unfortunately was delayed and sat three hours on the runway in Lilongwe with master photographer Brigitte Lacombe while waiting for Bill Clinton to arrive from Johannesburg, so we could proceed to Neno and be greeted by five hundred women, many of whom wore bright blue dresses embossed with a photograph of their president, singing, essentially: *Welcome to our village! Welcome, sincerely, to our village!*

Then it gets hot on the runway and I move into the executive lounge, which is done up like a Chicago rec room circa 1971: purple rugs, overstuffed red chairs, framed photo of the president of Malawi where the velvet nude of a woman-with-Afro should be. I sit with Diana Noble, director of the Clinton HIV-AIDS Initiative. Diana's elegant, articulate, and funny — a perfect example of the kind of talent the foundation attracts — and modest, so modest, in fact, that even now I don't know much about her other than that she gave up a high-powered career in venture capital (Rupert Murdoch was on her board; she was the youngest partner in what was then the most successful private-equity fund in Europe) and took a huge pay cut to join the foundation, in order to improve what she referred to as her "rocking-chair scenario," i.e., she wanted to be able, when old, to look back and feel she had done something worthwhile with her life.

As we wait, Diana shows me, on her laptop, some photos of AIDS patients the foundation has worked with in Rwanda.

Here's a near dead baby — a kind of corpse-doll — who weighs just three pounds, staring terrified at the camera as if afraid the camera is going to finish her off. If a U.S. newborn is three pounds, it's a crisis; this three-pound baby is *six months old*. It's a shocking photo: the baby looks simultaneously like a bald baby, a corpse, and a really old woman.

I find myself looking away, hoping for the After shot.

And here it comes, more shocking than the Before: the same kid, twelve weeks after the start of ARV therapy, now beautiful, frizzy-haired, and chubby, grinning like she knows she's just cheated death or has caught sight of a dog or a sunbeam or something else lovely enough to startle out such a smile.

"Wow," I say.

"Right," says Diana.

In Slow Motion Now, Let's See How That Was Done

The Clinton Foundation is eight hundred people, working in thirty-five countries around the world, on issues ranging from HIV to poverty eradication to global warming. It is best understood as a kind of *Mission: Impossible*–style team that drops into a country at the invitation of its government and addresses, per that government's desires, a specific problem, providing a kind of rocket booster of improved efficiency. It is made up mostly of business-consultant types — you hear a lot of talk about "baselining" and "system building" and "rubrics" — and the work they do is thus technical and iterative and efficiency-striving. If something works, they're glad; if not, they change it. While most NGOs identify areas of low-hanging fruit and ensure that the fruit gets plucked (treating AIDS patients in the cities, for example, where doctors and nurses are more inclined to work and where transportation of patients is easier), what the foundation does is ask the government what its *hardest* problems are — where is there a need that is not being addressed by existing donors (the treatment of rural and/or pediatric patients, say)? The foundation has Draconian hiring standards, and this exclusivity seems to have produced a kind of high-functioning all-star team that would, I suspect, be as effective at selling records or managing the redesign of a wastewater plant as they are at fighting global poverty and disease.

For example — let's look at what went into saving that baby above.

Before the foundation got involved, nearly every country in the world used pediatric ARV formulations that typically consisted of a third of a glass of terrible-tasting syrup, twice a day. (Think about that: your kid's going to die soon unless you can get her to drink a couple cups of sludge per day.) These medicines were not only a nightmare for kids to take but a pain for parents to obtain. Say you're the mother of our near dead baby: Once a month, you have to pick up the medications at the nearest clinic, which, if you're rural, could mean a five-hour walk each way. On the way back, you're lugging dozens of heavy, liquid-containing glass bottles. Once home you have to combine medicines from three or four of the bottles, in a weight-specific ratio that is difficult to measure precisely and will need to be continually adjusted as your child grows.

Fixed-dose combination pills exist but are too expensive for your government to afford (about triple the price of adult ARV drugs). Also, before the fixed-dose pill can legally be used in your country, a drug-specific registration has to be obtained by the manufacturers, via a rigorous, time-consuming, heavy-on-the-paperwork process.

Enter the Clinton Foundation. The foundation started out by approaching two generic manufacturers in India (Cipla and Ranbaxy) and asking these companies if they would consider increasing production and reducing prices. (Though the economic wisdom of this wasn't clear at the time, the companies felt it was the right thing to do, especially since children were involved.) At the same time, the foundation began approaching governments, asking that they switch their patient regimens from syrups to the fixed-dose pills, and then began working with these governments to speed up the odious registration process.

Did it work?

It did.

The price of pediatric fixed-dose combination pills dropped radically — from $600/person/year to the current level of around $60 — and are now the standard treatment for children in most of the countries in which the foundation works. Not only that, because of the increased volumes being sold (that low-margin, high-volume model again), Cipla and Ranbaxy are making a nice profit.

It does not suck for them.

It also does not suck for the approximately 100,000 kids in thirty-five countries (7,500 in Rwanda and Malawi) who, thanks to the foundation, went on ARVs for the first time this year, half of whom are already receiving the fixed-dose combination pills.

Clinton is fond of quoting Mario Cuomo's famous line, "We campaign in poetry, but we govern in prose." This, in essence, is what the foundation does: it governs in precise, efficient prose.

Long, Dull, Hot, Yet Incredibly Beneficial

As we approach Neno, Malawi, people down below cut loose from whatever it is they're doing and start hauling ass toward town. It's as if our chopper *knocks* them loose — from their fields, the walls they're building, their skinny goats. And then we keep flying at least another five minutes — which means they're coming from miles away to greet us.

We touch down, and the chopper creates a kind of horizontal dust flood, bending small trees nearly double, coating the leaves thick brown. Everything goes dark, and you expect to see Margaret Hamilton riding past on a bike.

Neno is nearly four hours' drive from the nearest city. It doesn't have a school or hospital. The water supply is problematic. The roads turn to mud when it rains. Farming is subsistence at best. If there were a village-motto-bearing sign at the edge of town, it might read: THE EARTH IS NOT NECESSARILY MADE FOR PEOPLE TO LIVE ON AND IS ALWAYS TRYING TO KILL US OFF.

Or anyway, that's how it used to be.

In Neno, the foundation is teaming with Paul Farmer (of Partners in Health and *Mountains Beyond Mountains* fame) and Scottish billionaire Tom Hunter in a more holistic approach to poverty reduction, in which health, clean water, agricultural assistance, fair trade, drought response, and carbon neutrality are all addressed at once, comprehensively. It's an incredibly ambitious project: building a sustainable village from the ground up. Hunter has pledged $100 million over the next ten years for this and similar work in Rwanda. This effort is intended to be pilot scale; the hope is that other NGOs will eventually adopt the approach.

Over the next four hours we visit: the hospital in progress, a school in progress, in-progress housing for the future staff of the in-progress hospital, the brick-making area where all the bricks for the various in-progress projects are being made by hand. The wild singing continues for hours from the roadside, singing that seems improvised, if six- or seven-part harmonies can be improvised for hours on end, periodically punctuated with mouth clicks and ululations. A wild crowd surges through the village with Clinton: local chiefs in box-shaped hats; a smattering of stylish, hot white women; a mysterious beautiful African lady wearing a fur stole in the heat, like some kind of Malawian Zelda Fitzgerald.

At one point, I'm standing in the shade watching Clinton stand in the headache-inducingly bright sun dressed all in black, his pale skin going red as he patiently listens to presentation after presentation by various local dignitaries, who introduce other local dignitaries, who introduce greater or lesser local dignitaries, who, it sometimes seems, introduce their cousins, just for the hell of it.

And I find myself wondering why he does it — what counterweights the heat, the hours of protocol-fulfilling chats and smiling for photos, the plodding from dusty building site to dusty building site?

I've heard the usual explanations (he's attention-hungry; he's eradicating memories of the impeachment; he's winning the presidency for his wife), but watching him endure this highly technical, minutia-engorged, science-fair-like day, these explanations seem grossly insufficient. Abstractions can't power a person through a day as grueling as this.

There is, of course, an element of ego in what he's doing. (What gets you up in the morning, or me?) There is an element of what we might call lineage pleasure in it, the pleasure he gets from seeing himself as part of a long line of workers-against-injustice (Gandhi, King, Mandela, etc). There is an element of simple self-expression, a sort of joy-in-closing-the-deal: a person with Clinton's abilities and proclivities coming up against the kind of problems that exist in Africa is like a strongman coming around a corner to find a heavy object, or a Lab racing into a vast field full of ducks — a chance to exercise one's God-given inclinations. There is, of course, also an element of empathy: he sees he can help, and wants to help, and takes pleasure in having helped.

A Clinton staffer tells me his theory. Think about Frank Sinatra, he says: born to sing. Think about Willie Mays: born to play ball. These guys got their power from living lives perfectly suited to their natures. Same with Clinton: his life is perfectly suited to his nature.

After one farmer talks him through a wall-size poster of project-related photos, Clinton has a question: if you succeed in growing more, won't you need storage so you can sell the extra crops you've grown?

The guy answers, nearly jumping out of his shoes with enthusiasm: Yes! That is exactly what we want, if we can be assisted!

Clinton nods, indicating: You will. You will be assisted.

Later, in Our Plane, Clinton will talk about this farmer:

"He was a smart guy. He was articulate, he had something to say, he was very specific about what he wanted us to do, he was well spoken, he was self-confident. So how come they're poor and I'm rich? If intelligence, ability, and effort are evenly distributed, as well as aspirations — why is the inequality so broad?

"Forget about Malawi for a minute; just think about your life.

Think about where you were when you were ten years old. And how did you get from being ten years old to sitting on this plane? Now, you may have had a lot of adventures, you may have been very brave, there may have even been some accidental opportunities, but one thing I'm sure of is that all of us, no matter how tough our lives were, no matter what misfortune befell us, at a critical point in our life, believed with all our hearts that there was a physical connection between the effort we exerted and the result we achieved. Think about it: If you go back there and use the restroom and you turn the sink on, you believe with all your heart that water will come out of the tap and that it is safe, and you take it for granted. There are all kinds of connections, all day long, for us, between the effort we exert and the results we achieve. What we're trying to do is get investment and opportunity and empowerment through education, and then structure society to make them believe that there is a connection between their dreams and aspirations and their efforts, and the consequences they achieve."

Still Going . . .

One of the things you always hear about Clinton is that he has amazing energy. This is true. Let me try to convey a sense of this, in the form of a Clinton to-do list for the remainder of our Neno day, July 20, 2007:

Approx. 7 P.M.: Take helicopter back to Lilongwe. Whole way back, engage in lively conversation with two Malawian ministers. Press — dirty, hot, ready for some downtime, tired of watching people work tirelessly on behalf of poor — dozes in back.

Approx. 8 P.M.: Arrive in Lilongwe. Board Press Plane. Although Press expects you to nab bed and sleep, proceed instead to pisser, emerge immediately, then give two-hour talk on subjects ranging from microfinance ("There's no question in my mind that now, the aggregate impact of the Grameen bank, in Bangladesh, is discernible on the national economic front") to Millennium Development grants; from recent progress in Malawian banking to the academic success of Chinese American kids; from Bangladeshi politics ("It's like a great soap opera, because Bangladeshis will vote dynastically") to Pierre Omidyar's empowerment network, whatever that is. During talk, clearly exhausted, run hot coffee cup back and forth over forehead, as if implementing some kind of Arkansas exhaustion-headache home remedy.

Approx. 10 P.M.: Arrive in Lusaka, Zambia. Make joke about own black clothing, i.e., say you feel like an extra in *West Side Story*. Burst into very passable version of "Maria." Get off plane. Greet president of Zambia. Staffer jokes: Ah Christ, another freaking red carpet?

Approx. 10:30 P.M.: Proceed to hotel.

Approx. 11 P.M.: While Press is showering/changing clothes/drifting down for a late dinner, attend, unbeknownst to Press, big-ass dinner-dance, with Donors, in hotel restaurant.

Approx. midnight: Surprise Press, who are standing by pool watching weird batlike creature fly in and out of pool, by robustly exiting big-ass Donor dinner-dance and striding into elevator. Press shocked you are still up, since you are not only older than they are and have had heart surgery and all of that, but got almost no sleep the first night in Africa, because you got up early to do *Good Morning America*, and have had little or no sleep since then, as far as they can tell.

While in elevator, send, via your right-hand man, who is in elevator with you, text message to another staffer, who has been hanging out with Press by the pool, waiting for reappearance of weird bat-bird.

Message reads: "Come play cards."

Stay up playing cards with this and other staffers until 3 A.M.

Speak, Memory

Next day we attend a soccer tournament in Lusaka cosponsored by the foundation. AIDS denial is a huge problem in Zambia, and the purpose of the tournament is to encourage openness by fielding teams made up of both HIV-positive and HIV-negative players, to send the message that people with HIV are not pariahs. The kids play fiercely, some wearing shoes, some barefoot, at least one in just his socks. Clinton comes over, watches the kids play fiercely. When he leaves, they continue to play fiercely, until it's time for the speeches and the awarding of trophies, and they walk off the field, little chests heaving.

There's something electric in the air — a sense of shared fear and of shared resolve to lean together en masse against that fear — that I've never felt before: something like what the Texans might have felt at the Alamo, had there been a chance they could have pulled it out by really *focusing*.

A young woman named Memory comes to the podium. She's nineteen. When she was ten, she was raped by an HIV-positive cab driver, presumably acting on the belief that a man can be cured of AIDS by having sex with a virgin. Also, her parents are dead, and she is now raising her three young brothers while trying to get caught up in school — she's now in the tenth grade. She's here to tell the other young people: life does not end with diagnosis. Therefore, young people should not be afraid to be tested; it is not a death sentence.

"Look at me now!" she says. "Here I am. Why should I die when others are living? There are very few of you who are standing up, speaking out. What about us? Where are we? Us youth? Through music, through dancing, we can really fight this disease! This virus is just in my body. It does not *rule* my body. I have to *control* my body. I have lived for eight years with this disease. I don't get sick. I'm *all right!*"

If it takes drugs to control her body, she says, she's going to take them. The disease does not rule her, will not be *allowed* to rule her.

"It is not who I am!" she says, and what breaks your heart is that she does not sound entirely sure — you hear it more as a noble statement of intent than as a fact.

That day, recalled these several months later, presents itself as a kind of joyful anti-AIDS bacchanal: a soccer coach sprinting across a lawn, leading the crowd in cheers; some Donor moms lazing in the grass with the soccer kids; Ira Magaziner beaming from a green lawn chair at the back of the crowd as Clinton speaks; Arpad Busson, hedge-fund millionaire, ex of Elle Macpherson, founder of ARK, a British charity dedicated to, among other things, improving inner-city schools, striding across the field in high boots, like a lover in a Jane Austen movie.

Have we ever, in our lifetimes, in our country, had to hold a gathering like this, a desperately inflected mini Woodstock, the subtext of which is: Brothers, Sisters, We Must Work Like Hell or This Pandemic Will Kill Us All?

No, because we are lucky and were born in the right country.

Off the Record

That night in Lusaka we attend the first of two "off-the-record" Press dinners in a restaurant that reminds me of a highbrow Olive Garden, if the highbrow Olive Garden was in a mini-mall in Zambia and was guarded by a series of sentrylike wood-burning outdoor space heaters. We Press are seated at a long table in a secluded part of the restaurant.

What happens at these dinners is: Clinton comes in, sits down. There's a moment of awkward silence. Then someone asks a question ("Have a good day, Mr. President?") and he starts to talk. He talks the way an ice trawler breaks through ice, the way a mountain stream runs downhill. It happens because it must. You think of some immense and previously inert thing starting to roll forward.

One question and you're off to the races.

Now, as someone trying hard to work on my listening skills, and my being-sensitive-to-others skills, and my trying-not-to-dominate-things-with-my-constant-urge-to-pontificate-in-my-too-fast-voice skills, I have to admit that, at first, this gave me pause. During these talks, he's not the Bill Clinton you hear about — probing people for their stories, asking where they're from, listening intently as they talk about their dreams, their hometowns, their long, epiphany-filled journeys through life. He's *talking*. He's talking, I think, because he (1) loves to talk, (2) does his thinking via talking, and (3) is easily the most interesting person at the table, and knows this, and knows you know it, and so is, in a sense, generously trying to fulfill his obligations as the most interesting person at the table.

Because when Bill Clinton's at your table, you don't really want anyone else talking, and that includes you. When you do talk, you feel stupid. I mean, you *are* stupid. You are suddenly short of facts and full of intuition. You lack the conversational zing that comes with having once been leader of the free world. Have your previous dinner partners included Gorbachev, Mandela, Bono, Liz Hurley, Stephen Jay Gould? Were you instrumental in bringing peace to Ireland? Were your personal foibles broadcast at a cringe-inducing level of detail into every home in America? Did you sign into law the Family and Medical Leave Act, already used by some three million Americans to be with a dying parent or at home after the birth of a child? Do people routinely accuse you and your wife of Macbethian levels of intrigue and ambition, levels that no actual living person is diabolical or efficient enough to attain? Have you ever made a speech to 50,000 people? Do people look at you and think: *should have done more in Rwanda?* Have you started a foundation that has saved, by even the most conservative estimates, hundreds of thousands of lives and set the stage, through a series of price cuts and the stabilization of markets, for millions more to be saved?

Well, right, me neither.

I was going to but then suddenly I was old and had failed to consolidate sufficient power.

So why not sit quietly, and Clinton will tell us (leaning over, performing constant eye-lock) what he thought of Gabriel García Márquez when he met him (lovely, lovely man, a kind of South American leprechaun), or what he said to Newt Gingrich last time he saw him, re a nasty shot Gingrich had taken at Hillary (it made him happy, because he knows Newt wouldn't take a shot at anyone but the front-runner).

Sometimes you sense a deep well of anger. Sometimes you sense a deep well of love. Sometimes as he recounts, with increasing heat, the slights and perceived cheap shots and misunderstandings-of-his-record he's endured, you think: this stuff *still* hurts him. And then you think: hell, why wouldn't it?

His supersized fondness for life, humans, activity, accomplishment, makes you aware of your own negative mind. His seemingly boundless energy makes you aware of how prematurely you habitually pronounce yourself tired. A hopeful, almost naive quality he has ("On this continent, under the most adverse circumstances, you find the highest percentage of the people that go through every day with a song in their heart") feels somehow generational: vestigial evidence of the Summer of Love. His drive, his fame, the public nature of everything he does, makes you giddily grateful for the humble scale of your own life.

When someone asks a question on a touchy subject — a question that elicits a collective intake of breath that would have put out the candles on the table had there been candles on the table — Clinton gives a brisk bring-it-on sort of nod and says, "All right, come on, let's talk about that."

And then he does.

When asked about his wife, he talks about her in a way that is fond, respectful, even reverent. His way of speaking about her reminded me of — well, it reminded me of the way I speak about my wife, the way any man married a long time to a woman who is beloved to him speaks about her: as if they have been on a long trip together, a sometimes complicated trip, for which he's grateful.

To observe Clinton up close is to get a mini seminar in the deficiencies of the media in conveying the real scale of our public figures. Comparing the man in person with the media-accreted version you have in your head, you feel the way you might if, having watched Michael Jordan on TV all those years, and having thus reduced him to *great quickness + fall-away jumper + excellent clutch-shooter*, you suddenly found yourself defending him one-on-one.

My guess is that, if you rated a million people on the basis of aptitude and verbal skills and powers of persuasion and retention and simple physical energy, Clinton would come out near the top in all categories.

And now, in this later stage of his public life, he's decided to put those abilities to use in Africa.

The reasonable response to this decision, it seems to me, given the intractability and cruelty of Africa's problems, regardless of how you might feel about Bill Clinton, is gratitude: if our boat were leaking and an additional bailer appeared, we'd be glad, and gladder still if his powers of bailing were prodigious.

No One Should Die of This (and Yet They Do)

Malaria kills 100,000 people a year in Tanzania, most of them children. A person dies of malaria in Tanzania nearly every five minutes. Walk into any hospital in the countryside, a Clinton staffer tells me, and you'll find it overflowing with comatose kids, IVs running into arms or scalps in a last-ditch effort to kill the malaria parasites that are killing them.

The real tragedy is: a cure exists. It consists of six pills taken over three days and results in complete recovery.

In a little village a couple of hours from Dar es Salaam, we Press crowd into a tiny, closet-size pharmacy with mirrored walls and watch multiple versions of ourselves watch multiple versions of Clinton listening to the pharmacy owner explain that the problem in Tanzania is that the most commonly available antimalarial drug, the one people have been taking for years (SP, a.k.a. Fansidar), no longer cures the disease in most cases, because malaria parasites have developed an immunity to it. There is a more effective drug available (artemisinin combination therapy, or ACT), but at current prices — about a week's earnings for most Tanzanians — it's too expensive for most families. Also, ACT has typically only been available in high-end pharmacies or health facilities; this fact, together with the relatively high price, means that while wealthier urban patients can get ACT, the rural poor can't.

Clinton listens patiently. He knows all of the above and, in fact, is about to go outside and make a speech to the 7,000 people gathered there (mobbing the pharmacy, extending back across the dirt road and a huge field, clambering up several sets of wobbly bleachers, standing on the peaked roofs of huts and, in at least one case, balanced on the seat of a kickstandless bike), the gist of which is: The foundation, working with the Tanzanian government and the Tanzanian affiliate of an American NGO called Population Services International, is launching a program to make ACT available in rural pharmacies like this one, at a subsidized price very close to that charged for the ineffective drug. The price has been driven down from around $8 to $10 to around *twenty to ninety cents.* The lower-cost ACT will initially be distributed in about 150 of these small shops, benefiting, it is estimated, approximately 450,000 people. The foundation's expectation is that a national scale-up by the Tanzanian government will follow, to eventually include all of the more than 5,000 small pharmacies in the country.

The crowd listens quietly during Clinton's speech. It's stat-heavy at first, a little wonky; the syntax is complex, and, in places, I'm not sure they can really understand him. But then it gets simpler, and a sort of wave of *getting it* passes over the sea of faces. No one should ever have to die of this disease again, is what he's telling them.

One on One

Next day, in the presidential suite of our hotel in Dar es Salaam — which I'd describe as Soviet-era austere with a glam, Ian Schrager-ish overlay — I sit down with Clinton for a one-on-one interview.

He's reading as I come in, glasses low on his nose, drinking coffee. He doesn't say hello or look up — just keeps reading. He is, it strikes me, extremely *presidential* — in his bearing, his discipline, the way he bends a moment to his will. Presidential and a little scary, especially if your first question is lame and tautological, essentially: Sir, so why do you think people tend to, you know, do good things and all?

But pretty soon he's rolling, speaking in thousand-word bursts — about how he first realized he had an extra dollop of empathy; about whether he's thought any about Buddhism ("A *lot*. I've thought about it a *lot*"); about the effect of his early reading life on his view of the world ("I learned to think about Shakespeare in terms of the people I knew; I learned to see [in them] the qualities of tragedy and greatness that he wrote about"); about dealing with criticism ("You have to realize, if you're in public life especially, that not everyone who criticizes you will be wrong. I mean, you can't live under that much pressure and make that many decisions for that long without making mistakes. Certainly public mistakes, and often private ones, too — you just can't do it, you can't. Nobody can live at that sustained level of activity, under that much pressure, and never make a mistake. In the words that Hillary used to give me, it's important to learn to take criticism seriously but not *personally*, because if you start taking it personally then you're *incapable* of taking it seriously, and you can't sort through what's accurate and not. That requires an enormous amount of discipline"); about the power of forgiveness ("Absolutely essential for a healthy life. It's nice for the people you forgive, but it's life's blood for you"); about his admiration for a speech Bill Gates gave at Harvard ("He says that if you believe all lives have equal value, you must recognize that the marketplace in the world doesn't treat them that way, and they don't have enough political clout for the political system to treat them that way, and therefore someone needs to step into the breach"); and about the Christian basis for the work he's doing in Africa:

"There are an enormous number of admonitions in the Christian New Testament where Jesus says we should pay attention to the plight of the poor, the ill, the imprisoned, those with physical handicaps; that we should not judge, but extend a helping hand to, people who have done things that society considers wrong, whether they're abusive tax collectors or prostitutes. That, you know, we should not look upon any person as less human than we are.

"The Book of James says faith without works is dead," he says. "'Show me your works and I will know your faith,' you know? While there is no explicit reference to, let's say, homosexuality in the New Testament, no explicit reference to abortion, there are hundreds and hundreds of references to the imperative of acting to help people who are in genuine need, who are less fortunate than you, whom you can help, and you're supposed to do it without regard to your own economic or social standing. The only test is whether you can make a difference in someone else's life without disadvantaging or really hurting someone in your circle of primary responsibility, you know, your family."

And then he closes this thought with something that might, in fact, be his mantra:

"It's fascinating," he says.

Clinton Spares My Ass and That of a Small Teen in the Cradle of Life, or Near It

That afternoon, the last of the trip, we go on safari at the Ngorongoro Crater.

As we drive down, it's like Eden, or an outlet store called All Beautiful Things Made by God: sunflowers, yellow-barked acacia trees (once thought to cure yellow fever), an immense cloud-covered valley, baboons standing by the roadside like jumpy naked tollbooth attendants.

After an hour or so we stop to stretch our legs and use the bathroom. I find myself standing near Clinton. Some monkeys appear in a nearby bush. He recently read, he says, an interesting fact about bonobo apes: they are very social and celebrate a kill by having group sex.

The moment seems rich with chummy comic potential; I respond by blurting out something that, even as I say it, I realize makes absolutely no sense.

"Heh, heh," I say. "Sounds like college."

Ouch, ouch, ouch, I think in my head. You did *not* just say that, to Bill Clinton, on the last day of the trip. In what way, moron, does killing + group sex = COLLEGE?

Clinton just lifts an eyebrow.

"I guess I must have missed that part," he says, and if there were ever a moment in my writing career when I would temporarily lift the embargo on the phrase *his eyes twinkling*, now would be it.

Then, a family approaches: Mom, Dad, two daughters, and a son, a nice-looking kid, beaming, but with legs disproportionately short relative to the rest of his body, about half the normal length. He looks about eighteen but is the height of a little kid.

The family poses with Clinton, who indulges them. They decide to be photographed individually with Clinton, one at a time. He indulges them. When it's the son's turn, Dad takes the picture — but it's odd. The kid comes up to Clinton's waist. There's a kind of circus feel to it — Tall Guy/Short Guy. Dad winces as he looks at it on the camera screen. But it's, you know, fine, what are you going to —

Clinton drops to one knee, his head right there beside the kid's head — they are now the same height — and smiles a big, goofy, clownish smile, one long arm draped around the kid's shoulders.

Dad gets the shot.

Where're you from? Clinton asks.

Holland, the father says.

What part? Clinton asks.

The mother gives the name of their town.

The father says, being funny: And you are, I think, from the U.S.?

This gets a laugh. Suddenly Dad's a hero. He — who, I get the feeling, has been rendered a little tender and timid and brittle by his son's disability — has scored a laugh, right there in front of his family and the famous American President, who smiles, as if pleased for

Dad, and doesn't rebut but lets the joke and the laughter and the conferred glory resonate.

Of all the things I saw Clinton do on this trip, and all the things I heard him say, this dropping to his knees now looms largest. Why? I suppose because it was so *minor*. And private. And essentially unobserved. He could easily have skipped it. I might have. But something in Clinton's psychological makeup wouldn't *let* him skip it. He reacted to the inherent discomfort of the moment as naturally as a person might stoop to pick up something important he'd dropped.

Simba! Don't Molest That Warthog Till the White-Haired One Arrives

Driving across the crater, we begin accumulating animals. I log them in my notebook like celebrities: buffalo, warthogs, Thomson's gazelles, wildebeests, crowned plovers, flamingos, a bustard, hippos. Zebras become commonplace. Multiple species mingle on the shore of a shallow lake, reminding me of the *Peaceable Kingdom* paintings, except some of the animals are eating others or nipping ravenously at their own asses. In the shallows, a hyena crunches the rib cage of a wildebeest at the volume of a bat hitting a baseball, then lets loose a kind of Three Stooges whinny, the creepiest sound I've ever heard, so creepy it actually inspires hatred: hatred for all hyenas, forever, no exceptions, the bastards.

We see a hippo pond. Some cheetahs sit placidly on a rock overlooking a rushing stream. We pass two ostriches standing in a field, like an all-ostrich production of *Waiting for Godot*. One walks over to the other, looking, as it walks, from the knees down, like a naked woman walking backward. The other one, as if in response, does a kind of Stevie Wonder thing with its head.

We pass some female lions who will, once Clinton arrives, kill some warthogs, right in front of his jeep. But as we pass, they just lie there, as if they know we are only Press.

Someone asks where we're going for lunch.

Our guide says: It is a surprise.

And boy, it is.

Lunch is set up in a clearing, under a huge strangler fig tree: the biggest tree I have ever seen, period. It is, say, one hundred feet by one hundred feet, looks like a leaf-covered apartment building. Nearby are a group of singing Masai elders; some long, elegant, white-clothed tables; and a serving line: We're having Masai barbecue. It's an insane, mythic scene, like something out of *Vogue*, but *Vogue* from the 1930s. I expect Hemingway to be sitting there or Teddy Roosevelt, with Isak Dinesen on his lap.

A couple hundred yards away, in the bright sunlight, a herd of zebras stand, as if hired for the occasion.

Some of us get on our cells.

There's decent coverage in the crater.

At lunch I'm seated next to Clinton. Across from me is the earlier-mentioned Arpad Busson, philanthropist and ex of Elle Macpherson. He is startlingly good-looking and startlingly rich but works, conversationally, to be liked and likable, by being, in spite of his beauty and wealth, interested in you and eager to convince you that the Clinton Foundation is a good thing, by humbly downplaying his own good works. (He has recently purchased ARVs for 20,000 people in South Africa and has donated $8 million to the Clinton Foundation, for use in the struggle against AIDS in Mozambique.)

The Masai start singing, and Clinton talks — about Lucy, the first hominid; about the history of life; about DNA tracing; about how all of us can trace ourselves back to Africa, where all human life is thought to have begun.

A Tanzanian guest, with the Park Service, chimes in: "And, therefore, we are all Masai."

Our waiter comes over, tells the President there are two choices for soup: pumpkin and chicken.

"Were the pumpkins grown in Tanzania?" Clinton asks.

They were.

"I'll have that," he says.

I have that. Busson has that. We are not copying; it just sounds good is all.

Clinton starts talking about the foundation, about the efficiency of their approach, his passion embodied, as it often is, in a flurry of well-marshaled facts. With a normal NGO, he says, half the donated money ends up staying in the United States. Even PEPFAR is not as efficient at getting money to Africa as the foundation is; it costs the United States government $400,000 just to get one worker on the ground in a foreign country, because of new, post-9/11 building standards for government offices. One hundred percent of the foundation's staff costs for the Harlem and Little Rock offices are covered by admissions and gift-shop sales from the Presidential Library. Any shortfall is covered by donations from his friends. Attrition? Sure, yes, attrition's high. They hire young people at very low pay and ask them to work long hours, fully expecting most to stay a year or so, then go on to something more lucrative. The ethos seems to be: the problem is huge, let us exert ourselves insanely.

If there's one problem with the foundation, he says, it's that there's so little bureaucracy, he doesn't always know what's going on. If Ira Magaziner started hitting the sauce and absconded with a bunch of money, Clinton jokes, it might be six months before he even heard about it. But this is the cost of having a streamlined organization with minimal internal reporting. It's important that the organization stays light on its feet. . . .

A staffer steps over, says: Mr. President, this gentleman would like to give you some presents.

Clinton takes a breath, smiles, rises to accept the presents.

A foundation, it occurs to me, like any NGO, is in essence a little country, conducting its own mini foreign policy. That policy tells you who that country is and what it believes in — by its fruits, in other words, you shall know it. And the fruits of this 800-person nation are good (hundreds of thousands of people getting much-needed medicine; a Tanzanian warehouse full of AIDS and malaria drugs; a new hospital in Neno, Malawi; a global-warming emissions program that brought together four of the largest energy companies in the world, five international banks, and sixteen of the world's largest cities). Their approach is a model for any country: Come in respectfully, ask what's needed, provide what's needed with ruthless efficiency, work with the intention that eventually the local government will take over, then exit quietly, leaving things better in their wake.

Shock and awe for grown-ups.

Once More around the Mountain, Thanks So Much

Then it's time to go home.

We fly out of Arusha. The sun goes down. Word comes from the cockpit: The pilots will circle Kilimanjaro for our viewing pleasure.

We rush to the windows. I end up kneeling in the corridor near the bedroom. I can't get the light off and so cup my hands to look out.

We are circling freaking Kilimanjaro. Why? Because we want to. We want to and are traveling with the former President.

Who gets to do this? I think.

You do, I answer myself, just this once.

Down below I can see long deep vertical crevasses in the glacier. Nobody appears to be overnighting.

"Every happy man should have an unhappy man in his closet," wrote Chekhov, "to remind him, by his constant tapping, that not everyone is happy, and that sooner or later, life will turn on him, and show him its claws."

Here all my undeserved good luck — my health, my family, the relative absence of trauma in my life, the causal relation between work and good fortune that exists in our non-chaotic culture, this beautiful moment up here in this plane — comes crashing against a sudden imagining of the many unlucky people (sick, poor) below us, right now, to whom this moment would seem like some insane dream.

A friend's grandmother, on her deathbed, said: *I should have forgiven more.*

What I'm afraid I'll say on my deathbed is: *I should have done more to help other people and less to feed my own ego.*

Up here, my ego has been good and fed.

Looking down at the mountaintop, I say a little prayer that all this luck will make me more compassionate instead of more full of shit.

The plane completes one lap, veers away.

We retreat to our respective couches, recliners, and beds for a little quiet time.

Then, somewhere between the predinner snack and actual dinner, a creeping sense of yuck goes full-blown, and I realize I'm getting sick. My head's burning. I've got a hacking cough. I look on in awe as my colleagues perform amazing feats of endurance: sitting up straight, typing, having dinner, watching a movie. It seems I'm surrounded by superheroes. I drop into fetal position at the curve of the couch and stay there, hour after hour. If I hold my head just so, I don't feel nauseous.

Then, no matter how I hold my head, I feel deeply nauseous.

Out the window of the master bathroom, hoping to throw up, I see frozen vignette: white wing and blue sky absolutely still, no apparent motion.

Just like that, I've fallen out of the God Realm.

Jesus, I think, what a thing it is to be trapped in a body. The things that can go wrong, and still there you are, inside yourself, forced to experience all the things going wrong, for as long as they persist, for as long as you persist, no limit to your misery, until you die. Malaria, I think, you must really suck. Dying while shitting out one's guts, with a high fever, no comfort in sight, must be enough to make any good thing you've ever known seem like a trick played by a malicious God, who's just been setting you up all this time, for death. Wasting away via AIDS must hurt like hell. There you are, you, so recently strong and happy, now weak and miserable, in a filthy bed in your village, say, or sprawled on some dirt floor, or in some little clinic if you're lucky, and all around you people are bickering, laughing, making plans that will come to nothing, or to something, looking forward naively to an endless string of days, joys, breezes, meals — but not you. You're finished. You, who you've known all your life, are done. That beloved body of yours is going to start looking fucked-up very soon. Even those you love are no longer yours; they've begun to distance themselves, as they must.

They'll go on, but you won't.

Insanely, there's a drug that could stop all this, give you back your life, but because you can't afford it, because of where you were born, you can't get it.

And then one day, some people from far away do something, and you can, you can get it.

And you get it, and take it, and it makes you feel better, and you live.

In Which I Succumb to the Analytical Urge

A childhood is a smelter. What got made in Clinton's childhood smelter? Well, resolve, probably, to get clear of the heat; guilt for wanting so badly to get clear of the heat; an animating urge to do good, so as to escape from the heat while simultaneously performing a kind of elevation by association for his smelter-mates; an ability to compartmentalize the negative so as to keep it from contaminating the positive he'd be needing for his ascent; some dark, self-confounding urges. But what also got made, it seems to me, is something central to who he is, and why he's drawn to the kind of work he's doing in Africa. When he was a kid, let's imagine, people he knew and loved were flawed, and those flaws cost them (and him) and so they (and he) suffered; and yet he loved them (in spite of their flaws and the suffering/squirming they sometimes caused him), and in so doing, learned, in his gut, that a person who is troubled — who is poor, sick, anxious, addicted, ignorant — wants to be, and can be, with help, something more: dignified, productive, at ease.

I predict that years from now, when people talk about Bill Clinton, they'll see him as the embodiment of a certain strain of ornery, compassionate, complicated American energy. And what they'll think of him will depend on what happens between now and then. He will either be a harbinger of the good turn we shortly took, toward compassionate/competent action in the world, or a reproach, a reminder of what we could have been, before we got mastered by our own fear, and forgot our own legacy.

PATRICK TOBIN

◼

Cake

FROM *The Kenyon Review*

ANNETTE THE FACILITATOR PRETENDED to be Kate, a woman in our chronic pain support group who killed herself. We went around the circle, Annette in the middle, each of us given the opportunity to tell "Kate" what we were feeling.

Gail with fibromyaglia: "How could you give up?"

Stephanie with the botched spinal fusion: "You should have reached out for help!"

Liz with diabetes-related neuropathy: "What about your children?"

There were a lot of tears. A lot of hugging. Then it was my turn.

"I have a question," I said.

"For Kate?" Annette asked. "Or for me, Annette."

"Makes no difference," I said. "Is it true she jumped off the San Pedro Bridge?"

"Yes. But —"

"Is it also true that she landed on a Maersk cargo ship headed out to sea?"

Annette shifted uncomfortably. "Claire, we should focus on our feelings —"

"And is it also true that Maersk sent back what was left of her body in a Rubbermaid cooler, that the cooler was stuck in customs for a week before Kate's husband could take custody of it, that the cooler was stolen on the way to the funeral home because a homeless guy thought it contained a picnic?"

Annette looked around the circle at the horrified faces. When she looked back at me, she nodded.

I started applauding.

"Why are you clapping?" Annette asked, her big fat cow eyes filled with confusion.

"For a job well done. Personally, I hate it when suicides make it easy on the survivors."

When I got home there were two messages. On the first one, Annette said the group had stayed late after I left, that it had been a difficult session for everyone and she didn't want to minimize my feelings, but —

She and the others feel it's in everyone's best interest if I find another support group — perhaps one specifically to deal with my "anger issues."

The second message was from my ex-husband Jason. He said he wanted to come by and pick up the last of his things. He asked me to call his assistant with a time when I won't be home, because he feels it's prudent that we don't see each other right now.

I'm sure his mother told him exactly what to say on the message because he never used to say things like "prudent." He always was a big mama's boy.

With all the excitement it was no wonder I was experiencing breakthrough pain. Breakthrough pain is my worst nightmare because it means the meds aren't working right.

Imagine the most excruciating thing you ever experienced. A migraine. A kidney stone. Giving birth.

All of these I've experienced, by the way.

Now try to imagine that the nerves involved in that pain are being pulled out by a sadistic fuck, one by one. No matter what you scream to make the sadistic fuck stop, he won't. The sadistic fuck just keeps laughing at you because he's enjoying your agony.

That, in a nutshell, is breakthrough pain.

Guess who got a private room at Cedars with her very own morphine drip?

Morphine is like being wrapped up in warm towels fresh from the dryer. Morphine is like your mother rubbing your back when you have the flu. Morphine is like drinking cold water from a hose on the hottest day of the summer.

Who am I kidding? Morphine's even better than all that.

Thank you morphine.

Thank you.

Thank.

You.

Morphine.

Drug Induced Hallucination #1:

There was a boa constrictor slithering under my sheets. The snake tried to convince me that *As You Like It* is Shakespeare's most unjustly criticized play. I stared at the mound under my sheets and didn't move a muscle for hours. I knew if I made any movement the snake was going to stop arguing literary theory and devour me.

Drug Induced Hallucination #2:

A group of young kids was standing outside my room, talking loudly. They didn't go away. I got angrier and angrier.

I finally rang the nurse and told her to tell those fucking brats to move it somewhere else, if that wasn't too much fucking trouble. Or was I interrupting her goddamned fucking break?

That's when the kids started throwing a basketball against my door.

"Don't you hear that?" I asked the nurse.

She pulled the drip out of my arm and started jabbing the needle in her eyes. "I can't hear a thing."

Drug Induced Hallucination #3:

Kate walked into my hospital room carrying a cake with a bunch of candles on it. I told her I liked her new look.

"Thanks," she said. "I wish I could say the same about you."

"The morphine makes it kind of hard to fix myself up."

"You're probably wondering about the cake."

"I didn't want to be rude, but yes."

"Remember that time when Annette asked us what our dream would be if we didn't have chronic pain?"

"I always hated her drippy little exercises."

"You said your dream involved the Brazilian soccer team." Kate crinkled her nose in disapproval.

"And you said you wished you could bake your kids a birthday cake."

Kate lit the candles. "Everyone in the group cried after I said that. You didn't though."

"I had my reasons."

"I know that now."

"To be honest, I wasn't that impressed with the whole Saint Kate thing."

"Saints don't jump off the San Pedro Bridge onto a Maersk cargo ship."

"Nice touch."

"I thought you'd like it."

Kate brought the cake over to me. "Make a wish," she said.

I closed my eyes and blew out the candles, even though I couldn't think of anything to wish for. When I opened my eyes, Kate threw the cake out the window and jumped out after it. There was a sickening thud and someone started screaming from the street below. A nurse ran into my room.

It took me awhile before I realized that the person screaming was actually me.

The remote didn't work so my TV had been stuck on the Discovery Channel the whole time. No wonder I was having nightmares about fucking boa constrictors. I told the mousy Filipina nurse to change the channel manually.

"No problem, your highness," she said.

"Ooh," I said, "somebody developed a spine while I was out of it."

She left the TV on the History Channel after I told her to turn it to HBO. Touché, Imelda.

I watched a documentary about the demise of drive-in theaters in America. Apparently there aren't any left in California except for one in Barstow.

Jason took me to a drive-in theater when we were dating, back when we were both in law school at UCLA. He'd been mortified when I found the *Carpenters: Greatest Hits* in his glove compartment. I teased him about it, until he cued the tape up to "Close to You." He held me in his arms while we listened to the song — I'd never felt as safe as I did at that particular moment.

It was only the second time I'd ever gotten drunk. Captain Morgan's Spiced Rum and Coke, on top of a large carton of buttered popcorn. After I threw up, his car smelled like sour cinnamon toast. He gently stroked my hair and told me everything would be okay.

I was stupid enough to believe him.

When I got home I made two phone calls. First I called Rosalva, my cleaning lady, and asked if she had a driver's license. When I found out she did, I asked her if she wanted to make an extra couple hundred bucks.

Then I called Jason's office. I told his assistant to tell him I was going to be out of town tomorrow, so he could come by the house then.

I told her to tell Mama's Boy I'd changed all the locks, but I'd leave a key in the bottom of the deep end of the pool for him.

For the road trip:
1. Vicodin.
2. Oxycontin.
3. Methadone.
4. A nasal opiate from Glaxo that's still in the trial phase.
5. The phone number and Mapquest directions for a pharmacy in Barstow. Just in case.
6. A fifty-dollar ergonomic travel pillow I bought at Sharper Image.
7. A two-hundred-dollar lumbar support pillow I bought off the Internet.
8. Orange juice.
9. Chips.
10. My sunglasses.
11. A change of clothes. Just in case.
12. A bottle of Captain Morgan's Spiced Rum.
13. A six-pack of Coke.

*

The drive to Barstow should normally take two hours, not five. I had to get out every twenty minutes to stretch. I felt like my breaks were starting to get on Rosalva's nerves.

"No, no, no, Mrs. Fine. Is okay," she said.

I told her I was still freaked out by the crow we killed near San Bernardino, the way it dived head-on into our car like a kamikaze pilot.

Rosalva acted like she was about to cross herself. "No more please."

"Sorry. We don't have to talk about the crow." I offered her some chips and a Coke and that seemed to improve her mood.

The pain got bad near Apple Valley. That annoyed me. It also annoyed me the way Rosalva looked at me when I took my pills.

"Could you do me a favor?" I asked.

"Yes, ask me what you need."

"Don't call me Mrs. Fine," I said. "I'm divorced now so I don't want to be called Mrs. Fine."

"But what to call you?"

"How about Claire. That's my name."

"Okay, Mrs. Claire," she said.

With a sweet smile. Oh, fuck it. She'll get it right one of these days.

Rosalva loved *The Passion of the Christ*. I found it kind of weird to listen to all the torture through the small, tinny speaker. I started chipping off the polish on my toenails.

"You must be seeing this," Rosalva said, her eyes filled with tears.

"I *am* seeing this," I told her, as chunk number forty-five flew off Jesus' body. "I'm also seeing we're out of Coke."

She seemed relieved when I offered to go to the concession stand so she could keep watching the movie. It's okay, I get it: The Jews killed Jesus, so we should have to go to the concession stand during *The Passion of the Christ*.

The desert night sky is dreamy this time of year — a deep purplish blue and stars that look like Christmas lights. The cold air hurt my lungs, but in a good way.

I crawled under the low wire fence behind the concession stand and walked through shrubs and gravel down to the train tracks.

What would Jesus do? I think if he were in my shoes he would lie down and wait for the next Union Pacific freight train.

When you think you're going to die imminently, you choose your final thoughts carefully. I tried to think of beautiful things, like Michelangelo's *David*. A Bach cantata.

That got me thinking about the *Nutcracker Suite*. When I was a little girl, I danced as a mouse two years in a row. It's still one of my favorite pieces of music.

My thoughts turned to Jason.

I hated to admit it, but I did understand what he meant when he said I wasn't the only one suffering — right before he handed me the divorce papers he'd personally drawn up. It was hard at the time to react graciously to what he said, because, after all, he'd walked away from the accident with only a sprained shoulder.

But now — I can see.

I can see that we were both the wrong kind of people to deal with this kind of situation. Problems that could be solved by money: *that's* the most we could handle. Not the loss. Not the pain. Not all the thousands and thousands and thousands of pills.

Too bad Jason's such a mama's boy that he'd never take methadone, because it really does help take the edge off life.

I felt the low rumble of a train. Then I heard a voice, getting closer and closer.

"Mrs. Claire! *Ay Dios mío!* Mrs. Claire!"

I struggled to sit up and saw Rosalva scrambling toward the tracks. I tried to gauge how far the train was in relation to her distance from me.

"It's okay, it's okay," I said, "I just got tired and needed a rest."

During the drive back Rosalva kept looking at me like I was going to jump out of the car.

"Knock it off with the attitude already," I said.

She scolded me in Spanish. I think she said something about how it was a good thing Jesus told her I went "loco."

I was thinking of the most profane thing I could say when the car started making a grinding noise. Right before the "service engine" light went on.

The guy at the garage in Barstow said it was going to take at least three days to fix the car. He tried to explain the problem to me.

"I don't need to understand what a head gasket is," I said. "Just make the arrangements for a rental car."

Blank stare.

"Okay," I said, "maybe you don't understand Triple A. I have the *platinum* coverage that gets me a free mid-size rental if repairs are going to take more than twenty-four hours."

"There's nothing open now," he said.

"Why? Is it a holiday?"

"It's nearly midnight. People have to sleep."

Now it was my turn for a blank stare.

Inside a dark Greyhound bus, strung out on opiates, traveling through the high desert in the middle of the night, I started to feel like I was in a rocket flying through outer space. I stared at Rosalva while she slept next to me. She opened her eyes.

"Gracias," I said.

"Why?" she asked.

"For putting up with me," I said. "I wish I knew how to say that in Spanish."

"Sleep, Mrs. Claire." Rosalva closed her eyes again.

I heard muffled laughter from the back of the bus. I turned around and saw a group of teenagers passing around a joint. Everyone else on the bus was asleep. I waited a few minutes, the smell of pot becoming stronger.

I made my way to the back. The leader of the group, a girl with a bad tattoo of a python on her arm, glared at me.

"Toilet's broke, bitch."

Her friends laughed.

"I don't need to use the toilet."

She sneered. "Then beat it."

Her friends were enjoying the show. I leaned down into her face.

"I used to be married to a federal prosecutor in L.A. Even though I hate his guts, I have no problem getting on my cell phone and asking him to send a marshal to the bus station."

The sneer disappeared.

I pointed to the joint in her hand. "Is that just pot or did you morons cut it with something else?"

I'd hoped the girl — Becky, a runaway from Idaho — wouldn't want to talk, but once we started on the second joint she wouldn't shut up.

"I want to be an actress," Becky said.

"Can I give you some unsolicited feedback?"

"Hell no."

"You're going to end up doing porn. Or worse. That's what happens to girls from Idaho like you."

"Gross! I won't do porn!"

"Right. Do any of these stars ever say in an interview, 'I ran away from Idaho when I was sixteen and ended up doing Hollywood movies'? No. That's what porn actresses say. Not Hillary Duff."

"I hate Hillary Duff," she said.

"If I had your body I would too."

"At least I don't look like you." She pointed at my face and arms with a vicious little smile.

"Give it time, honey. You'll get your own scars someday."

I asked if she had another joint.

"I hope you know these weren't free," she pouted.

I pulled out a hundred dollar bill. "Let's skip the soul baring. It's starting to get on my nerves."

Becky finally passed out. The bus was absolutely quiet as we went down the Cajon Pass. The sun was just coming up. The San Gabriel Valley glowed from under an ozone shroud.

Rosalva woke up. She panicked when she didn't find me next to her. I waved from my seat next to Becky.

"Who is this?" she asked, eyeing Becky's tattoo.

"I'm starved. I want a yellow cake with lots of fudge frosting."

"I make one tomorrow."

"I want one the minute we get home."

"Mrs. Claire, I must go to my home. Later I come to your home."

I realized I had no idea where Rosalva lived.

"Downey," she answered. "You do not know this place I am sure."

"Isn't that where the Carpenters were from?"

"I have not met them."

When we sat down in our seats Rosalva pulled out a brush and started combing my hair. I began to sing.

"Why do birds . . . suddenly appear . . ."

Rosalva smiled. "This is very pretty song."

"Every time . . . you are near? Just like me . . . they long to be . . . close to you."

At the L.A. bus station I sent Rosalva to Downey in a cab. While I waited for my own cab, I noticed Becky's friends had deserted her. She walked up to me with a shy look on her face.

"What are your big plans?" I asked. "Oh that's right, you're going to be a star."

"Shut up."

"Want to make an easy hundred?"

She gave me a look of disgust. "I knew you were a dyke."

"I don't want to fuck you. I just want you to bake me a cake."

"You're a freak. You know that, right?"

"Can you follow directions on a package, or are you illiterate?"

"Am I what?"

"Jesus. Can you read? Do they still teach that in Idaho?"

A cab pulled up. I opened the door and waited for Becky. She studied my face, trying to decide if I was a good risk or not. I felt bad for her until my legs started killing me again.

I sighed. "Do I look like someone who could hurt you?"

"You're mean enough."

"You outweigh me by at least fifty pounds."

"Fuck you."

"Fine."

I got inside and gave the cabbie my address. We were driving off when I heard Becky's voice.

"Wait!" she yelled, running after the cab.

I didn't look at her when she got in the car. "Offer's fifty now."

"What?"

"You heard me."

"That's not fair."

"Life's not fair. Any more lip and it goes down to twenty five."

Becky decided to make the cake from scratch. We were at the grocery store right by my house, in the baking section. I'd become distracted by the Disney-themed birthday candles.

"Do you have baking powder?" Becky asked.

"I'm not sure." I was starting to lose focus. "Is that the stuff you put in the fridge to keep it from smelling?"

Becky rolled her eyes. "That's baking soda."

"Then I don't think I have baking powder."

"Who doesn't have baking powder?"

"People who order out, that's who."

"You're pathetic," Becky said while were standing in the checkout line.

"You're only just now realizing that? God you *are* stupid."

"What about booze?" Becky asked.

"Can you handle liquor? I don't want green puke all over my carpet after you drink a whole bottle of Midori."

"Why are you such a cunt?" she hissed.

"Paper or plastic?" the clerk nervously asked.

*

While Becky made the cake, I went through the house. The last of Jason's clothes was gone. All the tools were missing — not that I'd ever use them. All his books were out of the den. With his collection gone it really exposed my intellectual laziness — Clive Cussler no longer propped up by *The Collected Works of Shakespeare*.

I found the picture on the desk, the framed photo of Jason and me and the twins. We'd hired an expensive photographer, a guy who does fashion spreads for *Los Angeles* magazine. The year before the accident, for our holiday greeting card.

I picked it up and studied our faces, until none of us was recognizable. I thought I'd made it clear to Jason he could keep the picture.

I called his office.

"Mr. Fine's not in. Would you like to leave a message?" his assistant asked.

"Tell him he won."

"Won what?" The assistant sounded nervous.

"He'll know," I said, before I hung up the phone.

I took so much methadone I just barely made it to my bed. Becky yelled from the kitchen.

"Where's the fucking booze?"

"Be resourceful!" I yelled back. "You need to be resourceful!"

My last thought before I passed out was that maybe primitive cultures are right — I think the camera did steal my soul.

When I woke up, Rosalva was wiping my face with a cold washcloth.

"What time is it?" I asked.

"Too many hours," she said.

"Is the girl still here?"

"No. I think she stealed."

Rosalva helped me get up. We discovered that Becky had taken my purse, all of my jewelry, all of the liquor, and the entire stash of pain medication, including the methadone.

How did she find the methadone? I'd completely underestimated her.

"I call the police," Rosalva said.

I stared at the frosted cake on the kitchen counter, covered in plastic wrap. "No."

"She does wrong when you are sick! This is bad girl!"

I dabbed my finger on the top of the cake and tasted it. Homemade fudge frosting. A little on the sweet side, but definitely homemade.

It's impossible in L.A. to find out where someone lives if they haven't given you the information. The white pages are useless; 411 is a fucking joke. I needed to talk to a human being and not Verizon's annoying computer, so I called Annette.

"And how are we doing, Claire?"

"We're doing *great.*"

"Well, that's super. Did you find another support group?"

"Funny you should mention that. Ever hear of Gloria Allred?"

"Uh, well, yes, I have."

"Because I've decided to sue you for discrimination."

"Goodness. A lawsuit?"

"Just kidding. I'm calling to get Kate's address."

"I don't think I'm allowed to give out that information. Was there something I could help you with?"

"That's hardly possible."

"Well, I'm certain I can't give you that information. I'm sorry."

"Remember when I said I was kidding about the lawsuit?"

"Uh huh."

"Now I'm not kidding."

The address was in Palos Verdes, for a house that looked like the bastard child of a mansion and a small hotel. Rosalva, bless her heart, drove me there in the mid-size rental. I told her to wait for me in the car.

"I help you, Mrs. Claire."

"Thanks, but I need to do this by myself."

I wonder what Kate's husband will say. I have to remember his name before I ring the doorbell. Ken? Ben?

Fuck it. I'll just mumble something.

I hope he doesn't freak out and think I'm a crazy person for bringing a cake with cheap Disney-themed candles. Will I actually tell him it was something Kate had wanted to do for the kids? Jesus, I hope he doesn't start crying, or worse, ask me to come in to meet the family.

I stand outside the front door, my hand ready to press the bell. I hear children's voices inside. Lots of children.

I take a deep breath.

LAURA VAN DEN BERG

∎

Where We Must Be

FROM *Indiana Review*

SOME PEOPLE DREAM OF being chased by Bigfoot. I found it hard to believe at first, but it's true. I was driving back from Los Angeles in late August, after a summer of waiting tables and failed casting calls, when I saw a huge wooden arrow that pointed down a dirt road, ACTORS WANTED painted across it in white letters. I was in Northern California and still a long way from Washington — which wasn't really home, just where I had come from. I followed the sign down the road and parked in front of a silver Airstream trailer. It was dark inside and I felt the breeze of a fan. The fat man behind the desk said he'd never hired a woman before. And then he went on to describe exactly what happens at the Bigfoot Recreation Park. People come here to have an encounter with Bigfoot. Most of their customers have been wanting this moment for years. I would have to lumber and roar with convincing masculinity. I can do that, I said, no problem. And I proved it in my audition. After putting on the costume and staggering around the trailer for a few minutes, bellowing and shaking my arms, I stopped and removed the Bigfoot mask. The fat man was smiling. He said I would always be paid in cash.

Today I'm going after a woman from Chicago. She's small and sharp-shouldered, dressed in khaki slacks and a pink sweatshirt, her auburn hair held back with a tortoiseshell clip. I'd be willing to bet no one knows she's here. For a brief time, this woman will be living in another world, where all that matters is escaping Bigfoot. People say the park is great for realigning their priorities, for reminding them that survival is an active choice. I'm watching her from behind a dense cluster of bushes. The fat man has informed me that she wants to be ambushed. This isn't surprising. Most people crave the shock.

My breath is warm inside the costume. The rubber has a faintly sweet smell. I like to stroke my arms and listen to the swishing sound of the fake fur. The mask has eyeholes but blocks my peripheral vision. I can only see straight ahead. The fat man says this is an unexpected benefit of not having more advanced masks. According to him, Bigfoot is a primitive creature, not wily like extraterrestrials or the Loch Ness Monster, and only responds to what's directly in front of him. Two other people work at the park, Jeffrey and Mack, but our shifts never overlap. The fat man thinks it's important for us to not see our counterparts in person, to believe we are the only Bigfoot.

I wait for the woman to relax, watching for the instant when she begins to think: maybe there won't be a monster after all. I can always tell when this thought arrives. First their posture goes soft. Then their expression changes from confused to relieved to disappointed. More than anything, the ambush is about waiting the customer out. I struggle to stay in character during these quiet moments; it's tempting to consider my own life and worries, but when the time comes to attack, it will only be believable if I've been living with Bigfoot's loneliness and desires for at least an hour.

The woman yawns and rubs her face. She bends over and scratches her knee. She stops looking around the forest. Her expectations are changing. She checks her watch. I start counting backwards from ten. When I reach zero, I pound into the clearing and release the first roar: a piercing animal sound still foreign to my ears.

Jimmy and I are sprawled out in his backyard, staring through the branches of a pear tree. Earlier I found him sitting on the front porch, trying to stop a nosebleed. I told him to tilt his head back and then pressed the tissue against his nostrils and watched the white bloom into crimson. It's not love. Or at least not what I thought love would feel like. It hurts to be near him and it hurts to be away.

"What do you dream of?" I ask.

"Of a time when the world was nothing but cool, blue water."

I spread my legs and arms and imagine floating in an enormous pool. Jimmy lives across the street from the one-bedroom bungalow I've been renting since early September, a long structure with low ceilings, the paint a chipped turquoise. When I first moved into the neighborhood, he dropped by and offered to give me a hand. I told him I didn't really have anything to unpack, but invited him inside anyway. He grew up in Oregon and after high school drifted down to California where he took a job as a postman. He was willowy and pale, dark hair and bright blue eyes. He didn't look like anyone else I knew. I pulled a bottle of Jim Beam out of my suitcase and he ended up staying the night.

He rolls toward me, leaving a silhouette of flattened grass. "What about you?"

"I dream of a room with empty white walls," I say. "Someplace quiet and clean."

He tickles my nose with a blade of grass. I laugh and try to snatch it from his hand, but he drops the grass and returns to lying on his back. He has a slightly crooked nose and long eyelashes.

A hawk with white-tipped wings crosses the sky; I wonder where the bird is headed. It's mid-October. The weather is cool and breezy. "I wish we could keep winter from coming," I tell him.

"Yeah," he says. "It's a real shame."

Jimmy told me he was sick the morning after we met. We were sitting on the floor of my living room, drinking water to ease the hangover. I raised my glass and pointed at the grit pooled in the bottom. He shrugged and said the water has always looked that way. And then he told me about the cold that lasted for three months and the clicking sound of the X-ray machine and the spot on his lungs. When I asked if he had help, he said he'd lost touch with his friends in Oregon and hadn't made any new ones in the postal service. His father was dead and his mother had remarried, a carpet salesman that drank too much and smoked Dunhills, and moved east a few years back. His mother tried to arrange a nurse once his outcome became definite, but he refused, saying he didn't want a stranger in the house. He stopped delivering mail months ago and was collecting disability checks. He told me all of this and then said he'd understand if I minded and we could go back to just being neighbors. But I told him I didn't mind at all. When I was young, my mother worked in a hospice center, although I didn't mention that to Jimmy. Most of the people who worked at the center got depressed from being close to so much death, but it never seemed to bother her. Sometimes, out of nowhere, I remember the scent of rubbing alcohol and ointment on her hands, a strong sage smell that made my skin itch.

"How was work?" he asks.

"Not bad." I stretch my legs and bump against a browning pear. At the end of the summer, the branches were heavy with fruit. We picked as many as we could and made huge bowls of fruit salad, but eventually the pears began to rot and fall onto the ground. "I gave a woman from Chicago a good scare."

"You can practice your roar today if you want," he says. "Since we're already outside."

"I can only do it when I'm in costume." I kick the pear and listen to it roll through the grass. "It's impossible to get into character if I'm not wearing it."

He moves closer and smushes his face into my neck. "You would've made a wonderful actress," he mumbles into my skin.

He often asks about my months in Los Angeles. I tell him how difficult it was to make enough money, how alien I felt carrying trays through a chic bistro that boasted a fifteen-page wine list and thirty-dollar desserts. And when he wants to know about the acting, I tell him the casting directors said I wasn't talented enough. I don't tell him how they often praised my poise and personality, but in the end all said the same thing: you just aren't what we're looking for. I don't tell him this felt worse than having them say I wasn't pretty or gifted, because it gave me a dangerous amount of hope.

I touch the back of Jimmy's head. His dark hair feels damp. In my mind, I list the things I need to help him with over the weekend: wash the sheets, mop the floors, gather all the rotten pears. Just when I think he has gone to sleep, he looks up and asks me to stay with him tonight. I tell him that I will. He lowers his head and we both close our eyes. The late afternoon sun burns against us.

I wake to the boom of a loudspeaker. *We are running tests. Please don't be alarmed if your water is rusty.* I glance out the window and see a truck from the water company inching down the street. The water has never looked right here. People complain and the company comes out for an inspection, but it never seems to get any better.

Jimmy is still asleep, one spindly arm draped above his head. I don't wake him before I go, even though I know he'd like me to. I want to be alone now, although as soon as I'm on my own, I'll only want to be back with him. I leave a glass of murky water and his pills on the bedside table. He doesn't stir when I kiss the side of his face and whisper a goodbye.

I walk across the street to my house, where I undress and take a shower. The water is a cloudy red. The color makes me uneasy and I get out before rinsing all the shampoo from my hair. My hair is light without really being blond and the dry climate has made the skin on my knees and elbows rough. I have an hour before work, although I wish I could go in early. I'm starting to realize I can't stand to be anywhere, except stomping through the forest in my Bigfoot costume. That's the reason I always wanted to be an actress: when I'm in character, everything real about my life blacks out.

In my living room, which is still more or less unfurnished, I do lunges and Pilates in preparation for my role. It's essential my muscles stay long and supple, so I can skulk with persuasive simianess. The little furniture I do have came from the Salvation Army across town and since I spend most of my time with Jimmy, I haven't had the incentive to acquire more than the necessities. The place could be nice, I sometimes think, walking through the sparsely decorated rooms and observing the patterns the sunlight makes on the wood floors, abstract and pointed shapes that remind me of origami.

The phone rings and it's Jimmy. He wants me to come over for breakfast. I tell him I'm late for work, which is about thirty minutes away from being true.

"And I have to finish rehearsing," I add.

"I thought you just do stretching exercises." The connection is bad, and his voice pops with static.

"It's more complicated than that," I reply. "And any actor will tell you it pays to do your homework."

He relents and makes me promise to come over after work. When I ask what he has planned for today, he says he's going through the jazz records in his closet.

"There's a guy from high school I'd like to mail some of them to."

"Don't you want to talk to him or try to visit?" I ask. "If you've already gone to the trouble of getting his address."

"No," he says. "I really do not."

I walk over to the window and look across the street. Jimmy is standing in his living room window, waving and holding the phone against his ear. He's still only wearing his boxers and through the glass, his figure is pale and wavy.

"I was wondering how long it was going to take you," he says.

"Doesn't it feel weird to see the person you're talking to?" I ask. "The whole point of the phone is long-distance communication."

"Talking to you isn't the same when I can't see your face," he says. "It's impossible to tell what you're thinking."

"Do I give away that much in person?"

"More than you know." He presses his face against the pane, so his features look even more sallow and distorted. I giggle into the phone and stick out my tongue.

"Okay," I tell him. "Now I'm really going to be late for work."

"All right." He pulls away from the window. "Go if you must."

After we hang up, we stand at our windows a little longer. His hair is disheveled and sticking up in the back like dark straw. He gives me one last wave, then disappears into the shadows of the house. I wait to see if he'll come back, but the sun has shifted and the glare now blocks my view. I imagine him watching me from another part of the house, through some secret window. I return his wave to let him know I'm still here.

The fat man says my client wants to kill Bigfoot. The customer is a man from Wisconsin who came equipped with his own paintball gun. He tells me not to ambush, but to let the man sneak up on me and then moan and collapse after he fires.

"I didn't know killing Bigfoot was part of the deal," I tell him.

As always, the fat man is sitting behind his desk. He leans back in his chair and picks something out of his teeth with the corner of a matchbook. "It's a recreation park," he says. "They get to do whatever they want."

"How do people even find this place?"

"I take out ads in magazines for Bigfoot enthusiasts," he says. "It was important to open the park in this part of California, since there have been lots of sightings around here. My cousin claims he saw Bigfoot behind his house, just a few miles down the road. He was standing in the backyard, going through a garbage can." He flips open the matchbook and rubs his thumb against the rough strip. "Some shit, I'll tell you."

I open the closet and take out my costume. "So this guy is going to shoot me with paintballs?"

"To be honest, you might feel a little sting," he says. "But I've banned any other kind of weapon after an old Bigfoot got shot in the face with a pellet gun."

"Ouch."

"It was at close range too. He was covered in welts and bruises for days." He runs a hand across his bald head. "If the weapon doesn't look like a paintball gun, then shout your safe word."

I step into the costume. "I have a safe word?"

"I don't like to tell people when they first start the job," he says. "In case they scare easily."

"I don't." I seal myself inside the rubber skin. "So what's my safe word?"

"*Jesus,*" he says. "It's really more for the customers, but this is a different kind of situation."

"How'd you come up with *Jesus*?"

"You'd be surprised at how religious some of these people are," he says. "I always thought screaming *Jesus* would get their attention."

I lower the Bigfoot mask onto my head and inhale the sweet scent of the rubber. Through the eyeholes, I can only see the fat man and his desk.

"And what if this guy doesn't believe in God?"

"Then you've still got the element of surprise."

I've been pretending to not see the man from Wisconsin for over an hour. He's positioned in the branches of a cedar: back pressed against the tree trunk, nose of the paintball gun angled toward the ground. He's wearing sunglasses and a baseball cap, so I can't see his face or eyes. He paid for two hours and I can tell most of our time has passed. He must be saving the killing for the very end.

In the meantime, I've been trying to do all the things Bigfoot might actually do. I ambled around, rubbed my back against a tree, ripped up some wildflowers. I sniffed the air and gave two magnificent roars. But the whole time I felt myself slipping out of character and soon I was only a person in the woods, waiting for something painful to happen. I wonder if this is how Jimmy feels when he wakes in the morning — alone and waiting to be hit.

One night we had a long talk about the days when he was first diagnosed and receiving treatment. He was in a hospital with a cancer center, two hours away from our houses and the Bigfoot park. He's young — twenty-nine, only two years older than me — and says he's never even held a cigarette; it wasn't until the hospital that he began to overcome the shock, to look ahead and weigh all that did and did not await him. He would sit around with the other patients and talk about what they would do if the chemotherapy and radiation and surgeries failed — if their hand was called, as he put it. Some wanted to travel to exotic places, islands for the most part, while others wanted to find lovers they had let go or to make amends with children they had neglected. Jimmy said he wanted to drive to the Grand Canyon and stay until he was no longer impressed with the view. He couldn't say why he chose that destination, only that it was the first thing that came to him. But he didn't go to the Grand Canyon and he couldn't say why that happened either. It wouldn't have been so hard, he told me, only a long car ride and a little money. After that night, I thought a lot about why he never went out to Arizona and finally decided it was fear — of having the experience fall short, of realizing too late that he should have made a different choice. For him, it was better to not know for sure what the Grand Canyon looked like, to retain the splendor of his dreams.

I'm so caught up in my waiting and thinking and not being Bigfoot that the shots come as a terrible shock. Two red splats in the center of my brown chest. I fall on my back, my furry legs and arms rising and then hitting the ground with a thump. Air rushes out of my lungs; I gasp underneath the mask. I feel the point of a rock digging into my back, a sharp pain in my forehead. I hear branches snapping and footsteps. Soon the man is standing over me, still holding the gun. He's shorter than he looked in the tree, with pasty skin and knobby elbows, a white smudge of sunscreen on the tip of his nose. He's wearing a t-shirt with a bull's-eye on the front and camouflage pants.

He nudges me with the toe of his boot and, forgetting I'm supposed to be dead, I squirm to the side. He frowns and raises the gun. I remember my safe word, but I'm able to stop myself. I want this to be as good as he hoped. If this man is dying, I want him to walk away feeling satisfied with his life.

He shoots me once in the neck and again in the shoulder. I shriek and press my rubber paw against my arm. I hear quick footsteps, then nothing at all. When my breathing steadies and I'm able to stand, I take off the mask and touch the hard lump on my neck. The ground is speckled with red paint. The man is gone.

"I was always one of those people who assumed I had my whole life to do whatever I wanted," Jimmy says without any prompting. He talks like this all the time now. I call them philosophy spells.

"Like what?" I'm sitting at his kitchen table, drinking a whiskey and Coke. The welt on my neck has swollen to the size of a date. The bumps on my chest and arm are smaller, but still bright pink. Jimmy has yet to notice my wounds — or perhaps he has and just decided not to ask.

"I don't know," he says. "See the Great Wall of China. Climb a mountain. Get married. Have a kid." He opens a beer and joins me at the table. "The point is I never felt much urgency."

"The last two aren't exactly the kind of things you'd want to rush into."

"I guess," he replies. "But maybe the only reason we tell ourselves that is because we think we have all this time." He spreads his arms and turns his palms upward; the skin on his wrists is as translucent as tracing paper. I remember him telling me about his last day of work, how the weight of the mailbag bruised his shoulder and he carried it until he couldn't anymore, how he dumped all the envelopes onto the sidewalk and began tearing them open: bills, love letters, subscription renewal notices, credit card offers. He told me that even though he'd never become close with anyone on his route, he was suddenly overcome with a desire to know what their lives contained. Because of his condition, he didn't get into much trouble but was talked into resigning with a year of disability compensation. They only agreed to the disability because they knew the payments would outlive me, he says whenever the checks come, but I take them to the bank and make his deposits all the same.

We're quiet for a while. I finish my drink and make myself another. When I offer to get Jimmy a second beer, he shakes his head and squeezes the can until the metal dents. I stand behind him and rest a hand on his shoulder. The ceiling light flickers. Earlier in the evening, I washed all the dishes and scrubbed the floor. The room looks dull and empty. He lets me do what I know best: acquiesce, accommodate, allow my desires to melt like wax around someone else's life.

"It's almost a relief to not consider the future," he says. "To not wonder how my life will turn out, if I'll find what I was looking for or just be disappointed. Everything falls away in the face of this." He tips his head back and looks at me. His eyes are bloodshot. "So it doesn't really matter if you love me or not, does it?"

"Of course it does," I tell him, because I think it's the right thing to say. With Jimmy it seems more important to say the right thing than to be honest. Or maybe I have it backwards. But it does matter in a way, although not in the sense that it could change what's going to happen to him.

"What did you do at work today?" I can tell he wants to change the subject.

"I got killed."

"They can do that?"

"Apparently."

"Is that why you've got that lump on your neck?"

"Yep." I brush a clump of hair from his forehead. "Shot dead with a paintball gun."

"There was a woman in the hospital who had cancer in her lymph nodes and when they swelled, it kind of looked like that," he says. "We kept in touch for a while after leaving the center. She died last winter."

He hunches over the table and hangs his head. I prepare myself to comfort. He surprises me with laughter.

At two in the morning, I'm woken by a barking dog. I kick away the covers and sit up, but the sound has already faded. Jimmy is curled underneath the sheets, his breathing nearly imperceptible. I watch him until my eyes adjust to the darkness and I can make out the rising and falling of his chest. His face is pressed into the pillow, his lips parted so I can see the wet bulge of his tongue.

I get out of bed and wander through the kitchen. I can still smell the cleaning products I used on the floor. The house seems much smaller in the night and I suddenly want to be outside. I go out the back door and sit on the concrete steps. The sky is black and starless. I'm wearing a pair of Jimmy's boxers and one of his t-shirts. Both fit me perfectly. Before we went to bed tonight, he came into the bathroom while I was brushing my teeth. He didn't say anything for a while, just stood in the doorway and stared. And then, as I was rinsing the spearmint toothpaste from my mouth, he asked if I would like to have some of his clothes. It was the first time he'd mentioned anything about his belongings, and I'd been happy to avoid the subject altogether. I spit green liquid into the sink and watched it swirl into the drain. I mean when we're not doing this anymore, he continued. After it's all over. I turned from the sink and told him I'd take whatever he wanted me to have. He didn't say anything else, just nodded and walked into the bedroom.

I notice a rotten pear sitting on the bottom step. I reach down and pick it up. This one is really far gone, dark and sticky in my hand like an exposed organ. A kidney, perhaps. Or some kind of decayed heart. When I look ahead, I see the trunk of the tree. I throw the pear and it smacks the bark, exploding with a sound like a muffled gunshot. I sit in the stillness of the yard for a moment longer, then wipe my palm on the steps and go inside.

"You don't have to stay here," Jimmy says when I return to bed. "If you're having trouble sleeping."

"I've been sleeping fine," I reply. "Something just woke me. That's all."

"What were you doing in the backyard?"

I tell him about finding the pear and the noise it made when it splattered against the tree. I tell him how I've always had good aim, ever since I played in my first softball game as a kid. I flex my arm and he squeezes the small swell of muscle, pretending to be impressed.

"Maybe that's what I'll do tomorrow," he says. "Smash the rest of the pears against the tree." He takes my hand and places it on his chest. "Pop, pop, pop."

"That's one way to get rid of them." I swing my legs over his and ask if he finished sorting the records in his closet, which ones he ended up sending to his friend.

"I mailed him both my Django Reinhardt's."

"Why did you pick those?"

"Because Django has the most interesting story," he replies. "Do you know it?"

I shake my head, my hair rustling against the pillow.

"Django's first wife made paper flowers for a living and one night they all caught on fire. It's said Django knocked over a candle, but of course no one knows for sure. Half his body was badly burned, including his left hand, his guitar hand. His doctors thought he would never play again. But he did. And he became the greatest."

"What does that have to do with your friend?"

"Nothing, really." He brings my hand to his mouth and kisses my fingertips. "I just wanted to share the story with someone. And he lives too far away to drop by for one of those final visits. All the way out in Hawaii, if you can believe it."

A light rain begins to fall. We both turn quiet. I hear the barking dog again. I can't tell which end of the street it's coming from, the noise all at once distant and immediate. Soon Jimmy's breathing becomes hushed, and I know he's drifted off. I keep my hand on his chest. His bones shift beneath his skin.

When I get to work the next day, the fat man says we need to talk. I stand in front of his desk, since there are no other chairs in the trailer. The welt on my neck is still large, and the color has deepened into a purplish red. I wonder if he's giving me another customer with a special request.

"Jean," he begins, and I realize it's the first time he's ever said my name. I know right away that this isn't about a new assignment. It's always a bad sign when someone who never says your name suddenly starts. "Your last customer wasn't satisfied with his Bigfoot experience."

I tell him how difficult it was to wait for so long, how I kept dipping in and out of character, how I was so used to being the attacker, I couldn't keep the same momentum while pretending to be prey. I promise to work on this angle, to stand in my backyard and practice waiting.

He shakes his head, round and pale as a cantaloupe. "No," he says. "That's not the problem."

"What did the man say?"

"He said you fell like a girl."

I tell him that's impossible. I explain how I deliberately let my torso hit the ground first, the way Bigfoot would, and refrained from shoving out an arm to lessen the impact. "I know how to fall," I tell him.

"The man said you flailed your arms and squealed. He said the moment you fell, he knew it was a woman in costume, not Bigfoot. And the dream was broken."

I point at the welt on my neck. "He shot me two more times while I was on the ground."

The fat man shrugs. "Maybe he doesn't like women."

I open the closet and push through the other Bigfoot costumes, looking for mine. It's smaller than the rest and has my initials written on the tag. The fat man had it specially made for me, with lifts in the feet and extra padding sewn into the body. When I don't find it, I shut the door and press my lips together.

"I almost had to give him a refund." He rises from his chair. "Sorry, Jean."

He's being nice enough to not fire me directly, to let me figure it out for myself, so I don't give him a hard time. I don't yank the other costumes from the hangers. I don't swipe my arm across his desk. I don't strike a match and set the whole place on fire. I nod and thank him for giving me a chance, then open the door and go outside. The sky is a deep, cloudless blue. The winds are high, and gray dust rises around me, as though I'm standing in the quiet center of a storm.

*

I've been walking for twenty minutes and haven't seen a single person on the road. It's three miles from the park to my house. The wind keeps blowing specks of dirt into my eyes. Normally I drive, but today I felt like being outside. And after getting fired, I'm glad I have to walk; parts of my body feel so heavy, I worry if I sat down for too long, I'd never get up.

I find myself thinking of things that haven't come into my mind for months. Like how I was married once, to a guy who lived in my neighborhood in Tacoma. We eloped to Las Vegas and were married in a tiny white chapel. It lasted for less than a year. I always knew he was seeing another woman when I asked why he was late or who was on the phone and he began laughing uncontrollably and tugging the collar of his shirt. He had such a terrible game face, it was almost charming. He kept a stack of pornography underneath our bed and one time I sat on the carpeted floor and looked at the magazines, nothing but pages and pages of women kissing each other. I tried to not let his collection bother me, but, of course, it always did. Once I asked him to explain why he insisted on keeping all those magazines, but he wasn't able to give a reason that made sense. It's just what we do, he told me.

I worked in a bottle factory back then and painted houses on the weekends, so I know there are other things I can do for money. Maybe I can get a job at the local fairgrounds, transform myself into one of the clowns or magicians I've seen roaming the weekend carnivals, paint stars around my eyes and drape a black cape across my shoulders. What I really want is someplace balmy and hillless. Someplace where it never rains and the dirt smells like salt and seagrass. That is, of course, if it weren't for Jimmy.

It's occurred to me that part of his appeal is the guarantee — as much as anything can be guaranteed — that he will love me and only me for the rest of his life. He will die loving me. By default, of course — he doesn't have the time or energy to find someone else. But if I could grant him more years, enough time to make it likely that he would abandon me for another woman or at least have a brief dalliance, probably with the college girl that lives down the street and likes to ride her bike in shorts and a bikini top, I would do it. I said this to him one night, when we were in the backyard, underneath the tree, telling the truth for once. Then you do love me after all, he replied, a smile spreading across his hollowed face. And I wondered if he might be right.

A red truck passes on the road, flecking my skin with gravel. The wind has settled. The sky is still a clear blue, the brightness of the sun muted by some transparent sheet of cloud. It isn't long before I see the low peak of Jimmy's house in the distance.

"I need to get in the water," he tells me when I turn up at his door. His eyes are wild and determined. I worry he's beginning to get delirious, which the doctors told him might happen toward the end.

"You're cracked," I say. "You get tired after picking up a few pears in the backyard."

"There's a lake twenty minutes down the road," he says. "I need you to drive me." He steps onto the porch and closes the door behind him.

"But you could get a cold," I protest. A cold for Jimmy could be deadly. "And then you'll be back in the hospital, which is exactly where you don't want to be."

"I had that dream again," he says, glossing over my practical concerns. "Where the world is a pool of cool water. I woke knowing I had to go to the lake today." He looks longingly across the street, at my dented gray car. "And anyway, my body is where I don't want to be, but there's no changing that, now is there?"

"I'm really low on gas."

He steps off the porch. "There's a station on the way."

"Remember when you told me you never learned to swim?"

"I don't know how to swim," he says. "But you do."

He walks across the street and, knowing I usually leave my car unlocked, opens the door and eases himself into the passenger seat. When I hesitate, he honks the horn. I wonder if he's just trying to make everything go more quickly and has decided to enlist my help. Today it's swimming, tomorrow skydiving. The thought paralyses me. It's an effort for him to sit at the kitchen table or on the porch for a few hours. After we make love, which we're doing less and less, he rolls onto his side and plunges into a deep sleep, as though he's been drugged. I hear the engine start, which means he's found the keys in the cupholder. I consider telling him I've just been fired and don't feel like swimming, but he wouldn't care. And he shouldn't. He honks the horn again. I sprint across the street and join him.

I park underneath a sequoia and toss the keys into the glove compartment. I watch Jimmy get out of the car and walk to the edge of the lake, moving with all the speed he can muster. The late afternoon sunlight pours through the windshield, illuminating the ridge of dust on the dashboard. I lean forward and blow; the particles scatter and hang in the air like the petals of a molting dandelion.

I leave the car and stand with Jimmy on the bank of the lake. He removes his shoes and t-shirt, then begins to unbutton his jeans. He asks me to take off my clothes. The lake is half a mile from the main road and surrounded by trees and dark green bushes. I feel emboldened by the enclosure and slip out of my shorts and blouse. I fold our clothes and place them on the knotted roots of a tree, align our shoes so they're side by side. Once he's naked, Jimmy slowly wades into the lake, extending his arms for balance. I wait until his knees disappear into the water, then follow. It's cold at first and my skin goes numb after just a few minutes.

"This is too shallow," he says. "Let's go out there." He points to the thick darkness in the center of the lake.

"That will be too deep," I tell him. "You won't be able to stand."

"I don't want to feel anything underneath me." He tucks a loose strand of hair behind my ear. His wet hand slides down my throat and rests against my collarbone. "Will you teach me to float?"

"I'll do my best," I say, meaning it. "But we have to start in the shallow water."

He nods. I tell him to let his body go slack. He relaxes a little, but it's not enough. I tell him to let himself sink and when the water rises over his shoulders, I place my hands underneath his back and turn his body horizontal. We manage this in one graceful movement, like synchronized swimmers rehearsing a number.

"The trick is to let your arms and legs dangle, but keep your back firm."

"I can do that," he says.

I take away my hands and after he's floated on his own for a while,

I grip his upper arms and swim into the deep water. I tell him to close his eyes, to not think about trying to stay above water, to pretend my hands are still pressing against his spine. The muscles in my thighs burn from treading and holding onto Jimmy. His hair is glossy and black, his eyelashes long and curved. I can see the teardrop shape of his cheekbones, the green and purple veins in his face. He looks so delicate I almost consider dragging him back to shore, but I know that's simply not possible now. After we reach the center of the lake, I release his arms. His position in the water doesn't change, a good sign. I drift backwards and tell him to open his eyes.

"The sky is spinning," he says.

I tilt my head back and the water swallows the ends of my hair. I see a huge cloud that resembles a mountain range and recall his wish to visit the Grand Canyon. Perhaps the failure to make that journey explains his persistence today, his refusal to grant himself the opportunity to be dissuaded. Maybe he has grown tired of seeing things only in dreams.

"How far out are we?"

"All the way in the center," I reply. "But don't look. It will break your focus." For once, he listens to me.

The sun is beginning to drop, a brilliant orange disc with liquid borders. Jimmy is floating on his back, staring up at the sky. His lips are turning blue, but I don't say anything. I've never seen anyone learn to float so quickly before, but maybe people learn faster when they don't have much time. Time. I've grown to hate that word. I think of it often, how much is wasted, how freeing it would be if we weren't always counting. I look at Jimmy, his skin excruciatingly white against the dark water, and wonder if he's stopped paying attention to time, if he's resigned himself to allowing the days to pass until they don't anymore. I think of what he said back at the house, about how his body is where he doesn't want to be, how neither of us are where we want to be, yet somehow, at this moment, we are.

"Will you roar for me?" he asks.

I shift in the water, creating small ripples that push his body farther away.

"Your Bigfoot roar," he continues. "I want to hear an echo."

"I can't."

"Why not?"

"I was fired today." I touch the bump on my neck; it's down to the size of a grape.

He's quiet for a minute. He doesn't move in the water and I'm proud of him for maintaining his concentration. "That doesn't matter," he finally says. "You can still be Bigfoot."

"It's not as convincing without the costume. I've told you this before."

"Then imagine it," he says. "You're supposed to be an actress, right?"

I shut my eyes and picture Bigfoot lumbering through the forest, more alone than any human could grasp. I imagine the weight of his solitude. I open my mouth and fill my lungs with air, then arch my back and push it all out. The noise that comes from my body is unlike anything I've ever heard before. It beats against the thinning branches and the fall air, shoots toward the clouds like smoke. The echoes last for a long time, the vibrations moving across my skin like electrical currents. When I open my eyes, the lake and treetops are washed in a blue darkness.

Jimmy has floated out of my reach, but I don't swim after him. When the crescent moon turns luminous, he asks to be taken back to the car. I guide him to the shore and once he's on dry land, he crouches and begins to shiver violently. I scold myself for not bringing a blanket or towels and try to get him to at least put on his clothes. But he shakes his head and asks me to help him wait it out. It will pass, he tells me. I'm being tested, I realize, to see how long I can endure suffering in another person. I bend over and press my hand between his shoulder blades, feeling all the slender ligaments and bones a healthy body conceals. The moonlight makes the lake glow like an enormous black pearl. The soft skin on my stomach hardens with goosebumps. The night is quiet, save for the sound of Jimmy's rapid breath. I kneel next to him, the damp leaves sticking to my knees. I look down at Jimmy's thigh, at the dirt smudged across the pale stretch of skin; I brush it away, the grit damp and cool on my fingers. I bring my hand to my lips and let the dirt melt off my fingertips, tasting the bitterness and metal. The moon shifts and the grass ahead catches silver, the light passing over us and away.

■

Pearls Before Breakfast

FROM *The Washington Post*

HE EMERGED FROM THE Metro at the L'Enfant Plaza Station and positioned himself against a wall beside a trash basket. By most measures, he was nondescript: a youngish white man in jeans, a long-sleeved T-shirt and a Washington Nationals baseball cap. From a small case, he removed a violin. Placing the open case at his feet, he shrewdly threw in a few dollars and pocket change as seed money, swiveled it to face pedestrian traffic, and began to play.

It was 7:51 A.M. on Friday, January 12, the middle of the morning rush hour. In the next forty-three minutes, as the violinist performed six classical pieces, 1,097 people passed by. Almost all of them were on the way to work, which meant, for almost all of them, a government job. L'Enfant Plaza is at the nucleus of federal Washington, and these were mostly mid-level bureaucrats with those indeterminate, oddly fungible titles: policy analyst, project manager, budget officer, specialist, facilitator, consultant.

Each passerby had a quick choice to make, one familiar to commuters in any urban area where the occasional street performer is part of the cityscape: Do you stop and listen? Do you hurry past with a blend of guilt and irritation, aware of your cupidity but annoyed by the unbidden demand on your time and your wallet? Do you throw in a buck, just to be polite? Does your decision change if he's really bad? What if he's really good? Do you have time for beauty? Shouldn't you? What's the moral mathematics of the moment?

On that Friday in January, those private questions would be answered in an unusually public way. No one knew it, but the fiddler standing against a bare wall outside the Metro in an indoor arcade at the top of the escalators was one of the finest classical musicians in the world, playing some of the most elegant music ever written on one of the most valuable violins ever made. His performance was arranged by the *Washington Post* as an experiment in context, perception, and priorities — as well as an unblinking assessment of public taste: in a banal setting at an inconvenient time, would beauty transcend?

The musician did not play popular tunes whose familiarity alone might have drawn interest. That was not the test. These were masterpieces that have endured for centuries on their brilliance alone, soaring music befitting the grandeur of cathedrals and concert halls.

The acoustics proved surprisingly kind. Though the arcade is of utilitarian design, a buffer between the Metro escalator and the outdoors, it somehow caught the sound and bounced it back round and resonant. The violin is an instrument that is said to be much like the human voice, and in this musician's masterly hands, it sobbed and laughed and sang — ecstatic, sorrowful, importuning, adoring, flirtatious, castigating, playful, romancing, merry, triumphal, sumptuous.

So, what do you think happened?

Hang on, we'll get you some expert help.

Leonard Slatkin, music director of the National Symphony Orchestra, was asked the same question. What did he think would occur, hypothetically, if one of the world's great violinists had performed incognito before a traveling rush-hour audience of one-thousand-odd people?

"Let's assume," Slatkin said, "that he is not recognized and just taken for granted as a street musician. . . . Still, I don't think that if he's really good, he's going to go unnoticed. He'd get a larger audience in Europe . . . but, okay, out of one thousand people, my guess is there might be thirty-five or forty who will recognize the quality for what it is. Maybe seventy-five to one hundred will stop and spend some time listening."

So, a crowd would gather?

"Oh, yes."

And how much will he make?

"About $150."

Thanks, Maestro. As it happens, this is not hypothetical. It really happened.

"How'd I do?"

We'll tell you in a minute.

"Well, who was the musician?"

Joshua Bell.

"NO!!!"

A onetime child prodigy, at thirty-nine Joshua Bell has arrived as an internationally acclaimed virtuoso. Three days before he appeared at the Metro station, Bell had filled the house at Boston's stately Symphony Hall, where merely pretty good seats went for $100. Two weeks later, at the Music Center at Strathmore, in North Bethesda, he would play to a standing-room-only audience so respectful of his artistry that they stifled their coughs until the silence between movements. But on that Friday in January, Joshua Bell was just another mendicant, competing for the attention of busy people on their way to work.

Bell was first pitched this idea shortly before Christmas, over coffee at a sandwich shop on Capitol Hill. A New Yorker, he was in town to perform at the Library of Congress and to visit the library's vaults to examine an unusual treasure: an eighteenth-century violin that once belonged to the great Austrian-born virtuoso and composer Fritz Kreisler. The curators invited Bell to play it; good sound, still.

"Here's what I'm thinking," Bell confided, as he sipped his coffee. "I'm thinking that I could do a tour where I'd play Kreisler's music . . ."

He smiled.

". . . on Kreisler's violin."

It was a snazzy, sequined idea — part inspiration and part gimmick — and it was typical of Bell, who has unapologetically embraced showmanship even as his concert career has become more and more august. He's soloed with the finest orchestras here and abroad, but he's also appeared on *Sesame Street*, done late-night talk TV, and performed in feature films. That was Bell playing the soundtrack on the

1998 movie *The Red Violin*. (He body-doubled, too, playing to a naked Greta Scacchi.) As composer John Corigliano accepted the Oscar for Best Original Dramatic Score, he credited Bell, who, he said, "plays like a god."

When Bell was asked if he'd be willing to don street clothes and perform at rush hour, he said:

"Uh, a stunt?"

Well, yes. A stunt. Would he think it . . . unseemly?

Bell drained his cup.

"Sounds like fun," he said.

Bell's a heartthrob. Tall and handsome, he's got a Donny Osmond–like dose of the cutes, and, onstage, cute elides into *hott*. When he performs, he is usually the only man under the lights who is not in white tie and tails — he walks out to a standing O, looking like Zorro, in black pants and an untucked black dress shirt, shirttail dangling. That cute Beatles-style mop top is also a strategic asset: because his technique is full of body — athletic and passionate — he's almost dancing with the instrument, and his hair flies.

He's single and straight, a fact not lost on some of his fans. In Boston, as he performed Max Bruch's dour Violin Concerto in G Minor, the very few young women in the audience nearly disappeared in the deep sea of silver heads. But seemingly every single one of them — a distillate of the young and pretty — coalesced at the stage door after the performance, seeking an autograph. It's like that always, with Bell.

Bell's been accepting over-the-top accolades since puberty: *Interview* magazine once said his playing "does nothing less than tell human beings why they bother to live." He's learned to field these things graciously, with a bashful duck of the head and a modified "pshaw."

For this incognito performance, Bell had only one condition for participating. The event had been described to him as a test of whether, in an incongruous context, ordinary people would recognize genius. His condition: "I'm not comfortable if you call this genius." *Genius* is an overused word, he said: It can be applied to some of the composers whose work he plays, but not to him. His skills are largely interpretive, he said, and to imply otherwise would be unseemly and inaccurate.

It was an interesting request, and under the circumstances, one that will be honored. The word will not again appear in this article.

It would be breaking no rules, however, to note that the term in question, particularly as applied in the field of music, refers to a congenital brilliance — an elite, innate, preternatural ability that manifests itself early, and often in dramatic fashion.

One biographically intriguing fact about Bell is that he got his first music lessons when he was a four-year-old in Bloomington, Indiana. His parents, both psychologists, decided formal training might be a good idea after they saw that their son had strung rubber bands across his dresser drawers and was replicating classical tunes by ear, moving drawers in and out to vary the pitch.

To get the Metro from his hotel, a distance of three blocks, Bell took a taxi. He's neither lame nor lazy: he did it for his violin.

Bell always performs on the same instrument, and he ruled out using another for this gig. Called the Gibson ex Huberman, it was handcrafted in 1713 by Antonio Stradivari during the Italian master's "golden period," toward the end of his career, when he had access to the finest spruce, maple, and willow, and when his technique had been refined to perfection.

"Our knowledge of acoustics is still incomplete," Bell said, "but he, he just . . . *knew*."

Bell doesn't mention Stradivari by name. Just "he." When the violinist shows his Strad to people, he holds the instrument gingerly by its neck, resting it on a knee. "He made this to perfect thickness at all parts," Bell says, pivoting it. "If you shaved off a millimeter of wood at any point, it would totally imbalance the sound." No violins sound as wonderful as Strads from the 1710s, still.

The front of Bell's violin is in nearly perfect condition, with a deep, rich grain and luster. The back is a mess, its dark reddish finish bleeding away into a flatter, lighter shade and finally, in one section, to bare wood.

"This has never been refinished," Bell said. "That's his original varnish. People attribute aspects of the sound to the varnish. Each maker had his own secret formula." Stradivari is thought to have made his from an ingeniously balanced cocktail of honey, egg whites, and gum arabic from sub-Saharan trees.

Like the instrument in *The Red Violin*, this one has a past filled with mystery and malice. Twice, it was stolen from its illustrious prior owner, the Polish virtuoso Bronislaw Huberman. The first time, in 1919, it disappeared from Huberman's hotel room in Vienna but was quickly returned. The second time, nearly twenty years later, it was pinched from his dressing room in Carnegie Hall. He never got it back. It was not until 1985 that the thief — a minor New York violinist — made a deathbed confession to his wife and produced the instrument.

Bell bought it a few years ago. He had to sell his own Strad and borrow much of the rest. The price tag was reported to be about $3.5 million.

All of which is a long explanation for why, in the early morning chill of a day in January, Josh Bell took a three-block cab ride to the Orange Line and rode one stop to L'Enfant.

As Metro stations go, L'Enfant Plaza is more plebeian than most. Even before you arrive, it gets no respect. Metro conductors never seem to get it right: "Leh-fahn." "Layfont." "El'phant."

At the top of the escalators are a shoeshine stand and a busy kiosk that sells newspapers, lottery tickets, and a wall full of magazines with titles such as *Mammazons* and *Girls of Barely Legal*. The skin mags move, but it's that lottery ticket dispenser that stays the busiest, with customers queuing up for Daily 6 lotto and Powerball and the ultimate suckers' bait, those pamphlets that sell random number combinations purporting to be "hot." They sell briskly. There's also a quick-check machine to slide in your lotto ticket, post-drawing, to see if you've won. Beneath it is a forlorn pile of crumpled slips.

On Friday, January 12, the people waiting in the lottery line looking for a long shot would get a lucky break — a free, close-up ticket to a concert by one of the world's most famous musicians — but only if they were of a mind to take note.

Bell decided to begin with "Chaconne" from Johann Sebastian Bach's Partita No. 2 in D Minor. Bell calls it "not just one of the greatest pieces of music ever written, but one of the greatest achievements of any man in history. It's a spiritually powerful piece, emotionally powerful, structurally perfect. Plus, it was written for a solo violin, so I won't be cheating with some half-assed version."

Bell didn't say it, but Bach's "Chaconne" is also considered one of the most difficult violin pieces to master. Many try; few succeed. It's exhaustingly long — fourteen minutes — and consists entirely of a single, succinct musical progression repeated in dozens of variations to create a dauntingly complex architecture of sound. Composed around 1720, on the eve of the European Enlightenment, it is said to be a celebration of the breadth of human possibility.

If Bell's encomium to "Chaconne" seems overly effusive, consider this from the nineteenth-century composer Johannes Brahms, in a letter to Clara Schumann: "On one stave, for a small instrument, the man writes a whole world of the deepest thoughts and most powerful feelings. If I imagined that I could have created, even conceived the piece, I am quite certain that the excess of excitement and earth-shattering experience would have driven me out of my mind."

So, that's the piece Bell started with.

He'd clearly meant it when he promised not to cheap out this performance: He played with acrobatic enthusiasm, his body leaning into the music and arching on tiptoes at the high notes. The sound was nearly symphonic, carrying to all parts of the homely arcade as the pedestrian traffic filed past.

Three minutes went by before something happened. Sixty-three people had already passed when, finally, there was a breakthrough of sorts. A middle-aged man altered his gait for a split second, turning his head to notice that there seemed to be some guy playing music. Yes, the man kept walking, but it was *something*.

A half-minute later, Bell got his first donation. A woman threw in a buck and scooted off. It was not until six minutes into the performance that someone actually stood against a wall, and listened.

Things never got much better. In the three-quarters of an hour that Joshua Bell played, seven people stopped what they were doing to hang around and take in the performance, at least for a minute. Twenty-seven gave money, most of them on the run — for a total of $32 and change. That leaves the 1,070 people who hurried by, oblivious, many only three feet away, few even turning to look.

No, Mr. Slatkin, there was never a crowd, not even for a second.

It was all videotaped by a hidden camera. You can play the recording once or fifteen times, and it never gets any easier to watch. Try speeding it up, and it becomes one of those herky-jerky World War I– era silent newsreels. The people scurry by in comical little hops and starts, cups of coffee in their hands, cell phones at their ears, ID tags slapping at their bellies, a grim *danse macabre* to indifference, inertia, and the dingy, gray rush of modernity.

Even at this accelerated pace, though, the fiddler's movements remain fluid and graceful; he seems so apart from his audience — unseen, unheard, otherworldly — that you find yourself thinking that he's not really there. A ghost.

Only then do you see it: He is the one who is real. They are the ghosts.

If a great musician plays great music but no one hears . . . was he really any good?

It's an old epistemological debate, older, actually, than the koan about the tree in the forest. Plato weighed in on it, and philosophers for two millennia afterward: What is beauty? Is it a measurable fact (Gottfried Leibniz), or merely an opinion (David Hume), or is it a little of each, colored by the immediate state of mind of the observer (Immanuel Kant)?

We'll go with Kant, because he's obviously right, and because he brings us pretty directly to Joshua Bell, sitting there in a hotel restaurant, picking at his breakfast, wryly trying to figure out what the hell had just happened back there at the Metro.

"At the beginning," Bell says, "I was just concentrating on playing the music. I wasn't really watching what was happening around me . . ."

Playing the violin looks all-consuming, mentally and physically, but Bell says that for him the mechanics of it are partly second nature, cemented by practice and muscle memory: it's like a juggler, he says, who can keep those balls in play while interacting with a crowd. What he's mostly thinking about as he plays, Bell says, is capturing emotion as a narrative: "When you play a violin piece, you are a storyteller, and you're telling a story."

With "Chaconne," the opening is filled with a building sense of awe. That kept him busy for a while. Eventually, though, he began to steal a sidelong glance.

"It was a strange feeling, that people were actually, ah . . ."

The word doesn't come easily.

". . . *ignoring* me."

Bell is laughing. It's at himself.

"At a music hall, I'll get upset if someone coughs or if someone's cell phone goes off. But here, my expectations quickly diminished. I started to appreciate *any* acknowledgment, even a slight glance up. I was oddly grateful when someone threw in a dollar instead of change." This is from a man whose talents can command $1,000 a minute.

Before he began, Bell hadn't known what to expect. What he does know is that, for some reason, he was nervous.

"It wasn't exactly stage fright, but there were butterflies," he says. "I was stressing a little."

Bell has played, literally, before crowned heads of Europe. Why the anxiety at the Washington Metro?

"When you play for ticket-holders," Bell explains, "you are already validated. I have no sense that I need to be accepted. I'm already accepted. Here, there was this thought: *What if they don't like me? What if they resent my presence . . .*"

He was, in short, art without a frame. Which, it turns out, may have a lot to do with what happened — or, more precisely, what didn't happen — on January 12.

Mark Leithauser has held in his hands more great works of art than any king or pope or Medici ever did. A senior curator at the National Gallery, he oversees the framing of the paintings. Leithauser thinks he has some idea of what happened at that Metro station.

"Let's say I took one of our more abstract masterpieces, say an Ellsworth Kelly, and removed it from its frame, marched it down the fifty-two steps that people walk up to get to the National Gallery, past the giant columns, and brought it into a restaurant. It's a $5 million painting. And it's one of those restaurants where there are pieces of original art for sale, by some industrious kids from the Corcoran

School, and I hang that Kelly on the wall with a price tag of $150. No one is going to notice it. An art curator might look up and say: 'Hey, that looks a little like an Ellsworth Kelly. Please pass the salt.'"

Leithauser's point is that we shouldn't be too ready to label the Metro passersby unsophisticated boobs. Context matters.

Kant said the same thing. He took beauty seriously: In his *Critique of Aesthetic Judgment*, Kant argued that one's ability to appreciate beauty is related to one's ability to make moral judgments. But there was a caveat. Paul Guyer of the University of Pennsylvania, one of America's most prominent Kantian scholars, says the eighteenth-century German philosopher felt that to properly appreciate beauty, the viewing conditions must be optimal.

"Optimal," Guyer said, "doesn't mean heading to work, focusing on your report to the boss, maybe your shoes don't fit right."

So, if Kant had been at the Metro watching as Joshua Bell play to a thousand unimpressed passersby?

"He would have inferred about them," Guyer said, "absolutely nothing."

And that's that.

Except it isn't. To really understand what happened, you have to rewind that video and play it back from the beginning, from the moment Bell's bow first touched the strings.

White guy, khakis, leather jacket, briefcase. Early thirties. John David Mortensen is on the final leg of his daily bus-to-Metro commute from Reston. He's heading up the escalator. It's a long ride — one minute and fifteen seconds if you don't walk. So, like most everyone who passes Bell this day, Mortensen gets a good earful of music before he has his first look at the musician. Like most of them, he notes that it sounds pretty good. But like very few of them, when he gets to the top, he doesn't race past as though Bell were some nuisance to be avoided. Mortensen is that first person to stop, that guy at the six-minute mark.

It's not that he has nothing else to do. He's a project manager for an international program at the Department of Energy; on this day, Mortensen has to participate in a monthly budget exercise, not the most exciting part of his job: "You review the past month's expenditures," he says, "forecast spending for the next month, if you have X dollars, where will it go, that sort of thing."

On the video, you can see Mortensen get off the escalator and look around. He locates the violinist, stops, walks away but then is drawn back. He checks the time on his cell phone — he's three minutes early for work — then settles against a wall to listen.

Mortensen doesn't know classical music at all; classic rock is as close as he comes. But there's something about what he's hearing that he really likes.

As it happens, he's arrived at the moment that Bell slides into the second section of "Chaconne." ("It's the point," Bell says, "where it moves from a darker, minor key into a major key. There's a religious, exalted feeling to it.") The violinist's bow begins to dance; the music becomes upbeat, playful, theatrical, big.

Mortensen doesn't know about major or minor keys: "Whatever it was," he says, "it made me feel at peace."

So, for the first time in his life, Mortensen lingers to listen to a street musician. He stays his allotted three minutes as ninety-four more people pass briskly by. When he leaves to help plan contingency budgets for the Department of Energy, there's another first. For the first time in his life, not quite knowing what had just happened but sensing it was special, John David Mortensen gives a street musician money.

There are six moments in the video that Bell finds particularly painful to relive: "The awkward times," he calls them. It's what happens right after each piece ends: nothing. The music stops. The same people who hadn't noticed him playing don't notice that he has finished. No applause, no acknowledgment. So Bell just saws out a small, nervous chord — the embarrassed musician's equivalent of, "Er, okay, moving right along . . ." — and begins the next piece.

After "Chaconne," it is Franz Schubert's "Ave Maria," which surprised some music critics when it debuted in 1825: Schubert seldom showed religious feeling in his compositions, yet "Ave Maria" is a breathtaking work of adoration of the Virgin Mary. What was with the sudden piety? Schubert dryly answered: "I think this is due to the fact that I never forced devotion in myself and never compose hymns or prayers of that kind unless it overcomes me unawares; but then it is usually the right and true devotion." This musical prayer became among the most familiar and enduring religious pieces in history.

A couple of minutes into it, something revealing happens. A woman and her preschooler emerge from the escalator. The woman is walking briskly and, therefore, so is the child. She's got his hand.

"I had a time crunch," recalls Sheron Parker, an IT director for a federal agency. "I had an 8:30 A.M. training class, and first I had to rush Evvie off to his teacher, then rush back to work, then to the training facility in the basement."

Evvie is her son, Evan. Evan is three.

You can see Evan clearly on the video. He's the cute black kid in the parka who keeps twisting around to look at Joshua Bell, as he is being propelled toward the door.

"There was a musician," Parker says, "and my son was intrigued. He wanted to pull over and listen, but I was rushed for time."

So Parker does what she has to do. She deftly moves her body between Evan's and Bell's, cutting off her son's line of sight. As they exit the arcade, Evan can still be seen craning to look. When Parker is told what she walked out on, she laughs.

"Evan is very smart!"

The poet Billy Collins once laughingly observed that all babies are born with a knowledge of poetry, because the lub-dub of the mother's heart is in iambic meter. Then, Collins said, life slowly starts to choke the poetry out of us. It may be true with music, too.

There was no ethnic or demographic pattern to distinguish the people who stayed to watch Bell, or the ones who gave money, from that vast majority who hurried on past, unheeding. Whites, blacks, and Asians, young and old, men and women, were represented in all three groups. But the behavior of one demographic remained absolutely consistent. Every single time a child walked past, he or she tried to stop and watch. And every single time, a parent scooted the kid away.

If there was one person on that day who was too busy to pay attention to the violinist, it was George Tindley. Tindley wasn't hurrying to get to work. He was at work.

The glass doors through which most people exit the L'Enfant Station lead into an indoor shopping mall, from which there are exits to the street and elevators to office buildings. The first store in the mall is an Au Bon Pain, the croissant and coffee shop where Tindley, in his forties, works in a white uniform busing the tables, restocking the salt and pepper packets, taking out the garbage. Tindley labors under the watchful eye of his bosses, and he's supposed to be hopping, and he was.

But every minute or so, as though drawn by something not entirely within his control, Tindley would walk to the very edge of the Au Bon Pain property, keeping his toes inside the line, still on the job. Then he'd lean forward, as far out into the hallway as he could, watching the fiddler on the other side of the glass doors. The foot traffic was steady, so the doors were usually open. The sound came through pretty well.

"You could tell in one second that this guy was good, that he was clearly a professional," Tindley says. He plays the guitar, loves the sound of strings, and has no respect for a certain kind of musician.

"Most people, they play music; they don't feel it," Tindley says. "Well, that man was *feeling* it. That man was moving. Moving into the sound."

A hundred feet away, across the arcade, was the lottery line, sometimes five or six people long. They had a much better view of Bell than Tindley did, if they had just turned around. But no one did. Not in the entire forty-three minutes. They just shuffled forward toward that machine spitting out numbers. Eyes on the prize.

J. T. Tillman was in that line. A computer specialist for the Department of Housing and Urban Development, he remembers every single number he played that day — ten of them, $2 apiece, for a total of $20. He doesn't recall what the violinist was playing, though. He says it sounded like generic classical music, the kind the ship's band was playing in *Titanic*, before the iceberg.

"I didn't think nothing of it," Tillman says, "just a guy trying to make a couple of bucks." Tillman would have given him one or two, he said, but he spent all his cash on lotto.

When he is told that he stiffed one of the best musicians in the world, he laughs.

"Is he ever going to play around here again?"

"Yeah, but you're going to have to pay a lot to hear him."

"Damn."

Tillman didn't win the lottery, either.

Bell ends "Ave Maria" to another thunderous silence, plays Manuel Ponce's sentimental "Estrellita," then a piece by Jules Massenet, and then begins a Bach gavotte, a joyful, frolicsome, lyrical dance. It's got an Old World delicacy to it; you can imagine it entertaining bewigged dancers at a Versailles ball, or — in a lute, fiddle, and fife version — the boot-kicking peasants of a Pieter Bruegel painting.

Watching the video weeks later, Bell finds himself mystified by one thing only. He understands why he's not drawing a crowd, in the rush of a morning workday. But: "I'm surprised at the number of people who don't pay attention at all, as if I'm invisible. Because, you know what? I'm makin' a lot of noise!"

He is. You don't need to know music at all to appreciate the simple fact that there's a guy there, playing a violin that's throwing out a whole bucket of sound; at times, Bell's bowing is so intricate that you seem to be hearing two instruments playing in harmony. So those head-forward, quick-stepping passersby are a remarkable phenomenon.

Bell wonders whether their inattention may be deliberate: If you don't take visible note of the musician, you don't have to feel guilty about not forking over money; you're not complicit in a rip-off.

It may be true, but no one gave that explanation. People just said they were busy, had other things on their mind. Some who were on cell phones spoke louder as they passed Bell, to compete with that infernal racket.

And then there was Calvin Myint. Myint works for the General Services Administration. He got to the top of the escalator, turned right and headed out a door to the street. A few hours later, he had no memory that there had been a musician anywhere in sight.

"Where was he, in relation to me?"

"About four feet away."

"Oh."

There's nothing wrong with Myint's hearing. He had buds in his ear. He was listening to his iPod.

For many of us, the explosion in technology has perversely limited, not expanded, our exposure to new experiences. Increasingly, we get our news from sources that think as we already do. And with iPods, we hear what we already know; we program our own playlists.

The song that Calvin Myint was listening to was "Just Like Heaven," by the British rock band The Cure. It's a terrific song, actually. The meaning is a little opaque, and the Web is filled with earnest efforts to deconstruct it. Many are far-fetched, but some are right on point: It's about a tragic emotional disconnect. A man has found the woman of his dreams but can't express the depth of his feeling for her until she's gone. It's about failing to see the beauty of what's plainly in front of your eyes.

"Yes, I saw the violinist," Jackie Hessian says, "but nothing about him struck me as much of anything."

You couldn't tell that by watching her. Hessian was one of those people who gave Bell a long, hard look before walking on. It turns out that she wasn't noticing the music at all.

"I really didn't hear that much," she said. "I was just trying to figure out what he was doing there, how does this work for him, can he make much money, would it be better to start with some money in the case, or for it to be empty, so people feel sorry for you? I was analyzing it financially."

What do you do, Jackie?

"I'm a lawyer in labor relations with the United States Postal Service. I just negotiated a national contract."

The best seats in the house were upholstered. In the balcony, more or less. On that day, for $5, you'd get a lot more than just a nice shine on your shoes.

Only one person occupied one of those seats when Bell played. Terence Holmes is a consultant for the Department of Transportation, and he liked the music just fine, but it was really about a shoeshine: "My father told me never to wear a suit with your shoes not cleaned and shined."

Holmes wears suits often, so he is up in that perch a lot, and he's got a good relationship with the shoeshine lady. Holmes is a good tipper and a good talker, which is a skill that came in handy that day. The shoeshine lady was upset about something, and the music got her more upset. She complained, Holmes said, that the music was too loud, and he tried to calm her down.

Edna Souza is from Brazil. She's been shining shoes at L'Enfant Plaza for six years, and she's had her fill of street musicians there; when they play, she can't hear her customers, and that's bad for business. So she fights.

Souza points to the dividing line between the Metro property, at the top of the escalator, and the arcade, which is under control of the management company that runs the mall. Sometimes, Souza says, a musician will stand on the Metro side, sometimes on the mall side. Either way, she's got him. On her speed dial, she has phone numbers for both the mall cops and the Metro cops. The musicians seldom last long.

What about Joshua Bell?

He was too loud, too, Souza says. Then she looks down at her rag, sniffs. She hates to say anything positive about these damned musicians, but: "He was pretty good, that guy. It was the first time I didn't call the police."

Souza was surprised to learn he was a famous musician, but not that people rushed blindly by him. That, she said, was predictable. "If something like this happened in Brazil, everyone would stand around to see. Not here."

Souza nods sourly toward a spot near the top of the escalator: "Couple of years ago, a homeless guy died right there. He just lay down there and died. The police came, an ambulance came, and no one even stopped to see or slowed down to look.

"People walk up the escalator, they look straight ahead. Mind your own business, eyes forward. Everyone is stressed. Do you know what I mean?"

> *What is this life if, full of care,*
> *We have no time to stand and stare.*
> — from "Leisure," by W. H. Davies

Let's say Kant is right. Let's accept that we can't look at what happened on January 12 and make any judgment whatever about people's sophistication or their ability to appreciate beauty. But what about their ability to appreciate life?

We're busy. Americans have been busy, as a people, since at least 1831, when a young French sociologist named Alexis de Tocqueville visited the States and found himself impressed, bemused, and slightly dismayed at the degree to which people were driven, to the exclusion of everything else, by hard work and the accumulation of wealth.

Not much has changed. Pop in a DVD of *Koyaanisqatsi*, the word-less, darkly brilliant, avant-garde 1982 film about the frenetic speed of modern life. Backed by the minimalist music of Philip Glass, di-rector Godfrey Reggio takes film clips of Americans going about their daily business, but speeds them up until they resemble assem-bly-line machines, robots marching lockstep to nowhere. Now look at the video from L'Enfant Plaza, in fast-forward. The Philip Glass soundtrack fits it perfectly.

Koyaanisqatsi is a Hopi word. It means "life out of balance."

In his 2003 book, *Timeless Beauty: In the Arts and Everyday Life*, British author John Lane writes about the loss of the appreciation for beauty in the modern world. The experiment at L'Enfant Plaza may be symptomatic of that, he said — not because people didn't have the capacity to understand beauty, but because it was irrelevant to them.

"This is about having the wrong priorities," Lane said.

If we can't take the time out of our lives to stay a moment and listen to one of the best musicians on Earth play some of the best music ever written; if the surge of modern life so overpowers us that we are deaf and blind to something like that — then what else are we missing?

That's what the Welsh poet W. H. Davies meant in 1911 when he published those two lines that begin this section. They made him fa-mous. The thought was simple, even primitive, but somehow no one had put it quite that way before.

Of course, Davies had an advantage — an advantage of percep-tion. He wasn't a tradesman or a laborer or a bureaucrat or a consul-tant or a policy analyst or a labor lawyer or a program manager. He was a hobo.

*

The cultural hero of the day arrived at L'Enfant Plaza pretty late, in the unprepossessing figure of one John Picarello, a smallish man with a baldish head.

Picarello hit the top of the escalator just after Bell began his final piece, a reprise of "Chaconne." In the video, you see Picarello stop dead in his tracks, locate the source of the music, and then retreat to the other end of the arcade. He takes up a position past the shoeshine stand, across from that lottery line, and he will not budge for the next nine minutes.

Like all the passersby interviewed for this article, Picarello was stopped by a reporter after he left the building and was asked for his phone number. Like everyone, he was told only that this was to be an article about commuting. When he was called later in the day, like everyone else, he was first asked if anything unusual had happened to him on his trip into work. Of the more than forty people contacted, Picarello was the only one who immediately mentioned the violinist.

"There was a musician playing at the top of the escalator at L'Enfant Plaza."

Haven't you seen musicians there before?

"Not like this one."

What do you mean?

"This was a superb violinist. I've never heard anyone of that caliber. He was technically proficient, with very good phrasing. He had a good fiddle, too, with a big, lush sound. I walked a distance away, to hear him. I didn't want to be intrusive on his space."

Really?

"Really. It was that kind of experience. It was a treat, just a brilliant, incredible way to start the day."

Picarello knows classical music. He is a fan of Joshua Bell but didn't recognize him; he hadn't seen a recent photo, and besides, for most of the time Picarello was pretty far away. But he knew this was not a run-of-the-mill guy out there, performing. On the video, you can see Picarello look around him now and then, almost bewildered.

"Yeah, other people just were not getting it. It just wasn't registering. That was baffling to me."

When Picarello was growing up in New York, he studied violin seriously, intending to be a concert musician. But he gave it up at eighteen, when he decided he'd never be good enough to make it pay. Life does that to you sometimes. Sometimes, you have to do the prudent thing. So he went into another line of work. He's a supervisor at the U.S. Postal Service. Doesn't play the violin much, anymore.

When he left, Picarello says, "I humbly threw in $5." It *was* humble: You can actually see that on the video. Picarello walks up, barely looking at Bell, and tosses in the money. Then, as if embarrassed, he quickly walks away from the man he once wanted to be.

Does he have regrets about how things worked out?

The postal supervisor considers this.

"No. If you love something but choose not to do it professionally, it's not a waste. Because, you know, you still have it. You have it forever."

Bell thinks he did his best work of the day in those final new minutes, in the second "Chaconne." And that also was the first time more than one person at a time was listening. As Picarello stood in the back, Janice Olu arrived and took up a position a few feet away from Bell. Olu, a public trust officer with HUD, also played the violin as a kid. She didn't know the name of the piece she was hearing, but she knew the man playing it has a gift.

Olu was on a coffee break and stayed as long as she dared. As she turned to go, she whispered to the stranger next to her, "I *really* don't want to leave." The stranger standing next to her happened to be working for the *Washington Post*.

In preparing for this event, editors at the *Post Magazine* discussed how to deal with likely outcomes. The most widely held assumption was that there could well be a problem with crowd control: In a demographic as sophisticated as Washington, the thinking went, several people would surely recognize Bell. Nervous "what-if" scenarios abounded. As people gathered, what if others stopped just to see what the attraction was? Word would spread through the crowd. Cameras would flash. More people flock to the scene; rush-hour pedestrian traffic backs up; tempers flare; the National Guard is called; tear gas, rubber bullets, etc.

As it happens, exactly one person recognized Bell, and she didn't arrive until near the very end. For Stacy Furukawa, a demographer at the Commerce Department, there was no doubt. She doesn't know much about classical music, but she had been in the audience three weeks earlier, at Bell's free concert at the Library of Congress. And here he was, the international virtuoso, sawing away, begging for money. She had no idea what the heck was going on, but whatever it was, she wasn't about to miss it.

Furukawa positioned herself ten feet away from Bell, front row, center. She had a huge grin on her face. The grin, and Furukawa, remained planted in that spot until the end.

"It was the most astonishing thing I've ever seen in Washington," Furukawa says. "Joshua Bell was standing there playing at rush hour, and people were not stopping, and not even looking, and some were flipping quarters at him! Quarters! I wouldn't do that to *anybody*. I was thinking, *Omigosh, what kind of a city do I live in that this could happen?*"

When it was over, Furukawa introduced herself to Bell, and tossed in a twenty. Not counting that — it was tainted by recognition — the final haul for his forty-three minutes of playing was $32.17. Yes, some people gave pennies.

"Actually," Bell said with a laugh, "that's not so bad, considering. That's forty bucks an hour. I could make an okay living doing this, and I wouldn't have to pay an agent."

These days, at L'Enfant Plaza, lotto ticket sales remain brisk. Musicians still show up from time to time, and they still tick off Edna Souza. Joshua Bell's latest album, *The Voice of the Violin,* has received the usual critical acclaim. ("Delicate urgency." "Masterful intimacy." "Unfailingly exquisite." "A musical summit." "Will make your heart thump and weep at the same time.")

Bell headed off on a concert tour of European capitals. But he is back in the States this week. He has to be. On Tuesday, he will be accepting the Avery Fisher Prize, recognizing the Flop of L'Enfant Plaza as the best classical musician in America.

■

The Elegant Rube

FROM *Open City*

WALLETS, LADIES. NOW!

That's what the mugger said to Michael and Wade when he ambushed them. They had just come out of a late movie and were rounding the corner onto a residential block when he emerged from some shrubs. The teenaged assailant with lippy peach fuzz and a confusing accent called the brothers *ladies*. He held the grip of some weapon, stuck into his pants at the waistband. Michael dropped his popcorn, which flew up and then scattered onto the pavement. He tossed his wallet to the skittish kid, and then his brother did the same.

Turn around or I'll shoot off your face!

Michael and Wade turned and stood with their arms at their sides until the boy's staccato footsteps grew faint. Because it was late at night in Los Angeles, nobody was there to see them. They looked like life-size wooden soldiers who'd been positioned on the sidewalk and then abandoned. Michael, whose scarecrow body and tentative manner made some women think of poets, stood with his back straight and long. He maximized each distinct vertebra but he still felt delicate in the presence of his brother's much larger body, just inches away. He glanced over at the spiny orange birds-of-paradise that separated one duplex from the next. The flowers looked like plastic from the ninety-nine-cent store — odorless probably, and coated in a fine layer of dust. He conjured up the kid's voice. *I'll shoot off your face* is what he'd said, as though he and Wade shared one face — the meshing, hapless visage of a single victim.

The night on which a crime occurs is always the wrong night — always incongruous, inappropriate, charged with meaning. This night was no exception. It was the brothers' first encounter in nearly a year. In the early days of their estrangement, Michael had been optimistic. Because he couldn't trace it back to a decisive insult, it seemed like an adult's rift — a barely perceptible accumulation of subtle wrongs — rather than a brawl, beef, or blowup. He visualized it as an artery, occluded with the plaque of misunderstanding, until, after too many awkward phone calls and canceled breakfasts, the blood barely pumped.

He could still see the two of them as boys, falling back onto the couch with the loose-limbed ease of brothers. He saw Yoo-Hoo spewing out of each other's noses, he saw Wade spinning Nina Marsak's tiny, mysteriously obtained underpants around his forefinger, and he heard the echo of handballs against the garage. Their parents had believed in the sanctity of the fraternal bond. "When we're gone," they would say, "it'll only be you two." And the boys would answer, "yeah-yeah" as they chased the dog past the TV, slammed bedroom doors papered with raunchy bumper stickers, and slouched sullenly around on Sundays in mismatched socks.

And then their parents were gone — run off the road three years earlier, on their way to San Francisco. It happened north of San Simeon but below Big Sur, the point at which the viscous coastal fog wraps itself around the road like a big gray cat. On childhood car trips, Michael likened this misty stretch of Highway 1 to the Middle Earth in his books, where white cliffs arched and preened, like women getting dressed. It was their parents' favorite strip of the coast, which made Michael feel simultaneously better and worse that they had died there.

Attempts to stay in touch had been sporadic since then. After the accident, the brothers collaborated in the work of death, meeting in corner booths over french fries, cloaking their grief in logistics. Finally, after what felt like months but were in fact only weeks, the affairs of their short, round, easygoing parents had been streamlined into paper statements and reduced to receipts.

The brothers would make casual plans and then break them each time. It had been gnawing at Michael for a year. At home in his bed, after mixing sound for cartoons all day, he wondered about his brother. He'd allow himself one beer for two that were non-alcoholic, and then two reals for one fake and so on. He felt bloated and muzzy-headed, but he rarely got drunk. He spent his days wedged tightly between headphones and in front of screens — rising and falling to the manic, high-speed rhythms of big color and voice. This did sinister things to his nights, when the silence sounded loud and the stillness dizzied him — like sitting in front of a television that had just been turned off, the click and the blackness piercing the center of his forehead: a bindi of sudden quiet.

Michael doubted that Wade was as preoccupied with their estrangement as he was, not because Wade was a bad or callous person, but because his superpower was the ability to make himself slippery, so that nothing ever touched him. Michael assumed he was busy with his own life, which had always been somewhat mysterious. Wade had dropped out of law school and gone into "investments." Michael assumed he earned money making rich people richer. He was defensive and noncommittal when Michael asked.

Had one brother bullied the other or stolen a girlfriend, the situation would have been clearer. But Michael began to understand, during his bedtime alchemy of drinking, and not-drinking, and then drinking, that his problems with Wade were not fixable, and that Wade was a person he wouldn't have known had they not been related. They'd always been comfortable at home with their parents and on holidays in restaurants. They were good at being brothers. Boys. But the family made sense only as a foursome, and now the surviving two were thrust back into the world, maladroit on the skinny legs they'd inherited from their father. There were memories to unearth and stories to tell and retell, but without the parental glue, the brothers had come apart.

Michael called Wade on a Monday night. He made himself sound casual because Wade responded well to lightness. The ease of the call surprised him; they decided on Vincenzi's remastered 1948 triumph of leftist desolation, *The Elegant Rube*. A movie date might have been a strange choice for a potentially tense reunion, but for Michael and Wade it made sense.

Fifteen minutes before the show, Michael arrived to find Wade in his usual seat: middle section, five rows from the front, on the left aisle. It was just the two of them, save for a woman in the front row, with long, wild gray hair and a complicated scarf. The deco sconces that lined the walls were the same ones that stood watch over Michael and Wade's childhood matinees and teenage late shows. Their parents had never understood the boys' interest in revival house fare — often the same movies they'd watched when they were kids — but they were relieved that their very different sons had this in common. Michael's magic lessons and Wade's soccer practice began dwindling in exchange for Westerns and war films at age ten. And during teenage weekends, when Michael painted naked women (although he'd never seen one) and Wade played Atari, they'd line up late at night for the culty, bloody, and bawdy. They'd sit together in that blue-lit space — that timeless, placeless fish tank of shadow and sound. At sixteen, Michael wrote an essay entitled "Breathing Underwater: Ode to the Cinema," in which the viewer watches a movie while pleasantly submerged in the indeterminate space of the theater: a warm, undulating zone of contrast, a fusion of land and sea.

Michael didn't want to creep up on Wade and scare him, so he weighted his gait enough to make it audible as he walked down the aisle.

Wade turned and smiled. He'd gotten fatter.

There was a simian brushing of hands and bumping of limbs against shoulder and knee. Michael sat down.

Wade handed him a half-eaten bar of expensive-looking chocolate. "So?"

"So?" said Michael, who broke off three squares, already wondering where they'd go when the movie ended.

They finished the chocolate too fast. Michael wanted to slow everything down. He wanted them to take their time but he didn't know how to pause and linger in a way that wouldn't alarm Wade.

"You got fat," Michael said.

"I know. All I eat is meat and candy. Mirabelle's putting me on a diet."

Wade had always dated rich girls, who'd been carefully named:

Mirabelle, Tatiana, Tallulah. Whenever Wade mentioned a girlfriend, Michael sensed he'd never be allowed to meet her. He knew little about Mirabelle, even though she and Wade had been dating for some time. She was a rock critic whose not unimpressive trust fund allowed her to work on an extremely part-time basis. There was always a story about Mirabelle's disappointment when some rock legend turned out to be shockingly dull in person.

Michael tried to formulate a question about Mirabelle that would shepherd them past the small talk, but Wade maneuvered the discussion back to familiar territory.

"Remember when we tried to freeze our nose hairs, like dad?" he asked. He was referring to a story their father had told repeatedly: an army story. He was stationed at Fort Devins in the middle of a bad Massachusetts winter. While marching back and forth on the parade ground one frigid, windy morning, he felt his nose dripping. He reached up with a gloved hand and squeezed it, wincing at the sharp pain inside his nostrils: his nose hairs had frozen into glasslike shards. He began to bleed as he marched. It was a morning of bleeding and marching, bleeding and marching: a wretched moment in a relatively comfortable life. He thought the story might ensure that his boys chose college over the service, although there was never any real danger that they wouldn't. What the story did do was encourage the boys to freeze their own nose hairs by shoving crushed ice from the refrigerator up their nostrils.

"Popcorn?" Michael asked, and with Wade's mildly irritating double thumbs-up, he left for the concession stand.

In line in the lobby, Michael studied the posters for the Vincenzi retrospective. They were all pop art and primary colors, as if to dupe today's moviegoers into thinking that the bleak neo-realist world of Vincenzi might be kitschy and mod. And the films' English titles had all been changed. *Crime Tale* was now *Riotous Corpse,* and *God Is Here* became *The Boss of Us.* The strangest of all was the movie they were about to see; the gently wrenching *The Elegant Rube* had been renamed *Uncle Paolo Is No Criminal.* Michael paid for the popcorn, pumped it full of liquid butter, and told himself to tell Wade about the title.

There was no one new in the theater, still just the wild-haired woman. Her ragged attractiveness, coupled with the fact that she sat alone and in front, made her seem self-possessed, European, and a little morose. She had begun to read a book.

"But Uncle Paolo's a minor character," said Wade with a mouth full of popcorn.

"What I don't understand," said Michael "is why *Uncle Paolo Is No Criminal* is a better title than *The Elegant Rube*."

"It's his best film," said Wade.

"I like the later ones, after the stroke."

"But he was paralyzed. Dude couldn't even talk!"

"He said those were the movies he'd always wanted to make, that he wasn't a genius until he had the stroke."

The European woman whipped her head around as though startled by a loud noise and surveyed the brothers before returning to her book. Michael had mentally named the woman "Veronique," but then he changed it to "Simone."

The lights faded, which meant that in two minutes it would be dark. Michael stuffed a fistful of popcorn into his mouth and then rubbed his palms together so that the butter and salt stung the chapped grooves. He felt a fluid surge of trust in the next two and a half hours, as though he'd just taken a Valium on an empty stomach. He and Wade would sit there like they always had, snug in each other's idiosyncratic breathing and the periodic shifting of weight. They'd swell and break in tandem, like wrestling on the kitchen floor or kneeling over Tinkertoys, the stove popping with the first sounds of dinner. And after the movie they'd sit in silence for as long as they could stand it. They'd wait for the theater to empty and then they'd look at each other and smile — exhaling — slightly embarrassed at having just seen something great. They'd walk their identical hunched-over walk up the aisle, through the ancient lobby with its flocked wallpaper and whorehouse candelabras, and they'd rejoin the night. And before they began their postmortem, they'd look at each other again and just say, "Wow."

Wallets, ladies. Now!

Turn around or I'll shoot off your face.

They stood there until they believed the kid was really gone. Then they turned around and walked ten feet to the tub of popcorn and its splayed contents. The pieces of popcorn looked violated, as if they'd been alive before and now they were not.

"Great," said Michael, hands in his pockets.

Wade reached up and fingered the cartilage of his upper ear, a habit he'd had since he was a kid. "I think he was Latvian," he said. They weren't far from the Baltic section of town. "Lucky I only had a few bucks. Did you have cash?"

"None in my wallet. Five bucks in my pocket, which I kept," said Michael, kicking the tub of popcorn toward the gutter.

"He called us 'ladies.'"

"Ladies with no money," said Michael. "Little douche bag chose the wrong ladies."

They circled slowly around the pieces of popcorn, as though it might provide some insight into the situation.

"Now we have to cancel everything," said Wade. "I hate that."

"Like credit cards?"

"Credit cards, gas card, driver's license . . . my whole life was in there."

"If that's your whole life, Wade, I don't know. Not a good sign."

"Very funny."

"It takes five minutes to replace everything. You do it on the computer now. You'll have all your cards by next week."

"Okay. Relax."

"I am relaxed. You're the one who's worrying. Why do you care so much about your cards?"

"Jesus, Mike, calm down. If I irritate you so much, why'd you arrange this? Why'd you invite me out?"

"Because we're strangers, Wade. Because I don't know shit about your life after the age of eighteen."

"What do you want to know?"

"Come on."

"I'm serious. You've never asked about my life. When did you suddenly get interested in anyone besides yourself?"

"You have no idea what I'm interested in," said Michael, stunned at how suddenly their politeness had turned.

"Because you keep everything a secret. Your delicate little life, so sensitive. You think I'm some big dumb jock."

"You think I'm a depressed drunk."

"You are."

Michael began speed-walking up the middle of the street.

"Aren't you?" Wade yelled. He was a few paces behind Michael. Their loping gait was synchronized, their father's, something to do with those skinny legs and bad knees.

Michael stopped short and turned around. They were standing in the middle of the street, face to face, a foot apart. "At least I feel things, you bloated fucking robot."

They walked fast, heading toward the horizontal ribbons of light at the next big avenue. Tears crept down Michael's long face and Wade's broad one.

"If I'm a bloated robot, then you're a sullen teenager. If you're so unhappy, do something about it. You want to know who I am? Ask! You wait for the world to approach you, and when it doesn't, you pout. You're too old to feel so misunderstood, Mike. Unless you plan to die alone."

They passed a water-damaged apartment building with subtle metallic specks in its stucco façade, probably from the early sixties. On the grass in front, a young Filipino man was giving another young Filipino man — seated on a lawn chair and wearing a white smock — a haircut. It was jarring to see this after midnight, but the men on the lawn behaved as though it was the most natural thing in the world.

"You say I don't feel anything," Wade continued shrilly, wiping the tears from his face with the back of his hand. "You know *why* I'm pissed about my wallet? It's not the damn gas card. I had a picture of mom and dad in there. My favorite picture."

"Which one?" asked Michael, who felt all of a sudden responsible for what had happened, as if by orchestrating their reunion, he himself had taken the wallet from Wade's baggy, faded jeans.

The brothers stopped walking. They were in the middle of the street.

"A picture — from a long time ago. I just liked it."

"What were they doing? Where were they?"

"I think it was in the old backyard. You can't really tell. They're in bathing suits and they look like they're laughing at a dirty joke."

Michael saw Wade just then as a six-year-old wearing Mickey Mouse ears. The guy at Disneyland had mistakenly embroidered *Wayne* onto the hat, but Wade didn't mind. He was a happy child, easygoing even then. He wore his *Wayne* hat for an entire summer.

"What are we doing, Mike? Where are we going?" There was a pleading tone to Wade's questions.

"We're walking it off. I can't go home yet."

"Don't you feel like a target?

"We're not going to get mugged twice in one night," Michael said. "Oh man, can you imagine?"

"Jesus," said Wade, and they both laughed a little.

At that instant, Michael knew that the mugging had earned the stamp of official memory. He imagined the story they would tell, the pithy paragraph, the recounting. He didn't hear the words but he could feel the shape of them. The moment of the shared chuckle was the moment the mugging had become mutual, an event, another installment in the brothers' soft mythology. This incident, Michael knew with a prescient pang, would assume an unearned weight strictly because it was a memory — a memory for two people who existed for each other only in the world of memory.

They arrived at the honking bustle of a major east–west artery with the four usual corners: giant supermarket, giant bank, giant parking structure, giant hamburger drive-thru. Everything in Los Angeles had grown giant, mom-and-pop shops bulldozed away from high-profile intersections like this one. The garish display blew at the brothers like a gust of wind.

"I should go," said Wade.

"What?"

"I should go," he said. "Mirabelle's waiting up."

"Are you serious?"

"Yeah," he said, reaching up to finger his ear. "It's just starting to hit me. I don't want to be out in all this," he said, looking up and around at the lights and billboards and then down at the sidewalks and the pedestrians that weren't there. "If you want to spend your five dollars on a piece of pie, I'd split it, but I can't just traipse around."

Wade had always been an abrupt leaver, a fact that Michael only remembered during the mildly shocking moment of Wade's goodbye. His goodbyes seemed surprising and inevitable at the same time. Michael felt a twitching guilt about the night, but he didn't want to eat pie and he didn't want to reminisce. Memories offered little succor for him, perhaps because he and Wade always seemed to remember the same things. Didn't the power of memory lay in its ability to surprise and illuminate? Otherwise, wasn't it just an elaborate brand of small talk, starving the people in question while appearing, briefly, to feed them? Michael knew that a piece of pie with Wade would not feel like progress. Plus, there was nowhere to get pie after midnight, unless you were willing to drive, and what Michael needed was a beer.

"Okay," he said as he leaned in to his brother. They embraced like tin-men with unlubricated joints.

"I'll talk to you," said Wade. "Sorry." He walked back down the darkened street, toward the scene of the crime — or whatever it was — where his car was parked.

Michael sprinted through the blinking intersection and into the supermarket. It was painfully bright and operating-room-cold, but it was a familiar shock, and not unpleasant. He yanked a shopping cart out of the corral and began wheeling it through the meat aisle, which was far more populated than the street outside. The bustling aisle gave Michael the sensation of an approaching storm, of citizens stocking up on canned goods and butane, going about their business with the methodical American dread he'd seen on the news. He pushed his empty cart past the various meats. He passed at least three young women ogling lamb chops or pausing to consider a fillet or some other lonely cut. He wheeled past the breakfast meats and into the bread aisle, feeling well adjusted because, surely, he was the only person there who'd just been mugged and then immediately resumed his quotidian duties. But as he gained momentum down the pillowy aisle of muffins and pita and all the other starches, he felt in his stomach the possibility that he might be wrong. There was the chance, however slight, that others in the market had also just been mugged — or if not mugged, then accosted, attacked, held up, assaulted, shammed, scammed, humiliated, beaten up, shot at, or victimized in some way. It was possible. He checked his watch. It was 12:53 and they were all contained there in the bunker-like supermarket, wherever they'd been before.

He began filling up his cart. He took peanut butter and tomato soup and cans of tuna packed in oil, and he looked long at his late-night shopping companions, who maybe just didn't want to go home.

He pushed the cart, which now also contained a sports drink with electrolytes and some boxes of couscous, into the cereal aisle, where he saw the unmistakable gray rat's nest of a hairdo, simultaneously abject and sophisticated. Simone, still alone and wrapped up in her Euro-scarf, walked quickly down the aisle with a small red basket. There was a furtive grace to her gait, a hurried worry not unlike Alice chasing the White Rabbit. Here was a middle-aged, possibly European woman in a West Coast supermarket at one in the morning, but Michael saw the dewy, distressed heroine of a fairy tale. Maybe the night would end well. She — Simone — would be his reward for calling Wade and trying to repair things. This serendipitous detour could alter his life more profoundly than his well-meaning lump of a brother ever could. Maybe he was right to let Wade go, not agreeing to get pie but rather following his instincts.

He began trailing Simone, but he feared he'd make her nervous. He wanted to talk to her without seeming dangerous or desperate. He was too far away to make out the contents of her basket, but from a distance, her knee-length hem revealed a skinny ankle and a strong calf. They were at the edge now, near the verdant maze of produce, when she turned abruptly, a sudden jerk of impatience sending her to the express lane. She fished around in her well-worn leather bag, which looked like a baseball mitt. Michael got in line behind her. She leaned back against the metal railing, staring at something — or nothing — and maybe she sensed the jumbled intentions pulsing in him because she gazed out of her reverie and into his eyes, revealing, maybe, some tiny bit of recognition. And then she began placing her groceries onto the belt.

He grabbed a roll of mints from the display and tossed them into his cart when his stomach — which knew things before he did — turned a lumbering somersault as he remembered that his wallet had been stolen, and that he had no cards and no identification. His pockets were empty — save for the five-dollar bill and his car keys — but his cart was full. With his five dollars, he could afford to buy three of the beers in the six-pack in his cart, but he hated that guy, the one who buys three beers and nothing else, after midnight, alone. He scanned an imaginary list, mentally crossing off the things he would not do: he would not meet this brave and mysterious woman; he would not buy provisions for the imaginary storm; he would not call Wade to rehash the details of the mugging. He would excuse himself from the express lane, which had already filled up behind him, and he would leave his cart in the middle of some aisle, which is exactly what he did, and then he slipped a candy bar into his jacket pocket and he went to find his car.

CONTRIBUTORS' NOTES

Marjorie Celona has a degree in writing from the University of Victoria and is an MFA candidate at the Iowa Writers' Workshop, where she is working on her first collection of stories.

J. Malcolm Garcia has been published in the *Virginia Quarterly Review*, *Alaska Quarterly Review*, and *West Branch*, among other publications.

David Gessner is the author of six books of literary nonfiction, including *Sick of Nature, Return of the Osprey*, and *Soaring with Fidel*. His essay "Learning to Surf" won the John Burroughs award for best nature essay of 2006. His essays have appeared on NPR's *This I Believe* series and in many magazines and journals, including the *New York Times, Georgia Review, American Scholar, Orion*, the *Harvard Review*, and the 2006 Pushcart Prize anthology, for which his essay "Benediction" was selected. He has taught environmental writing as a Briggs-Copeland lecturer at Harvard and is currently a professor of creative nonfiction at the University of North Carolina at Wilmington, where he also edits the literary journal of place, *Ecotone*.

Andrew Sean Greer is the best-selling author of *The Confessions of Max Tivoli*, the story collection *How It Was for Me*, and the novel *The Path of Minor Planets*. His stories have been published in *Esquire*, the *Paris Review*, and *The New Yorker*. He lives in San Francisco, California.

Helon Habila was born in Nigeria in 1967. He studied literature at the University of Jos and worked in Lagos as a journalist. In Lagos, he wrote his first novel, *Waiting for an Angel* (2003), which has been translated into many languages, including Dutch, Italian, Swedish, and French. In 2002, he moved to England to become the African writing fellow at the University of East Anglia. After his fellowship, he enrolled for a PhD in creative writing. In 2005–2006, he was the first Chinua Achebe fellow at Bard College in New York. He is a contributing editor to the *Virginia Quarterly Review,* and in 2006, he coedited the British Council's anthology *New Writing 14.* His second novel, *Measuring Time,* was published in 2007. His writing has won many prizes, including the Caine Prize (2001), the Commonwealth Writers Prize (2003), and the Emily Balch Prize for Short Story (2007). He currently teaches creative writing at the George Mason University in Fairfax, Virginia, where he lives with his family. He is working on his third novel.

Paul Hornschemeier was born in 1977 in Cincinnati, reared in rural Georgetown, Ohio, and began self-publishing his experimental comics series *Sequential* in college. Graduating with a degree in philosophy, he moved to Chicago and began his series *Forlorn Funnies,* producing the graphic novels *Mother, Come Home, The Three Paradoxes,* and *Life with Mr. Dangerous* and the short story collection *Let Us Be Perfectly Clear.* Hornschemeier's work, translated into multiple languages, has won international acclaim and awards, including honors at the Victoria and Albert Museum in London. His prose stories have appeared in *Life* magazine, and he has worked with publications and programs ranging from the *Wall Street Journal* to *This American Life.* He currently resides in Chicago, where he is still at work on *Forlorn Funnies,* as well as various illustration, prose, and music projects.

Raffi Khatchadourian is a staff writer at *The New Yorker.* His first piece for the magazine, "Azzam the American," about Adam Gadahn, an American who joined Al Qaeda, was nominated for a 2008 National Magazine Award in profile writing. He has also written for the *Village Voice, The Nation,* and the *New York Times,* among other publications.

Stephen King was born in 1947 and has lived most of his life in Maine. He was teaching high school when his first novel, *Carrie*, sold to Doubleday and Company in 1973. He has since published over fifty books, most of them novels. Some have been made into movies, and some of the movies were actually pretty good. His latest novel, *Duma Key*, was published in early 2008. A new collection of short stories (of which "Ayana" is a part) is scheduled to be published in late 2008.

Barry McGee created the cover illustration for this book. He was born in 1966 in California, where he continues to live and work. In 1991, he received a BFA in painting and printmaking from the San Francisco Art Institute. McGee is also a graffiti artist, working on the streets of America's cities since the 1980s, where he is known by the tag name *Twist*. His work has been shown at the Walker Art Center in Minneapolis, the San Francisco Museum of Modern Art, the UCLA/Armand Hammer Museum in Los Angeles, and on streets and trains all over the United States.

Rutu Modan's first graphic novel, *Exit Wounds*, published by Drawn and Quarterly, was acclaimed by *Time*, *Entertainment Weekly*, and other publications, and topped the *Publishers Weekly Comics Week* Critics' Poll for 2007. *Exit Wounds* also won the France Info Prize for 2008 and was one of the winners of the Angouleme Essential Award. Rutu's illustrations have been published in the *New York Times*, *The New Yorker*, *Le Monde*, and many others. "Queen of the Scottish Fairies" is just one installment from her comics column *Mixed Emotions*, which appeared on the *New York Times* website during 2007. Rutu is nominated for the Eisner Award in 2008 for best new album and for best artist.

Emily Raboteau is the author of the novel *The Professor's Daughter*. She lives in Harlem and is working on a book of creative nonfiction about exodus movements throughout the African diaspora. She would love anyone with knowledge about groups of black folk who've left home to find home using the Old Testament's book of Exodus as inspiration to contact her at eraboteau@ccny.cuny.edu.

George Saunders is the author of six books (including the short story collections *CivilWarLand in Bad Decline*, *Pastoralia*, and *In Persuasion Nation*) and, most recently, the essay collection *The Braindead Megaphone*. He teaches at Syracuse University.

Jake Swearingen lives and works in San Francisco. He has been published in *Created in Darkness by Troubled Americans: The Best of McSweeney's, Humor Category*, and *The McSweeney's Joke Book of Book Jokes*. He is currently at work on his first self-help book, *You Need Help, Jake*.

Patrick Tobin's work has appeared in various journals, including *Agni*, the *Kenyon Review*, and the *Florida Review*. "Reunion," an essay about visiting his con-man father in prison, won PRISM International's 2006 literary nonfiction contest. His short story "Passage" was recently reprinted in the Ohio University Press anthology *New Stories from the Southwest*.

Laura van den Berg recently finished her MFA at Emerson College. Her fiction has appeared in the *Indiana Review*, the *Literary Review*, *American Short Fiction*, *One Story*, and *StoryQuarterly*, among others. The recipient of the 2007 Dzanc Prize, van den Berg's first story collection, *What the World Will Look Like When All the Water Leaves Us*, will be published by Dzanc Books in fall 2009.

Gene Weingarten, 57, is a syndicated humor columnist and staff writer for the *Washington Post*. He is the author of three books: *The Hypochondriac's Guide to Life. And Death.* (1998), *I'm With Stupid* (2004, with Gina Barreca), and *Old Dogs* (2008, with Michael S. Williamson). Weingarten won the 2008 Pulitzer Prize for feature writing.

Laurie Weeks lives in New York City. She was a contributor to the screenplay for *Boys Don't Cry* and is currently finishing her first book, *Zipper Mouth*, from which "My Massive Feelings" is excerpted.

Malerie Willens grew up in Nichols Canyon, a lush and mysterious area of Los Angeles. Her day jobs have required her to write as a man, a clairvoyant, and an Eastern European. She lives in New York, where she's writing a novel that's not about the end of the world or a family's secret pain. She has an MFA in fiction from Sarah Lawrence College. "The Elegant Rube" is her first published story.

THE *BEST AMERICAN*
NONREQUIRED READING
COMMITTEE

 Carlos Cheung is seventeen and attends Mission High School. He loves all sorts of food, especially homemade Chinese food. He likes to joke around a lot, but he can be mature and productive when necessary. He enjoys analyzing texts and figuring out their hidden meanings.

Carmen DeMartis attended Mission High School during her time with *Best American Nonrequired*. Carmen has a knack for picking up nicknames and will respond when called Bonqueesha. She will be a proud Banana Slug in the fall of 2008, at the University of California, Santa Cruz, where she will be reading, procrastinating, and hating mayonnaise with frightful and often baffling passion.

 A *BANR* veteran of two years, **Josh Freydkis** treasures every moment he spends in the secret sanctum that is the McSweeney's basement. He fervently enjoys bike rides, tree climbing, warm afternoons, and death metal. By the time you read this, Josh will be at New York University, trying to avoid — but pretending not to — all the other former *BANR* members also attending NYU. He loves them all, but enough is enough.

Yael Green is a senior in the creative writing department at School of the Arts in San Francisco. When asked about her plans for the future, she comes up with a different answer each time. Still, a good choice to take home to Mom. Yael is currently Jewish.

Katie Henry has been a member of the *Best American Nonrequired* Committee (or, as her friends call it, Junior Writers of the World Unite) for two years. She has an extensive collection of notebooks that are too pretty to write in, and her favorite animal is the giant isopod. In the fall of 2008, she will be attending NYU and majoring in something that will never make her any money.

Sayra Hernandez grew up in San Francisco and attended Mission High School. She is inspired by the arts. If she's not listening to music, writing, or busy with her art, then she's found releasing her stress to the tune of a piano.

Sophia Hussain is currently a senior at Redwood High School outside San Francisco. She writes for her school paper and aspires to be the next Woodward or Bernstein. She enjoys getting the *New York Times* on Sunday mornings and following the 2008 presidential election on the blogosphere. She likes everything except math.

In her free time, **Arianna Kandell** likes to dress up in power suits and join others who mumble suspiciously to themselves (known to some as debate tournaments). She also likes satsuma oranges, James Joyce, and the murals adorning alleyways between 18th and Valencia. Next year, she hopes to join others in their pursuit of tall, ivory buildings and copious amounts of books to slouch over. Or maybe she'll work for a human-rights firm in Ghana. Or fight tigers in Spain. Or learn how to walk on water. Or make computers that run off green tea and soybeans.

Bora Lee has most recently completed her third year at Lick-Wilmerding High School. She enjoys reading, playing the viola, and tending to her potted ferns and succulents. She spends most of her spare time snuggling/folding warm laundry and walking sidewalks in sets of three. This year she hopes to reduce her carbon footprint.

Terence Li of Mission High School has had his share of public schooling in San Francisco and so in the fall, he is going to Stanford University. He is overly neat and hopes to make a living in college by organizing others' rooms. During his spare time, Terence enjoys drinking water and pondering about how to efficiently squander his time.

In the fall of 2008, **Tanea Lunsford** will be a senior in the creative writing department at School of the Arts in San Francisco. She aspires to be a doctor, writer, firefighter, and helicopter nurse, preferably all in this lifetime. She goes to church every Sunday (by choice) and feels bad about Google-ing herself in her spare time.

Hey! My name is **Osvaldo Marquez**, and I will be a junior at Gateway High School in the fall. This is my first year with *The Best American Nonrequired Reading,* and I didn't know what to expect from it. I thought it was just going to be a book for the [826 Valencia pirate store] to have and show that we have been doing something. But NO! We read and talk and talk and talk and discuss and discuss and we pick the best of the best. But I guess it's all worth it when it comes to this book. Enjoy.

A girl with the soul of a troubadour, **Nina Moog** has been with the *Best American Nonrequired* Committee for what seems like decades. Nina enjoys dark chocolate, feather quills, and writing epic manifestos on a 1969 typewriter. Next fall, you will find this young'un attending St. Andrews University in

Scotland. She has loved her time with *Best American* and hopes you enjoy the collection.

My name is **Elizabeth Rodriguez**. I attend Metropolitan Arts and Tech High School, and I will be a junior in the fall of 2008. I was raised in San Francisco and have lived here all my life. I enjoy trying out new experiences and hanging out with my friends.

This fall **Marley Walker** will be a sophomore at San Francisco's School of the Arts. She is currently left-handed, a vegetarian, enjoys squeaking, playing the bass guitar, and eating mangoes. She took on writing because her friends told her there was no future in squeaking.

Naomi Krupitsky Wernham has thoroughly loved her tenure with *BANR*, but will be leaving this fall to attend NYU. She hopes to smush all of her interests into a cohesive major, as well as fill all the stamp pages of her passport with different trips to exciting places. She does not enjoy writing bios of herself.

Eli Wolfe is a senior at School of the Arts. He has worked previously on his high school's literary magazine, *Umlaut*. He plans to not live in poverty after college.

At the time of this writing, **Iris Zhang** was an eighteen-year-old Mission High senior. She will soon be a Cal Bear. Since she moved to the United States four years ago, she has been learning to appreciate English writings with the same love she has for Chinese literature. She really enjoys reading in the basement [the *BANR* offices] every Tuesday, as well doing drills on the badminton court, making rings out of daisies in the park, taking pictures of her latest knitting project, and carrying groceries on Irving Street.

This year's committee was helped enormously by the following editors and editorial assistants at McSweeney's: **Michelle Quint**, **Alexei Wajchman**, **Jesse Malmed**, and **Hallie Kutak**.

NOTABLE
NONREQUIRED READING
OF 2007

DANIEL ALARCÓN
  A Circus at the Center of the World, *The Virginia Quarterly Review*
WOODY ALLEN
  Calisthenics, Poison Ivy, Final Cut, *Zoetrope: All-Story*
JACOB M. APPEL
  Rods and Cones, *Southwest Review*
SONA AVAKIAN
  Artichoke Heart, *Instant City*

MATTHEW BALDWIN
  America's Next Top Model Democracy, *The Morning News*
JOSHUAH BEARMAN
  Heaven's Gate: The Sequel, *LA Weekly*
AIMEE BENDER
  Interval, *Conjunctions*
ELIZABETH BERNAYS
  Arthropods Molting, *Fence*
BARRIE JEAN BORICH
  Cities of Possibility, *Water-Stone Review*
T. C. BOYLE
  Hands On, *The Kenyon Review*
MICHAEL P. BRANCH
  The V.E.C.T.O.R.L.O.S.S Project, *Isotope*
AUSTIN BUNN
  The End of the Age Is Upon Us, *American Short Fiction*

ABOUT 826 NATIONAL

Proceeds from this book benefit youth literacy

A LARGE PERCENTAGE OF the cover price of this book goes to 826 National, a network of ten youth tutoring, writing, and publishing centers in seven cities around the country.

Since the birth of 826 National in 2002, our goal has been to assist students ages six to eighteen with their writing skills while helping teachers get their classes passionate about writing. We do this with a vast army of volunteers who donate their time so we can give as much one-on-one attention as possible to the students whose writing needs it. Our mission is based on the understanding that great leaps in learning can happen with one-on-one attention, and that strong writing skills are fundamental to future success.

Through volunteer support, each of the seven 826 chapters — in San Francisco, New York, Los Angeles, Chicago, Ann Arbor, Seattle, and Boston — provides drop-in tutoring, class field trips, writing workshops, and in-school programs, all free of charge, for students, classes, and schools. The 826 centers are especially committed to supporting teachers, offering services and resources for English language learners, and publishing student work. Each of the 826 chapters works to produce professional-quality publications written entirely by young people, to forge relationships with teachers in order to create innovative workshops and lesson plans, to inspire students to write and appreciate the written word, and to rally thousands of enthusiastic volunteers to make it all happen. By offering all of our programming for free, we aim to serve families who cannot afford to pay for the level of personalized instruction their children receive through 826 chapters.

The demand for 826 National's services is tremendous. Last year we worked with more than 4,000 volunteers and over 18,000 students nationally, hosted 368 field trips, completed 170 major in-school projects, offered 266 evening and weekend workshops, welcomed over 130 students per day for after-school tutoring, and produced over 600 student publications. At many of our centers, our field trips are fully booked almost a year in advance, teacher requests for in-school tutor support continue to rise, and the majority of our evening and weekend workshops have waitlists.

826 National volunteers are local community residents, professional writers, teachers, artists, college students, parents, bankers, lawyers, and retirees from a wide range of professions. These passionate individuals can be found at all of our centers after school, sitting side-by-side with our students, providing one-on-one attention. They can be found running our field trips, or helping an entire classroom of local students learn how to write a story, or assisting student writers during one of our Young Authors' Book Programs.

All day and in a variety of ways, our volunteers are actively connecting with youth from the communities we serve.

To learn more or get involved, please visit:

826 National: www.826national.org
826 in San Francisco: www.826valencia.org
826 in New York: www.826nyc.org
826 in Los Angeles: www.826la.org
826 in Chicago: www.826chi.org
826 in Ann Arbor: www.826mi.org
826 in Seattle: www.826seattle.org
826 in Boston: www.826boston.org

THE BEST AMERICAN SERIES®

THE BEST AMERICAN SHORT STORIES® 2008
Salman Rushdie, editor, Heidi Pitlor, series editor
> ISBN: 978-0-618-78876-7 $28.00 CL
> ISBN: 978-0-618-78877-4 $14.00 PA

THE BEST AMERICAN NONREQUIRED READING™ 2008
Edited by Dave Eggers, introduction by Judy Blume
> ISBN: 978-0-618-90282-8 $28.00 CL
> ISBN: 978-0-618-90283-5 $14.00 PA

THE BEST AMERICAN COMICS™ 2008
Lynda Barry, editor, Jessica Abel and Matt Madden, series editors
> ISBN: 978-0-618-98976-8 $22.00 POB

THE BEST AMERICAN ESSAYS® 2008
Adam Gopnik, editor, Robert Atwan, series editor
> ISBN: 978-0-618-98331-5 $28.00 CL
> ISBN: 978-0-618-98322-3 $14.00 PA

THE BEST AMERICAN MYSTERY STORIES™ 2008
George Pelecanos, editor, Otto Penzler, series editor
> ISBN: 978-0-618-81266-0 $28.00 CL
> ISBN: 978-0-618-81267-7 $14.00 PA

THE BEST AMERICAN SPORTS WRITING™ 2008
William Nack, editor, Glenn Stout, series editor
> ISBN: 978-0-618-75117-4 $28.00 CL
> ISBN: 978-0-618-75118-1 $14.00 PA

THE BEST AMERICAN TRAVEL WRITING™ 2008
Anthony Bourdain, editor, Jason Wilson, series editor
> ISBN: 978-0-618-85863-7 $28.00 CL
> ISBN: 978-0-618-85864-4 $14.00 PA

THE BEST AMERICAN SCIENCE AND NATURE WRITING™ 2008
Jerome Groopman, editor, Tim Folger, series editor
> ISBN: 978-0-618-83446-4 $28.00 CL
> ISBN: 978-0-618-83447-1 $14.00 PA

THE BEST AMERICAN SPIRITUAL WRITING™ 2008
Edited by Philip Zaleski, introduction by Jimmy Carter
> ISBN: 978-0-618-83374-0 $28.00 CL
> ISBN: 978-0-618-83375-7 $14.00 PA